IAN FLEMING'S WAR

IAN FLEMING'S WAR

THE INSPIRATION FOR **007**

MARK
SIMMONS

FOREWORD BY
ANTHONY
HOROWITZ

The
History
Press

First published 2020

The History Press
97 St George's Place, Cheltenham,
Gloucestershire, GL50 3QB
www.thehistorypress.co.uk

British Library Cataloguing in Publication Data.
A catalogue record for this book is available from the British Library.

ISBN 978 0 7509 9326 5

Typesetting and origination by The History Press
Printed and bound in Great Britain by TJ International Ltd.

Tiger was completely sent. He was back there again fighting the war. Bond knew the symptoms. He often visited this haunted forest of memory himself.

You Only Live Twice

CONTENTS

FOREWORD

BY ANTHONY HOROWITZ

Who is James Bond?

The question may seem an obvious one – he is by some distance the most famous fictional character ever created – but actually, there's no obvious answer.

If you start with the films, you have to sift through seven quite separate personalities from Connery to Craig, taking in Roger Moore with his exuberant puns (more *double entendre* than double-0-seven) and George Lazenby, who described Bond as 'a brute' and walked away from the franchise. Personally I've always admired the way the films have adapted themselves to whatever decade they've found themselves in: since 1962 and *Dr No*, Eon Productions have almost written a social history of the UK and its place in the world.

That said, some of the films have only a passing acquaintance with Ian Fleming's books. After *Dr No*, *From Russia with Love* and *Goldfinger*, the films went their own way, sending Bond into outer space, equipping him with an invisible car or pitting him against a villain with steel teeth. All very enjoyable but, as the author of two Bond 'continuation novels' (generously credited by Mark Simmons in this book), I've always found myself more drawn to Fleming's literary work.

But even here the question of Bond's inspiration is a tricky one.

Mark Simmons correctly draws parallels between Bond and his crea-
tor: they had the same taste for cigarettes, scrambled eggs and clothes.
They had the same rank of commander and, for that matter, the same
sexual drives. But Lionel Crabb, the Royal Navy diver, also appears
in these pages, as does Dusko Popov, the Yugoslavian double agent.
Fleming knew both of them and both have at one time or another
been suggested as the original Bond.

The pleasure of *Ian Fleming's War* – jammed with anecdote and
information I had never read before – is that it clearly demonstrates
how much James Bond owes to Naval Intelligence, to the Special
Operations Executive (SOE) and the fabled Room 39, and how some
of the hare-brained schemes thought up in Baker Street and elsewhere
ended up in the stories that would still be entertaining millions of
people seventy years later.

It's an extraordinary collision of fact, fiction and fantasy. I love the
way that Simmons starts with one of my favourite childhood stories –
Erskine Childers' 1903 classic, *Riddle of the Sands* – and suggests how
this may have given Fleming the idea for a wartime operation to spy
on enemy U-boats. Like so many of his schemes, this never actually
happened but years later it turns up, vaguely, as the plot of *A View to a
Kill*. So from fiction to fact and back to fiction again. Or what about
the completely bonkers idea of luring a Nazi leader to Britain on a fake
peace mission? It was inspired by a novella written not by Ian but by his
brother, Peter Fleming, and that might have been the end of it except
that, less than a year later, Rudolf Hess landed in Scotland and was captured in not entirely dissimilar circumstances – and when you add in the
fact that Fleming seriously investigated Hess's interest in the occult, even
(perhaps) meeting with the famous black magician and 'Great Beast',
Aleister Crowley, you begin to get a sense of the delirious mix of sense
and nonsense that make the Bond books so delicious. Simmons adds
that Crowley was the inspiration for Le Chiffre in *Casino Royale*, something I should have known but didn't.

Ever since I started writing *Foyle's War* for television, I have had a fascination with the intelligence organisations during the war. Everything
about them, from their larger-than-life personalities, their intense loyalty to the service and to each other, their imaginative schemes and, of

course, their gadgets are all … well, pure James Bond. I remember seeing a Sykes Fairbairn commando knife on display at the Special Forces Club in Knightsbridge and thinking of Bond in *Live and Let Die*, using 'a commando dagger of the type devised by Wilkinson during the war'. The limpet mine Bond uses in the same chapter could just as easily have been an SOE sticky bomb (thinking of later Bond films, SOE also invented a miniature submarine). I like the idea that, according to Simmons, Fleming travelled to Madrid with a fountain pen equipped with a cyanide cartridge and that a prototype of the briefcase with its various secret weapons used by Bond in *From Russia with Love* accompanied him on the same trip.

Watching the films as a boy, my favourite scenes were always the ones where Bond received his orders from M and I loved the relationship between them in the books: the bridge game at Blades, the health drive that leads to Shrublands, the lecture on diamonds that prompts M to growl: 'Don't push it in. Screw it in.' He's referring to a jeweller's magnifying glass but Bond has other uses of the dictum in mind. Kingsley Amis wrote of M as the analogue of 'a father and a father of pre-1939 vintage at that …' (*The James Bond Dossier*). But I think of him as the very exemplar of wartime intelligence.

Simmons provides us with ample proof that M was based on Rear Admiral John Godfrey, Director of Naval Intelligence and commander of Room 39. This has all been well rehearsed but I'm glad that he also mentions a personal hero of mine, the original Brigadier Colin McVean Gubbins as a possible influence. Gubbins was 'M' in real life, the head of SOE, and I've always wanted to write a drama about him. I even managed to meet Joan Bright Astley, who worked with him throughout the war and who also, incidentally, dated Ian Fleming. When I met her, she was in her late nineties but allowed me to take her out for a lunch, during which she firmly but politely made it clear to me that she had no interest in sharing any information about either man. Returning home, it occurred to me that I had met Miss Moneypenny but had not been buzzed through the green baize door.

Ian Fleming's War opens that door and I loved reading it. There was so much I didn't know. Is it really true that Fleming met a station chief called Wilfred 'Buffy' Dunderdale who was driven around in a bullet-proof Rolls-Royce by a Russian émigré called Gresev – and that this might have been the inspiration for Goldfinger and Oddjob? In my second Bond novel, *Forever and a Day*, I described the murder of a Japanese cyber expert in the Rockefeller Centre (which helped earn Bond his double-0 licence) without knowing that Fleming had actually broken into that very office in real life, tagging along with a Canadian spy. I'd have bought this book just to learn that Fleming decided to share his birthday – 28 May 1908 – with his arch villain, Blofeld.

So who was Bond? To Kingsley Amis he was a fantasy figure, a Byronic hero: 'Mr Fleming has brought off the unlikely feat of enclosing this wildly romantic, almost narcissistic ... hopelessly out-of-date persona inside the shellac of a secret agent.' He was, according to the first chapter of *The James Bond Dossier*, 'The Man who is only a Silhouette.'

By shining new light on Fleming's role in intelligence, the people he met and the adventures he had with them, Mark Simmons brilliantly illuminates the hero who was his greatest creation.

Anthony Horowitz
26 February 2020

INTRODUCTION

JAMES BOND THE MAVERICK

In the fifth 007 book, *From Russia with Love*, Bond bemoans the fact that: 'He was a man of war and when, for a long period, there was no war, his spirit went into decline.'[1] What war is he thinking about? Given that the book came out in 1957, could it have been Korea or Suez – a fiasco for Britain? Not either of these. It is the Second World War. It was the war of which Ian Fleming had direct experience; he had knowledge of a myriad of characters and operations, some of which he created himself when he worked at the Naval Intelligence Division (NID). Although the 007 books' time setting is the Cold War, James Bond is a maverick; he has more in common with John Buchan's Richard Hannay than he does with John le Carré's Alec Leamas. He is more akin to the Special Operations Executive's (SOE) sabotage and assassination, rather than the Special Intelligence Service (SIS) MI6's intelligence gathering.

The main motive behind Ian Fleming writing *Casino Royale*, the first Bond book, in 1953 was the deplorable state of Britain in the 1950s as he saw it. The Empire was in terminal decline: there was trouble in Egypt, Cyprus and Malaya, as well as with the Mau Mau in Kenya. Even worse for him, British Intelligence had been rocked to the core by the defection of Guy Burgess and Donald Maclean to Moscow, tipped off by the third man Kim Philby, who had been a Soviet spy since the

Spanish Civil War. This might explain why Fleming uses Vesper Lynd in *Casino Royale* as a double agent to reflect those times. Bond is suitably betrayed and telephones MI6 in London to report that '3030 was a double, working for Redland'.[2] In 1951, Peter Fleming's book *The Sixth Column* was published, which tells the story of a Soviet scheme 'Plan D' to undermine what was left of the British national character. It is foiled by his character Archie Strume, who has nothing in common with James Bond, but Peter dedicated it to his brother Ian. Perhaps it was a wake-up call to bring on James Bond, the supreme adventurer and tool of government.[3]

In 1958, Ian Fleming conducted a radio interview with Raymond Chandler in which they talked about thriller writing, comparing their two heroes James Bond and Philip Marlowe. In it Fleming defined what he felt Bond was:

> Your hero, Philip Marlowe, is a real hero. He behaves in a heroic fashion. I never intended my leading character, James Bond, to be a hero. I intended him to be a sort of blunt instrument wielded by a government department who would get into bizarre and fantastic situations and more or less shoot his way out of them, or get out of them one way or another. But of course he's always referred to as my hero. I don't see him as a hero myself.[4]

Yours truly first came across James Bond when my sister, three years my senior, managed to get me in to see the 1963 film *From Russia with Love*. I was 12 or 13 at the time, maybe my sister was underage as well but she looked older and passed muster. A few years after that in the late 1960s I read all the Ian Fleming Bond books one after the other and loved them. As far as the films are concerned, after Sean Connery stopped playing 007 I confess to losing interest.

In 1975, when I was a Cold War warrior myself, serving in the Royal Marine Commandos, I visited the Crown Colony of Gibraltar for the first time, one of the last of the 'pink bits'. Venturing up the Rock, via the cable car, you arrive at the viewing platform looking out over the sheer eastern face. If you move south, toward O'Hara's battery, away to the west across Gibraltar Bay is the sprawl of Algeciras. From here you begin to appreciate just how small Gibraltar is with an area of just 2.6 square miles. I wondered why Germany had not taken Gibraltar during the Second World War, especially considering Spain at the time was a fascist state.

My interest in this question continued for many years until I wrote my book about Spain and the Second World War. Over the years of my writing career often I came across Ian Fleming in my research and his wartime role in Naval Intelligence. He was one of those who played a leading role in keeping Spain neutral, thus the title of my book: *Ian Fleming and Operation Golden Eye: Keeping Spain out of World War II*. Little wonder he called his home on Jamaica Goldeneye after one of the most dramatic periods of his life. For that book I re-read *Casino Royale, Live and Let Die, Thunderball* and *On Her Majesty's Secret Service*. The plots of all four were clearly influenced by his time on the Iberian Peninsula. Yet it struck me at the time that all his books have their roots in the conflict. For this book I have re-read all Ian Fleming's other books, which has been a joy. A few other authors have taken up the mantle of writing the Bond books. Probably the best have been by John Gardner and Anthony Horowitz, the latter by using albeit small parts of Fleming's unpublished writing has really captured the flavour of the early books.

William Boyd also wrote a James Bond book, and has used the character of Ian Fleming in his memorable novel *Any Human Heart* when his character Logan Mountstuart joins Naval Intelligence in 1940. In my own novel *Room 39 and The Cornish Legacy*, the first of my reluctant MI5 agent Rob Nicolson's adventures, Fleming makes a cameo appearance.

By examining the work of Fleming in Naval Intelligence we come across a myriad of characters and events, many stranger than fiction, that influenced his writing. Such as Commander Lionel Kenneth Crabb, who sadly will forever be linked with the 1956 fiasco when he was sent on the mission to examine the hull of the Soviet cruiser *Ordzhonikidze* in Portsmouth harbour and was not seen alive again. The mission was ill-conceived, and Crabb far too old for it. His headless body was found off the coast fourteen months later. However, Fleming knew him long before that; in 1943 in Operation Tadpole he led the team in the waters around Gibraltar that took on the legendary Italian Tenth Flotilla to stop them sinking Allied shipping. This was a direct influence on *Live and Let Die* and *Thunderball*.

Was Fleming involved in the Rudolf Hess deception plan, which he could have worked on with Dennis Wheatley? Aleister Crowley, the occultist and sexual deviant called the 'wickedest man in England', was involved with NID at the time. He was likely to have been the inspiration for Le Chiffre, the villain of *Casino Royale*. Did Fleming bring him in to interview Hess knowing the German's obsession with the occult?

Then there is his close association with 30 Assault Unit, the Commando unit he helped create. Their exploits would provide the inspiration for *Moonraker*. And as we will see, the thread of Fleming's Second World War runs through all his Bond books.

GLOSSARY AND ACRONYMS

Abwehr	German military intelligence service, meaning 'defence' in German
30AU	30 Assault Unit Royal Marines, also known as 30 Commando
BSC	British Security Co-ordination, operating within North America
BUF	British Union of Fascists
'C'	Head of British Secret Intelligence Service (SIS) MI6
Camp X	Canadian training camp for SOE and OSS agents
Camp 020	British Interrogation Centre, Latchmere House, south London
CIA	Central Intelligence Agency, replaced OSS, USA
DNI	Director of Naval Intelligence, British
Enigma	German code machine system
FBI	Federal Bureau of Investigation, USA
FO	Foreign Office, British
GC & CS	Government Code and Cypher School, Bletchley Park, code name Station X
GCHQ	Government Communications Headquarters
GRU	Soviet Military Intelligence

HUB	Handelsverkehrbuch, German naval codes, First World War
JIC	Joint Intelligence Committee, British
KGB	Soviet Intelligence Service
Maiale	Italian two-man submarine (Pigs)
MoI	Ministry of Information, British
MI1	Military Intelligence Section 1 responsible for code breaking, First World War
MI2	Military Intelligence Section 2 responsible for geographic information, Second World War
MI5	Military Intelligence Section 5. British counter-intelligence service
MI6	Military Intelligence Section 6. British espionage service often known as SIS
17M	Signals section NID
MEW	Ministry of Economic Warfare, British
NID	Naval Intelligence Division, British. Also known as Room 39
NKGB	The People's Commissariat for State Security, Soviet Union, 1941–46
NKVD	Narodnyi Komissariat Vnutrennikh Del, People's Commissariat for Internal Affairs, Soviet Union
OIC	Operational Intelligence Centre, British
OKW	Oberkommando der Wehrmacht, German Armed Forces High Command
OSS	Office of Strategic Services, replaced by CIA, USA
PVDE	Portuguese Secret Police
RCMP	Royal Canadian Mounted Police
RM	Royal Marines
RNVR	Royal Navy Volunteer Reserve
Room 40	Cryptanalysis Section Naval Intelligence in the First World War, later renamed I.D.25
RSHA	Reichssicherheitshauptamt, *German* supreme state security department. Set up in 1939 to supervise the Gestapo and SD
Section D	SIS sabotage section

SD	*Sicherheitsdienst*, secret service branch of the SS
SHAPE	Supreme Headquarters Allied Powers, Europe
SIS	Secret Intelligence Service British, also known as MI6
SKM	Signal Book of Imperial German Navy, First World War
SMERSH	'Death to Spies', counter-intelligence service of the Red Army
SOE	Special Operations Executive, British, originally Section D of SIS
SO2	Sabotage Section SOE (Naval)
SPECTRE	Special Executive for Terrorism, Revenge, and Extortion.
Ultra	Decoded encrypted Axis radio communications, classified 'Ultra Secret'
Waffen-SS	Military arm of the SS
Werwolf	German resistance force operating behind Allied lines
XX Committee	Double Cross System, counter-espionage and deception, British
X MAS	*Decima Flottiglia Mas,* Tenth Light Flotilla, Italian Navy

1

LUNCH AT THE CARLTON GRILL

The Carlton Hotel London in 1939 stood on the corner of Haymarket and Pall Mall. It was there on 24 May in the Carlton Grill restaurant that the 31-year-old Ian Fleming met Rear Admiral John Godfrey for the first time. The restaurant was within easy walking distance of the Admiralty, where Godfrey had started work as the Director of Naval Intelligence (DNI) only four months before.

Godfrey had returned with his battlecruiser *Repulse* to the UK from the Mediterranean. The old ship was due to be paid off in December 1938 at Plymouth, but with the heightened tensions of the Munich Crisis it was saved from the breaker's yard and diverted to join the Home Fleet at Scapa Flow, where Godfrey's old friend Ernest Spooner took over command.[1] *Repulse* is directly referred to in *On Her Majesty's Secret Service*.[2]

Godfrey had been warned of his likely appointment in August 1938 by letter, which arrived while *Repulse* was in Malta; it was from the Naval Secretary to the First Lord and read: 'I expect you will be requested to come to the Admiralty early next year to relieve Troup (Vice Admiral James Troup) as DNI. I hope this will suit you. This is for your own personal information.'[3]

Godfrey was delighted by the prospect, the only concern he had was that few DNIs ever got a sea command again. He went ashore and consulted with his boss Admiral Dudley Pound, then the Commander-in-Chief (C-in-C) Mediterranean Fleet, who told him he saw no reason why later he could not return to sea duties, and he would help him when the time came. This ended Godfrey's one doubt about his new appointment, although later at the height of the war Pound had to renege on his assurance. However, Godfrey never regretted becoming DNI.[4]

John Godfrey had joined the Royal Navy as a cadet in 1903. His family had no tradition of service in the armed forces. Rather it appears that it was the idea of his older brother by fifteen years, Charlie, that he should join the Navy. In the entrance examination he passed fifteenth out of more than 200 applicants.[5] By the time he became DNI he had been in the Navy more than thirty-five years. During that time he served with distinction in many hotspots around the world. In 1910 he joined the river gunboat HMS *Bramble* on the China station, patrolling the Yangtze River on the eve of the revolution that overthrew China's last Imperial Dynasty. He spent most of the First World War in the Mediterranean, at first in the Dardanelles as a lieutenant navigating officer aboard the light cruiser *Charybdis*. In 1917 he became staff officer to Commodore Rudolf Burmester, Chief of Staff of the Mediterranean Command, mostly based in Egypt. There he met T.E. Lawrence on more than one occasion, who he found 'practical, logical, hard-working and amazingly knowledgeable about Middle East archaeology, topography and Arabic roots', and that much 'rubbish had been written about Lawrence ...'[6] Godfrey also recalled meeting Lawrence on the *Euryalus*, walking up and down the quarter-deck with him one evening between Jidda and Port Sudan while for an hour 'he [Lawrence] explained how and why there were twenty ways of spelling and pronouncing the word Cairo'. At the time Godfrey was trying to complete a survey on inshore place names for combined operations with Arab forces as the existing charts were inadequate but he had to retain names the Arabs would understand.[7]

After the war, in which he had twice been mentioned in dispatches, and awarded the Legion of Honour by France, he was appointed to the staff of C-in-C Home Fleet Sir Charles Madden. In 1921 he joined the Plans Division and in December of that year married Margaret Hope. In the 1920s he had two spells at the Royal Naval College at Greenwich, the second as Deputy Director. In 1931 he was appointed to command the heavy cruiser *Kent* on the China station. Returning home, he had another spell at the Plans Division, this time as Deputy Director, before early in 1935 being given command of the 32,000-ton battlecruiser *Repulse*, which had just undergone a major refit and was destined to join the Mediterranean Fleet.

Although Godfrey had often worked around the fringes of the intelligence world, he freely admitted himself to be a novice and that he was indebted to Admiral Reginald 'Blinker' Hall, nicknamed 'Blinker' because of his rapidly blinking eyes, the likely cause of which was sarcoidosis or dry-eye and the blinking a sub-conscious attempt to keep his eyes lubricated.[8]

Hall had been DNI in the First World War and came to see Godfrey on 27 March, only weeks after he had taken over his new department, and 'offered me full access to his great store of knowledge and judgement in this strange commodity intelligence, about which I then knew hardly anything'. He supplied many varied 'contacts'. And it was through Hall that Godfrey met Sir Montagu Norman, the Governor of Barings; Olaf Hambro, Chairman of Hambros Bank; and the two Rothschilds, 'all of whom helped me in a variety of fruitful and helpful ways, particularly in the recruitment of wartime staff'.[9]

When Godfrey asked Hall about the type of man he should appoint as his personal assistant, the former DNI thought he should try a stockbroker, as he had done in Claud Serocold. Godfrey had little knowledge of the City and so, 'I consulted Serocold and Admiral Aubrey Hugh-Smith and talked again with Hall about filling this appointment in war.' They advised him to consult with Montagu Norman and Edward Peacock, of the merchant bank of Barings.[10]

Shortly after this, Norman telephoned Godfrey to advise him that he had found his man. They met at the Admiralty to discuss the matter. There Norman told him about Ian Fleming, a stockbroker who was not as successful as Serocold but with many attributes.

The young man Godfrey was to meet for the first time at the Carlton Grill that warm spring day of 1939, Ian Lancaster Fleming, was only four days past his thirty-first birthday. It would be hard to say that Fleming had had a distinguished career up to that time. Out of four Fleming boys, Ian was the black sheep of the family. Peter won all the academic prizes at Eton, and in 1926 went on to Christ Church, Oxford. Richard became head of house, and the youngest, the popular Michael, sailed through everything with no trouble and was loved by everyone. There was only a year between Peter, the eldest brother, and Ian, and although they were devoted to each other there was an early air of competition that in some ways remained with Ian all his life. Although outclassed at Eton by the superior intellect of Peter, Ian was a far better athlete. Peter on the other hand never felt superior to Ian, mainly because he was smaller physically.[11]

Ian broke his nose while playing football, which his mother felt gave him an air of 'battered nobility'.[12] Yet he was far more adept at non-team games and in 1924 at Eton he swept the board in the junior athletics. As a senior he was Victor Ludorum (champion of the games) two years running, a feat that had not happened within living memory at the time.

This was a fact he would use on the blurb of *Casino Royale* more than twenty-five years later and again citing the superiority of his brother, 'he was educated at Eton, where he was Victor Ludorum two years in succession, a distinction only once equalled – presumably, he suggests, by another second son trying to compensate for a brilliant elder brother'.[13] However, on the whole Ian hated Eton, and he had his fictional hero James Bond expelled from the school 'after trouble with one of the boys' maids'. This was in *The Times* obituary for Commander James Bond in *You Only Live Twice*.[14]

His mother, Evelyn, was the first to call him the black sheep of the family. Ian's poor academic performance at Eton made her force him into the Army class, considered as the place for dunces, where they could prepare for Sandhurst Royal Military College. However, he was soon in trouble with motor cars and girls, both of which were banned in term-time. He shared a Morris two-seater known as William with his brother Peter, who by that time was at Christ Church, Oxford.[15]

He was removed from Eton by his mother shortly after he had won his second Victor Ludorum and to make sure he got into Sandhurst she sent him to a special crammer college, run by Colonel William Trevor; he was there only three months. He passed the Sandhurst entrance exam eleventh out of 120 candidates. Trevor wrote to Evelyn pleased with Ian's achievement and felt he should make a good soldier, 'provided always that the Ladies don't ruin him'.[16]

The life at Sandhurst, with its strong code of discipline, was not for Ian. He did not take the military life seriously and one of his reports advised that he needed to 'make the best of what is, to him, a bad job and settle down'.[17] During a night out in London at the 43 Club in Soho he contracted gonorrhoea from a hostess. On 1 September 1927, at his mother's insistence he resigned from Sandhurst. Evelyn felt that she and the family had been disgraced by Ian, and she thought about sending him to Australia with a one-way ticket. However, she did not wash her hands of him and instead sent him to the Villa Tennerhof in Kitzbühel, Austria, for further education. Peter had gone there in the summer of 1927 to improve his German; he disliked Austria and wrote: 'I simply loathe this place.'[18] The school was run by Ernan Forbes Dennis, a friend of Evelyn who was a former British diplomat and spy, assisted by his wife the author Phyllis Bottome. Forbes Dennis later recalled of Ian's arrival: 'all he could do successfully was to make a nuisance of himself. For he was a rebel like most second sons.'[19] Here the pupils were treated more like guests and there were few rules, which suited Ian.

Yet Ernan and Phyllis got Ian to buckle down and work. Phyllis in particular encouraged him to write some short stories. For his education, they set the main goal as the Foreign Office examination, for which competition was fierce, with most places being taken by Oxford and Cambridge students. The course he undertook with Ernan was much wider than any he could have acquired at a university. They instilled a love of books in him, and not just for reading but as an object in their own right, for he would become a keen collector. All these influences would lead him to make a living with his pen. Ian wrote in his book *Thrilling Cities* about his time in Kitzbühel:

I remember, in those days before the war, reading, thanks to the encouragement of the Forbes Dennises, the works of Kafka, Musil, the Zweigs, Arthur Schnitzler, Werfel, Rilke, von Hofmannsthal, and of those bizarre psychologists Weininger and Groddeck – let alone the writings of Adler and Freud – and buying first editions (I used to collect them) illustrated by Kokoschka and Kubin.[20]

Ian also found the freedom at Kitzbühel to explore the company of young women without his family breathing down his neck. One of his fellow pupils admired the effect he had on the female sex, calling him 'irresistible to women'.[21]

By now an old Standard Tourer he got while at Eton had replaced William the Morris. About this time he borrowed a three-litre Bugatti in which he exceeded 100mph on the open road for the first time. Ian would instil in his hero James Bond an equal love of cars, starting in *Casino Royale* where he describes his car as 'his only personal hobby'. It was a battleship-grey 4.5-litre Blower Bentley 'with the supercharger by Amherst Villiers'.[22]

The old Standard made it to Austria. Ralph Arnold, another pupil who would also become a novelist, remembered riding in the Standard with Ian, following a large lorry loaded with machinery up a narrow mountain road. Ian became impatient behind the slow-moving vehicle and began to invent a story of agents in the lorry being chased by gangsters. He explained to prevent their capture one would, 'Climb out on the back of the lorry and slice through the ropes. Just think what would happen to us now if those ropes went and that machinery came crashing down. We'd all be smashed to smithereens.'[23]

A similar scene would be used in *Moonraker*. When Sir Hugo Drax comes across a Bowater lorry carrying huge rolls of paper, his henchman Willy Krebs, who had served with him in the 150th Panzer Brigade, leaps from the Mercedes Drax is driving onto the lorry, cutting the ropes that go hurtling down Charing Hill and cause the chasing Bentley of James Bond to crash.[24]

The Standard was soon wrecked in a collision with a train at a level crossing. Fleming had been returning from Munich one dusk and a field of tall corn had obscured the railway track. Neither train driver nor Ian saw each other until it was too late. The train sliced off the front of the Standard, engine and all, depositing it 50 yards down the track. Ian was unhurt but badly shaken.

In another adventure he courted death by skiing in a known avalanche zone. He was buried to his shoulders but escaped with only minor injuries; a few bruises and a twisted ankle.[25] This was the likely source of the scene in *On Her Majesty's Secret Service* in which an avalanche misses Bond by feet. 'The ground shook violently under Bond's skis and the swelling rumble came down to him like the noise of express trains roaring through a hundred tunnels.'[26]

After a year at the Villa Tennerhof, Ian was sent to Munich to become a day student at the university while boarding with a German family. By the middle of 1929 he was back at Kitzbühel, and Ernan felt he would soon be ready for the Foreign Office exam, but first he was sent to Geneva to improve his French. In the Swiss city Ian acquired a black Buick two-seater sports car and a fiancée – Monique Panchaud de Bottomes, a slim, dark-haired beauty who lived near Lake Geneva. Back in London for Christmas, he found his mother hopeful he would become a diplomat. She even agreed to meet his Swiss girlfriend.

In September 1931 Ian sat the ten-day written Foreign Office examination. There were only three places available and an agonising four-week wait for the results. He came twenty-fifth, and got the lowest marks for his English essay – 20 out of 100.[27]

It was another disappointment for Ian, even worse than Eton or Sandhurst. His mother sent Monique back to Geneva in tears, blaming her as a distraction in Ian's career. It was through Evelyn that he obtained a trial post at Reuters, the news agency, for six months, and he started work there in October 1931. He had no journalistic experience but it was a job that suited him. He first worked in the news room but got out to cover motor racing events at Brooklands, the oval banked racing circuit.

Fleming was seen as being 'accurate, painstaking, and methodical' in his work by Bernard Rickatson-Hatt, the editor-in-chief. In July 1932 he was sent to Munich on his first assignment, a plumb job for Ian, to report on the Alpine motor trials.[28]

Even better, he was to navigate for the rally driver Donald Healey, who had won the Monte Carlo Rally the year before. He came from Perranporth in Cornwall and would later build the Austin Healey sports cars. For the Alpine trials he would drive a 4.5-litre Invicta with Ian on board; it would mean good publicity for Healey. Rickatson-Hatt, the monocle-wearing former Coldstream Guards officer, had a soft spot for Ian, knowing the jaunt would give him the opportunity to see Monique. The Alpine trial that year ran through Germany, Italy, Switzerland, France and Austria over a distance of 1,580 miles, much of it across mountain roads. Healey and Ian first had to drive the 700 miles to Munich, crossing the English Channel on the car ferry SS *Forde*. It took them two days to get to the capital of Bavaria.[29]

The rally started at 0400 on the morning of 28 July in the pouring rain, which suited Healey's driving style. For a week he led, winning the Coupe des Glaciers for completing the event without penalty points, and setting a new record for the ascent of the Stelvio Pass between Merano and St Moritz.[30]

Back in his beloved Alps, Ian was thrilled by international motor racing, pitting themselves against the likes of Mercedes Benz, Alfa Romeo, Lancia and Bugatti. It was a new, exciting world. The rally finished in San Remo on the Mediterranean coast. Straight away Ian sent in his copy to Reuters, and soon he was ensconced in the arms of Monique.

After a complaint from the *Telegraph* that Reuters were merely promoting British cars, Rickatson-Hatt took Ian to task, demanding an explanation. Ian explained in a five-page letter that the British victory had been complete as he had reported. Indeed, a team of three Talbot 105s won the Coupe des Alpes, the first time a British team had won it in eighteen years. Rickatson-Hatt accepted Ian's explanation, citing that he had only questioned his view as a piece of useful criticism.[31] Donald Healey would become another of Ian's long-term friends and after the war they would often meet on one of the *Queens* crossing the Atlantic, discuss cars and recall the rally they had taken part in.[32]

Then in 1933 Ian was sent to cover the trial of six British engineers in Moscow who were accused of espionage and sabotage. They worked for the Vickers Electrical Company installing and supplying heavy electrical machinery. Vickers was one of the few favoured foreign firms working in the Soviet Union.

He flew out from Croydon airport on the morning of 6 April on a Lufthansa flight to Berlin, and from there he took a train to Moscow. At around 1000 on 8 April the train pulled into Moscow's Belorussky station.[33]

Robin Kinkead, Reuters bureau chief, an American, met Ian at the station. Shaking hands, he told him he was booked into the National Hotel and that it was 'not the Ritz, but it's better than anywhere else in Moscow. At least they've got a bar, and you sometimes get hot water.' Kinkead then whisked him off to his hotel in a hired Lincoln. The streets of Moscow were drab, the shops empty, the trams overcrowded, the people scruffy. Ian felt overdressed in his check suit and explained to Kinkead that he had got it at a 'fifty shilling tailors' and had never had the nerve to wear it but, 'Somehow I thought I might get away with it out here.' Kinkead thought that a fine joke and added that 'everyone thinks that you English always wear check suits'.[34]

Through the seven days of the trial Ian gained much first-hand experience of the communist state at work, which would fuel his later fiction. At Reuters he became a good reporter and it was there that he learned how to write fast and precisely.[35] On 23 April he left the Soviet Union and on his return to London he was asked to appear at the Foreign Office to report his views on the Soviet Union to some mysterious unnamed officials. It was likely to have been his first contact with the Secret Intelligence Service. First though he had to deal with a huge tapeworm he had picked up in Moscow, which he attributed to bad Beluga caviar, which left him unable to work for three days. He nicknamed the tapeworm his Loch Ness Monster.[36]

Reuters were pleased with his work and offered him the plumb job of 'Far-Eastern Correspondent' working out of Shanghai. He was excited to go, even though the salary at £800 a year was not good given his lifestyle. Sir Roderick Jones, the head of Reuters, wanted him to go to Berlin first to see how a foreign office was run and put his good German to use. He might even be able to obtain an interview with Hitler. However, Ian turned the package down as he had been offered a job in a merchant bank. His ageing grandfather, Robert Fleming, was behind it, and he made plain that no special provision was to be made for Ian or his brothers in his will. Ian regretted his move into banking and later called it a 'beastly idea giving up all the fun of life for money', but that he had been 'pretty well pushed into it from all sides'.[37]

Thus began Fleming's six years as a merchant banker and then as a stockbroker. Unlike journalism, he had no real natural aptitude in the financial world, but still made a great deal of money from it. He spent it as fast as he could make it, on golf, gambling and women. He became known as a 'glamour boy' in the party set.[38] As one fellow stockbroker Hugh Vivian-Smith said of his efforts in that field: 'As a stockbroker, old Ian really must have been among the world's worst.'[39]

In 1939 he returned to Moscow, this time to cover a government trade mission for *The Times* and taking leave from his stockbroking firm. He found the Russian capital a depressing city. Sefton Delmer, covering the same event for another paper, thought Fleming was there not only for a newspaper but the government too, given Ian's thinly veiled comments about secret agents. On the train journey home, Soviet customs at the border went through Ian's luggage with a fine-tooth comb. They took particular interest in some Russian contraceptives Ian had.[40]

The Moscow talks produced little of benefit for Britain, although Ian produced three articles for *The Times,* and when back in London another two. He then wrote a longer treatise on the Soviet armed forces, concluding that the vast reserves of manpower might in any conflict with the Axis powers be of the 'greatest strategic value to the Allies'. However, *The Times* refused to publish it, not favouring his analysis. Instead he sent it to Philip Nichols, a friend of his at the Foreign Office. Later in early May he was interviewed by Lawrence Collier of the Northern Office about his experiences in the Soviet Union.[41]

★★★

As the taxi dropped Fleming off at the Carlton Hotel, he had little idea what the meeting might be about. He did not even know what Admiral Godfrey looked like, and Henri Mihaz, the grill room maître, had to show him to the table. There was an elderly man with a neatly trimmed white beard sitting at the table as well, Admiral Aubrey Hugh-Smith, who Ian knew. He was the brother of Lance Hugh-Smith, the senior partner where Ian worked at the stockbrokers Rowe and Pitman. It was Aubrey who introduced Fleming to their host, who thanked Ian for coming and began to order lunch.[42]

As a reserve subaltern in the Black Watch with the clouds of war gathering, Fleming no doubt found it strange sharing a table with a brace of admirals. Neither of the old sea dogs explained exactly the purpose of the meeting. The tables in the Carlton Grill were well spaced, so there was little chance of being overheard.

During the course of the meal, Godfrey told Fleming that he might like to be ready for a special post in the event of war. Ian was keen to help in any way he could.

The New Zealand High Commission now stands on the site of the Carlton Hotel. During the Blitz in 1940 it was hit by German bombs and one of the great landmarks of London was lost.

A few days after the meeting Ian received a letter from the Secretary of the Admiralty, Norman Macleod, who thanked him for the 'offer of your services' and that the Admiralty 'would probably desire to avail themselves of your offer should hostilities break out'. The letter assured him that he would be 'earmarked for service under the Admiralty in the event of emergency'.[43] A short time after the letter reached Fleming, Godfrey telephoned to arrange a meeting at his offices. He wanted him to start work on a part-time basis. This suited Ian well enough and he spent most weekday afternoons in July visiting the Admiralty after lunch.

2

NAVAL INTELLIGENCE DIVISION, 1912–39

The Naval Intelligence Division Ian Fleming started visiting in July 1939 was situated at the Admiralty buildings along the Mall close to Captain Cook's statue. To enter, he would have to show his pass to the retired sergeant of the Royal Marines who manned a small desk at the quadrangle leading off to the bowels of the building. He would follow the corridor on the left, which brought him to a black door with the number 39 on it in white numerals. The organisation he was about to join was not yet 30 years old and had reached its zenith of achievement so far in 1917.

The weather in London in January 1917 had been miserable, cold and unsettled. The war entering the fourth year seemed endless, grinding on in a bloody stalemate. It was consuming men at an alarming rate. Yet still the prospect of German unrestricted submarine warfare and the horrors of Third Ypres, better known as Passchendaele, lay ahead. Why then was a single event in Room 40 of the Admiralty building at Whitehall London, on the morning of Wednesday, 17 January, to mark a turning point in the war?

At 1030 that morning Nigel de Grey, a linguist and cryptographer working in Room 40, burst into the office of the Director of Naval Intelligence, Captain William Reginald 'Blinker' Hall, with the news.

'Do you want to bring America into the war sir?'

Hall was working with his assistant Claud Serocold on a pile of signals and correspondence needing his attention. Serocold was by profession a stockbroker like Ian Fleming, who came after him to fulfil a similar role at Naval Intelligence. In reply to de Grey's interruption Hall said, 'Yes my boy. Why?'

De Grey could hardly contain his excitement. 'I have got something here which – well; it is a rather astonishing message which might do the trick if we could use it. It isn't very clear, I'm afraid, but I'm sure I've got most of the important points right. It's from the German Foreign Office to Bernstorff.'[1]

Johann Heinrich Count von Bernstorff was the German Ambassador in Washington. The telegram de Grey had brought to Hall had been sent from Berlin via Sweden and Argentina to Washington and on to Mexico. This route had been uncovered by Room 40 in May 1916 and was known as the 'Swedish roundabout'.[2] De Grey and Dilly Knox had managed to decipher enough of the message to reveal its importance.

It was from the German foreign secretary Arthur Zimmermann, who proposed that Germany should ally with Mexico and conduct a war against the United States. When the contents of the telegram were revealed to the US public the clamour for war grew to a crescendo. It remains the single most famous signal decoded by British Intelligence in either war and would make 'Blinker' Hall a national hero. It was his father, Captain W.H. Hall, forty years before, who laid the foundations of the NID.

In the latter half of the nineteenth century Britain had come close to war with Russia twice and had no real intelligence about the enemy. In 1882 the Foreign Intelligence Committee (FIC) was formed as part of the Admiralty, yet the new formation had a tiny staff under Hall senior consisting of four and one overseas naval attaché.[3]

After another war scare, FIC was expanded into a larger department to cover intelligence and plans for mobilisation of the fleet. Lord Charles Beresford, known in the service as 'Charlie B', a junior naval lord at the time, had written a report on FIC recommending it should be expanded and developed by Hall, who was appointed to lead the enlarged NID. When Hall left to return to sea duties in 1889, NID had become a vital part of the Admiralty.

Ten years later responsibility for mobilisation was transferred to a new division, while NID in 1912 became part of the new Naval War Staff. Captain Henry Oliver (later Rear Admiral) was appointed DNI in September 1913, by which time the establishment of NID amounted to twenty-three staff. When Blinker Hall took over in December 1914 his staff consisted of twenty-nine, by the war's end this had ballooned to 360 men and women, and into not just a naval department but a worldwide organisation.[4]

Less than twenty-four hours after Britain declared war on Germany in the early hours of 5 August 1914, the cable ship *Telconia* out in the North Sea cut five cables linking the port of Emden with Spain, Africa and the Americas. The same day a Royal Navy cruiser cut two more German cables near the Azores. This forced the Germans to communicate by wireless with its overseas embassies and stations. Yet at the time many felt the newer technology of wireless telegraphy was secure.[5]

Franz von Papen was military attaché in Washington during the early years of the war and wrote of the effectiveness of the British actions. 'The German Embassy in Washington became completely ineffective. The Foreign Office in Berlin was so unprepared for war that they had not even reckoned with the possibility of cable communications being cut by the British …'[6]

With the loss of much of the cable systems, the increase in German overseas wireless traffic was huge, all being read by anyone who cared to listen. Thus the British Admiralty was overwhelmed by relayed messages sent from British naval stations, the Post Office and the Marconi Company. The war room at the Admiralty was swamped by thousands of telegrams littering rooms and not being recorded.[7] Captain Oliver was quick to address the problem. He brought in Sir Alfred Ewing, Director of Naval Education, who in turn recruited several of the Navy's language teachers. However, some of these were fairly quickly diverted to the War Office as the more pressing problem was the British Expeditionary Force coming under increasing pressure in Belgium and France. The Army needed all the help it could get in reading the huge volume of German Army wireless traffic; naval work was given a lower priority. Alastair Denniston, who became Ewing's deputy, was a German-language teacher. He observed that 'no time was lost in getting down to decipher'. In many cases the Germans were sending messages in plain language, so it was more a case of translation.[8] The poor use of ciphers by the German Army gave the British and French excellent knowledge of their movements leading to the First Battle of the Marne, which marked the defeat of the Schlieffen plan to knock France out of the war with one blow.[9] The two British cryptographic teams of the Admiralty and War Office worked together in teams to maintain a twenty-four-hour watch supplying the Army with accurate information, while the Navy got three lucky breaks in their own intelligence war at sea.

On 11 August, the Royal Australian Navy (RAN) captured the German steamship *Hobart* off Melbourne; her captain was even unaware war had been declared. The ship's documents were captured intact, including a copy of the Handelsverkehrbuch (HVB), the codes used by the German Admiralty, including those used to communicate with merchant ships. The RAN did not at first realise the importance of what they had and the information did not reach London until the end of October.[10]

In the Baltic on 23 August the Germans sent a small Flotilla into the Gulf of Finland to attack Russian shipping consisting of two light cruisers and three destroyers. Two days later the cruiser *Magdeburg*, at about 1230 ran aground in fog on the low lying Russian island of Odensholm near the lighthouse. Various efforts including a destroyer trying to pull off the *Magdeburg* failed to refloat the stricken ship.

The next day her Korvettenkapitän, Richard Habenicht, aware the cruiser had been spotted by the Soviets, ordered it to be blown up and all confidential documents destroyed. As the German destroyer *V26* was coming alongside to take off *Magdeburg*'s crew one of the charges went off prematurely and men began to abandon ship. *V26* stopped to fish these men out of the water but had to abandon the operation when Soviet ships arrived and opened fire. The *V26* escaped but some of *Magdeburg*'s crew were captured. The Soviets boarded the cruiser, which was still afloat, and found the captain's signal book, the Signalbuch der

Kaiserlichen Marine (SKM, Signal book of the Imperial Navy). The Soviets generously sent a dry copy to the British. Churchill, then at the Admiralty, received from 'our loyal allies' the 'priceless documents'.[11] Two days later, on the morning of 13 October, Blinker Hall was appointed DNI.

Four days later, the light cruiser HMS *Undaunted* was on patrol with four destroyers off the Dutch coast near the German border. North of the island of Texel they ran into four German destroyers steaming south to lay mines. The Germans were heavily outgunned and soon sent to the bottom. The senior officer on *S-119*, as per standing orders, dumped all the confidential documents overboard in a lead-lined chest as his ship was sinking. In November, a British trawler fishing off Texel dragged up the chest in her nets; this was sent to Room 40 and became known by NI staff as the 'Miraculous draught of fishes'.[12] In the chest was found a copy of the Verkehrsbuch (VB), a specialist codebook for communicating with warships and overseas naval attachés. Thus within five months of the outbreak of war Room 40 had copies of the German Navy's most important codes.

During the battles on the Western Front in 1914 NI had been kept informed about the success of breaking German Army ciphers, yet the Navy revealed nothing about their good fortune to the Army code breakers in MI1 (b). It was felt the capture of the SKM was too important to be revealed. In 1915 the close working relationship between the War Office and the Admiralty began to break down, and the two intelligence services went their own ways.[13]

With all their staff returning to the Admiralty, a bigger room was needed. A quiet secure place for the code breakers to work was found in the Old Admiralty Buildings and the section was moved into Room 40 (OB), which gave Ewing's team its home and its name.[14]

One drawback of Room 40 was that its activities were kept so secret that very few officers even within the Admiralty or the Fleets were aware of its existence.

Even though it knew more about the German Fleet's intentions than any other department, it was not allowed to communicate directly with operational commanders. Instead it passed on decrypted text to a handful of officers of the Operations Division, who were not experts in intelligence or signals traffic of the German Navy. They, as Patrick Beesly wrote, 'failed lamentably to make the best use of this priceless information with which they had been presented'.[15]

Only three months after Blinker Hall had been appointed DNI he had put into motion a plan to remove Turkey as an ally of Germany. Churchill and Admiral of the Fleet, the First Sea Lord John (Jacky) Fisher, were kept informed. Sir Maurice Hankey, a former intelligence officer of the Mediterranean Fleet who knew the Middle East well, had learned through Gerald Fitzmaurice of the British Embassy in Istanbul that Turkish public opinion was against the alliance with Germany. Here lay an opportunity to influence the Turks, coupled with bribery to oil the wheels, and make the break. On 4 March 1915 Hankey wrote in his diary: 'I saw Captain Hall, Admiralty War Staff, who said the negotiation had been opened to bribe the Turks to oust the Germans, as I had proposed earlier.'[16]

Hall's agents began secret negotiations with the Turkish Minister of the Interior, Talaat Pasha, to allow the Fleet free passage through the Dardanelles. Hall instructed them to offer £3 million and to go to £4 million if required. The stakes were raised by asking the Turks to hand over the German battlecruiser *Goeben*, which had been in Turkish waters since the outbreak of war. The Turks got cold feet when the Royal Navy started bombarding the forts at the mouth of the Dardanelles in mid-February. They also learned the British Foreign Office had offered the Soviets Istanbul. On 5 March, Hall put on the squeeze, reducing what was called a 'subsidy' to £500,000. Yet he was still prepared to go to £4 million provided agreement was reached at a meeting scheduled to take place at Dedeagach, Bulgaria, on 15 March.

A German message intercepted two days before the meeting by Room 40 sealed the fate of thousands of men and Hall's plan to pass through the straits in peace, resulting in the attack on the Dardanelles. It was from Admiral Georg von Muller, Chief of the Imperial Naval Staff, to Admiral Guido von Usedom in charge of the defences of the Dardanelles, and reported that: 'Everything conceivable is being done to arrange the supply of ammunition. And that it is under serious consideration to send submarines to the area.'[17]

Hall personally took the message to Fisher, who he found in Churchill's room. Both men became excited over the Turks' apparent lack of ammunition. Fisher, who had disliked the scheme to force the straits from the start, shouted: 'By God, I'll go through tomorrow, we shall probably lose six ships but I'm going through.' Churchill told Fisher to draft the orders.[18] The Allied Fleet attacked the Dardanelles narrows on 8 March 1915 but failed to break through.

As Hall was about to leave, Churchill asked him how the negotiations were going. When the amount of the possible bribe to be offered was revealed, both Churchill and Fisher were amazed. Churchill asked, 'who authorised this?' Hall admitted it was him, but defended his actions, believing a peaceful passage would be worth every penny. He was instructed to withdraw the offer, and later wrote this 'rendered any future discussions useless but also destroyed the belief in Turkish minds of our good faith'. Could it have worked? It is doubtful but it should have been tried. Bribery was used effectively in the Second World War, in particular to help keep Spain neutral.[19] NID signals intelligence was only part of the department's work. A large body of agents and informants was built up around the world particularly in the United States, Ireland and the Iberian Peninsula.

The naval attaché in Washington, Captain Guy Gaunt, Hall's main agent in North America, recruited a network of German-speaking Czechs and Slovaks with a strong anti-German bias. Emanuel Viktor Voska became Gaunt's principal leader of the group; he had been expelled from Bohemia as a political agitator and emigrated to the USA. Voska's group succeeded in infiltrating the German Embassy in Washington, the consulate in New York, as well as the offices of leading German commercial interests in the country. At its height Voska's network had eighty agents. Among the best placements were Bernstorff's chauffeur and his wife's maid. Also, the chief clerk in the Austrian Embassy was a Voska man.[20]

Via Gaunt, Voska supplied NID with information about repeated German violations of US neutrality. By mid-1915 they had found out that couriers travelling with neutral passports were carrying documents for the Germans and Austrians. In the last week of August, John Archibald sailed on *Rotterdam*. He was taken off the ship when it docked at Ramsgate and was found to be carrying 110 documents for the Austrian Embassy. Hall found further evidence of disruptive actions designed to affect the US economy. The Foreign Office was reluctant to reveal Hall's findings, feeling this type of thing was not quite 'cricket'. Hall had no such qualms: he was ready to use any and every weapon he could against Germany. He showed some of the documents to Edward Bell of the US Embassy in London, who passed the information on to Leland Harrison of the State Department.[21]

NI was instrumental in thwarting German attempts to aid an armed uprising in Ireland. The American Fenian leaders John Devoy and Daniel Cohalan had approached the Germans for support early in 1915. However, German Intelligence had concluded support in Ireland for an uprising was weak. Hall, on the other hand, was wary of the Irish Nationalists, Sinn Féin, who were known to have links to Germany. With his friend at Special Branch, Basil Thomson, they hatched a scheme to try and infiltrate the Nationalists and explore the possibility of German submarine 'beds' off the west coast of Ireland. There were also the more realistic activities of Sir Roger Casement to be explored. He had returned to Ireland in 1913 to join the Irish National Volunteers. Through Room 40 decrypts it was concluded he was trying to bring a consignment of arms to Ireland.[22]

The 581-ton steam yacht *Sayonara* was chartered from an American millionaire. A hand-picked naval crew of fifty were schooled in slang to pass off as American sailors. They were commanded by Lieutenant F.M. Simon of the Royal Naval Volunteer Reserve (RNVR), who had learned to mimic Americans during his service on the Cunard Line. The owner was played by Major Wilfred Howell, a soldier of fortune who had been wounded in the Boer War. His character was Colonel McBride, a rich pro-German American of Irish descent from Los Angeles, dressed to appear Teutonic with his upturned Kaiser-like moustache, Homburg hat and German accent. *Sayonara* sailed from Southampton on 15 December 1914. However, neither the Irish authorities nor the admiral commanding at Queenstown, now called Cobh, on the south coast of Ireland were aware of the yacht's mission, which was to gain information about German subversion and Sinn Féin activities and, more important, to intercept Roger Casement. *Sayonara* and her eccentric crew soon aroused suspicion with the naval patrols in the area. Captain F. Le Mesurier of HMS *Cornwallis* had the yacht and crew placed under arrest in Westport harbour when a concealed radio was found on board during a search. Hall had to intervene personally to get the yacht released. This may have convinced the Irish rebels of the authenticity of the yacht but in reality the mission achieved little, although Hall later insisted the cruise had been worthwhile in regard to the Easter Rising.[23] Christopher Andrew, in his history, felt there was little 'justification, that intelligence obtained by *Sayonara* had proved very valuable during the Easter Rising of 1916'. He added that Hall was overly fond of cloak and dagger capers.[24]

Hall gained far more reliable intelligence from Room 40 decrypted telegrams exchanged between the German Foreign Ministry and its Washington Embassy on Irish matters. He was able to follow Casement's attempts to obtain German support for an Irish uprising. NID gained advance warning that the Germans would land arms in Ireland in the spring of 1916, and that Casement would follow by U-boat. On 9 April the *Libau*, manned by a crew from the Kriegsmarine, disguised as the Norwegian steamer *Aud,* left Lubeck, a major port of the River Trave, with a cargo of 20,000 rifles. They were Soviet Mausers captured after the German victory at Tannenberg in 1914, plus ten machine guns and a million rounds of ammunition. Room 40 intercepted a German signal sent from the transmitting station at Nauen in Brandenburg on 15 April questioning the ship's position.[25]

Aud was intercepted by HMS *Bluebell* on 21 April and ordered to proceed to Queenstown. The next day, as the ship neared the port, the crew scuttled her. On 12 April, Casement and two companions sailed from Wilhelmshaven on *U-20*; however, the boat's rudder was damaged and she returned to port. The Casement party were transferred to *U-19*, which sailed three days later. Again signals between the U-boat and Submarine Command were intercepted. Casement landed at Tralee Bay on Good Friday and was arrested within hours of coming ashore.[26]

The Irish authorities were kept ignorant of the intelligence, and the Royal Irish Constabulary (RIC) was not informed of the likely impending rebellion. The police force was fully Irish and Basil Thomson felt they were not to be trusted with confidential information. Also, the

Army was kept largely in the dark. Thus the Easter Monday uprising of 24 April was a surprise to the RIC and the Army, while the Navy was fully aware.

Casement was taken to London and interrogated by Hall and Thomson. He asked them to appeal in his name to call off the Irish Rising. Hall refused and Casement wrote that Hall said: 'It is better that a cankering sore like this should be cut out.'[27] It is unlikely such an appeal would have dissuaded the Irish Republican Brotherhood leadership from going ahead. Casement said his trip to Ireland by submarine was in fact an attempt to stop the rebellion; rather an odd way to arrive in a U-boat if that was the case. He was sent to trial at the Old Bailey, where he was convicted and sentenced to death. Influential people in Britain, Ireland and the United States petitioned for the sentence to be reduced to life in prison. Even the United States Senate asked the British government for clemency, citing Casement's previous good works in the field of human rights.

However, Herbert Asquith, prime minister at the time, although worried about the anti-British feelings in the United States over the case, felt he could not get involved, for here was a man who had:

> visited Irish prisoners in German camps and tried to seduce them to take up arms against Great Britain – their own country. When they refused, the Germans removed them to the worst places in their Empire and, as a result, some of them died. Then, Casement came to Ireland in a German submarine, accompanied by a ship loaded with guns. In all good conscience to my country and to my responsibilities I cannot interfere.[28] [Casement was hanged at Pentonville Prison on 3 August 1916.]

Hall's weakness for covert operations was given more fulfilment in Spain. Early in the war Mansfield Cumming, head of the SIS, which had been given the vital role of monitoring U-boat movements around the Iberian Peninsula, left control of the secret service in Spain to NI. Hall recreated the cruise of *Sayonara* to better effect in Spanish waters in 1915 by sending the yacht *Vergemere* with Sir Hercules Langrishe, an Irish baronet from Kilkenny, attractive and gregarious and a skilled sailor, to play the role of owner. The C-in-C Portsmouth helped him assemble a naval crew. While *Vergemere* was loaded with crates of booze and Champagne, Langrishe was to appear to be an eccentric British gentleman. Lavish parties were given on board to convince all watchers and those invited that there were no shortages at home, and Hall instructed him to charm the ladies.[29]

It did not take Langrishe long to identify a German steamer playing the same game. From the extensive information collected, Hall was convinced he needed to maintain the yacht patrols, to aid the network of agents under the control of his assistant, Lord Herschell, who had personal links to the Spanish royal family. Command in the field was left to Major, later Lieutenant Colonel, Charles Julian Thoroton, who became known as 'Charles the Bold'. He was a career Royal Marine who had arrived in Gibraltar in 1913 to take up his post as senior Naval Intelligence Officer for the area. He built up a network that he divided into three groups: 'naturals', British nationals living in Spain; 'sympathisers', Spaniards supporting the Allies; and 'professionals', put mainly into ports to watch and gain information on shipping.[30]

Thoroton's most effective recruit was Juan March, who he liked to call 'The Pirate'. He was a Majorcan smuggler who had an income of £10,000 a year and a huge network of informants, some of them corrupt officials, all of which he enlisted as submarine watchers. The Germans made several attempts to induce March to work for them. After offers of money failed, they tried seduction. Basil Thomson wrote in his diary in June 1916:

> The Germans tried a lady from Hamburg, who first would and then would not, though he offered her 30,000 pesetas. This infuriated him [Juan March]. Thoroton had told him she was a spy. He said he did not care what she was. He meant to have her. Thoroton became nervous, but early this month he (the smuggler) returned triumphant from Madrid with a scratch across his nose inflicted by the lady, who resented having received only 1,000 pesetas. Now the smuggler is in harness again.[31]

March became a millionaire, and although he supported Franco and the Nationalists in the Civil War, he again supported Britain in the

Second World War, becoming one of Alan Hillgarth's, the naval attaché at Madrid, main agents during that conflict. He was interviewed by Admiral Godfrey in September 1939 when he visited NID.

In 1917 German Intelligence used the actress Beatrice von Brunner in an attempt to compromise Thoroton sexually, or to kill him, when he was in Paris, as his network was so effective against the U-boat campaign. It appears that while she was trying to poison him, he was attempting to turn her to work for the Allies. The wily Thoroton avoided the poison chalice, while Beatrice had to drink a small amount to avoid suspicion, becoming ill in the process.[32]

The prolific author Alfred Woodley Mason, perhaps best known for his novels *The Four Feathers* (1902) and *Fire over England* (1936), was one of Thoroton's agents. He served in the Manchester Regiment as a captain in 1914 but was transferred to the reserve list in 1915 when it was found he had lied about his age; he was 49 at the time. Hall, who knew Mason well, had him transferred to the Royal Marine Light Infantry and sent to Spain. He took up the role first played by Langrishe, cruising around the Spanish ports, the Balearics and Morocco, first in *Vergemere* and later in Lord Abinger's yacht, *St George*. Hall called him his 'star turn'; his flamboyant style did not fool the Germans for long, but he provided excellent cover for more covert operations conducted by Charles the Bold.[33]

Mason would claim after he left Spain in January 1917 that NI had frustrated 'German shipping policy' and intelligence on U-boat movements, 'on several occasions' saving potential targets from destruction. He cited, 'two English steamers and one Italian about to sail from Barcelona during the month, January 1917, were prevented because we had precise and definite information that submarines had instructions to sink these particular boats and were waiting for them'.[34] Thoroton wrote of Mason in a report: 'I feel I cannot let this opportunity pass without calling attention to the very excellent work which Captain Mason has performed.'[35]

Eddie Bell, of the American Embassy in London, who had worked closely with Hall, observed how effective NI had been on the Iberian Peninsula:

In Spain it became immensely powerful and used frequently to give information to the Spanish Government of disaffection and proposed strikes in Spain itself, and when a few months ago Admiral Hall started to cut down his organisation after the armistice the Spanish Government actually requested him not to do so on the grounds his organisation was to them a far more reliable source of information of what was going on in the country than their own police and civil authorities.[36]

Perhaps more important for Britain was Thoroton's legacy that lived on even after his death in 1939 through his surviving intelligence network in Spain, Portugal and Morocco, which was to prove of immense value to Ian Fleming and NI in the Second World War.

The academic Ewing controlled Room 40 for the first two years of its existence. He built it up from scratch, recruiting people mostly with a similar background to him, although Hall had some input. Yet for all his good work Ewing never seemed to comprehend the great weakness of his section: that it was not an integral part of NID. W.F. Clarke, one of the senior cryptanalysts, was exasperated by Ewing's management of Room 40, casting doubt on whether he had ever contributed anything important to its success, and later wrote that: 'Ewing never really understood the problems and wasted more of the valuable time on his subordinates than can be imagined.'[37]

By the summer of 1915, Hall began raising concerns over lack of co-ordination. Admiral Henry Oliver, as Chief of Staff, who had great respect for Ewing, tried to arbitrate between them and put in place a compromise, whereby Ewing retained control of Room 40, but Hall had direct access to it.

Yet Hall already had his man in Room 40, Commander Herbert Hope, whose job was to analyse the German intercepts and provide the naval experience required for correct interpretation that the largely civilian cryptographers lacked.

In effect, Hope took over Room 40. Clarke saw Hope and Paymaster-Commander Charles Rotter as the real power in the section, while most of his colleagues were indifferent to Ewing. Nigel de

Grey, who brought Hall the Zimmermann telegram, thought Ewing a 'chatterbox'.[38]

In May 1916, Ewing was offered the post of principal at his old university of Edinburgh, which he reluctantly turned down on the grounds his secret war work was too important. In the summer the offer was made again and, receiving only lukewarm support from the Admiralty to stay on, he accepted. He kept his position as Director of Naval Education and was retained as an advisor to Room 40, but Hall became responsible for running the section. In May 1917, Ewing left the Admiralty altogether. Room 40 was then formally incorporated into NID as section 25 of the department, I.D.25.[39]

Penelope Fitzgerald was Alfred Dillwyn Knox's niece. He was the epitome of the absent-minded professor, the most able if eccentric of Room 40's cryptographers. Penelope wrote of Hall's impact on Room 40:

Under his hypnotic blue gaze and furious energy, the work was reorganized and redivided, and the modest 50 personnel, keeping two-man watches round the clock, was greatly increased. Hall fore-saw the complications that were to come, and imperiously told the Treasury that he must have more money for more code breakers.[40]

She went on to describe the location of I.D.25, reached:

through two arches in the Old Buildings. The basement acted as a kind of telegraph office. Intercepted messages coming in by land-line were printed out and sent up by pneumatic tube of the kind that can still be seen in some old-fashioned shops. In the enormous Room 40 itself, the shuttles rattled in to wire baskets at the rate of two thousand a day, with a sound like a maxim gun. 'Tubists' sorted them into their time groups and put those aside beginning SD (very urgent). The signals were still in the familiar code, but this was super-enciphered by rearranging the letters in vertical columns under a keyword. The key, which in 1914, had been changed once every three months, now (1917) changed every twenty-four hours. At midnight the watch on duty set to work frantically to find the new key. It was alleged that if they solved it they fell asleep again immediately, if not, they hung their heads in shame as the new watch came on. But Room 40 was only the central cell of the hive-like organization.

It was surrounded by rooms, which were all marked NO ADMITTANCE. RING BELL; but there were no bells. In the rooms were specialised units; directional, diplomatic, Baltic Traffic, the Card Index, on which every signal was registered and so forth. There was also an administration staff, though much smaller than in most departments, but no tea ladies, and no cleaners. Room 40 was never dusted until the war was won.[41]

By the end of the war Room 40, renamed I.D.25, had developed its full potential working closely with other departments, and so provided the blueprint for the Operational Intelligence Centre (OIC) of the Second World War, which was at the heart of winning the Battle of the Atlantic.

Blinker Hall saw use of the Zimmermann telegram in 1917 as 'a huge gamble' and later wrote: 'I know of no other incident in my experience as an intelligence officer, which better illustrates at once the difficulties of using to the best advantage such information as is obtained and the great and sometimes grave risks which have to be taken to bring about the desired end.'[42]

The telegram was sent on 19 January 1917 in coded form by Arthur Zimmermann, a civil servant in the German Foreign Office, to the German Ambassador in Mexico, Heinrich von Eckardt, in anticipation of the American response to Germany resuming unrestricted submarine warfare on 1 February. It read in its fully decoded form:

We intend to begin on the first of February unrestricted submarine warfare. We shall endeavour in spite of this to keep the United States of America neutral. In the event of this not succeeding, we make Mexico a proposal of alliance on the following basis: make war together, make peace together, generous financial support and an understanding on our part that Mexico is to reconquer the lost territory in Texas, New Mexico, and Arizona. This settlement in detail is left to you. You will inform the President of the above most secretly as soon as the outbreak of war with the United States of America is certain and add the suggestion that he should, on his own initiative, invite Japan to immediate adherence and at the same time mediate between Japan and ourselves. Please call the President's attention to the fact that the ruthless employment of our submarines now offers the prospect of compelling England in a few months to make peace.

Signed Zimmermann.[43]

Hall saw three main problems in using the telegram to influence the United States. First, by releasing the telegram it would reveal to the Germans that their codes were broken. Second, it would reveal interception of the Swedish roundabout. Third, the Americans might guess NI was reading their own diplomatic traffic.[44]

For more than two weeks he wrestled with this dilemma while the telegram remained secret, known only within the walls of Room 40. He hoped the United States might join the war without his intervention. When unrestricted submarine warfare began on 1 February, two days later President Woodrow Wilson broke off diplomatic relations with Germany but still hoped to avoid war. He had a deep revulsion of war, for he had seen its horrors first hand in the American Civil War. As a small boy he had helped tend Confederate wounded in his father's church in Augusta, Georgia, and witnessed the desolation the war brought to the southern states.

Colonel E.M. House, Wilson's advisor on foreign affairs, told the British naval attaché, Gaunt, a close friend, two hours before it was made official, of the President's decision. Gaunt telegrammed Hall straight away using their personal code based on naval slang. Hall had no choice now but to use the telegram, the question was how?[45]

On the morning of Monday, 5 February, Hall went to see Lord Hardinge, the permanent under-secretary at the Foreign Office, and showed him the Zimmermann telegram. Hall asked that Edward Thurston, the British Minister in Mexico, obtain a copy of the telegram as he was sure that the message that had arrived in Mexico City would be easier to decrypt fully, rather than the one they had intercepted routed via Washington. Five days later, Hall was informed by Thurston that he had obtained a copy from the Mexico City Post Office. By 19 February, Hall had the telegram; this now made it possible to show it to the Americans without arousing suspicion that American cables had been tapped. Within a few hours the American diplomat Eddie Bell was in Hall's office reading the telegram. His reaction, other than fury, was: 'Why not offer them Illinois and New York while they were about it.'

There then took place at the US Embassy a debate about how best to present this officially to the United States and who should do it.

Eventually the US Ambassador Dr Walter Page, Eddie Bell and Blinker Hall agreed the effect on President Wilson would be enhanced if Arthur Balfour, the British Foreign Minister, was to hand it officially to Page. This took place at the Foreign Office on 23 February. Balfour called the moment he handed it over 'the most dramatic of my life'.[46]

The Zimmermann telegram did not alone bring the United States into the war, Wilson was already edging reluctantly to that position, but it did largely scupper the powerful anti-intervention lobby efforts and made Room 40's contribution decisive.[47]

It was published in the United States on 1 March, yet there still remained a minority who called it a fake. The State Department telegraphed Page in London asking if it was possible that 'the British Government would permit you or someone in the Embassy to personally decode the original message which we secured from the telegraph office in Washington'. This meant the State Department could claim it had been supplied by their own people. Hall was happy to oblige. Page came to the Admiralty and there deciphered the German code. In fact, de Grey did it for him. By mistake he brought along the wrong decode book, but by that time he knew the thing by heart and 'bluffed the thing out'.[48]

It has been suggested that James Bond's code number 007 was based on the German diplomatic code used to send the Zimmermann telegram from Berlin to Washington, which was 0070. Ian Fleming would have been well aware of Hall's great success in the First World War. However, as we will see later, there are other claimants to the origins of the 007 number.[49]

In the final analysis Ramsay put it well in his biography of Hall, whose actions in the case always most importantly had to safeguard Room 40. 'Hall had almost single-handedly influenced the course of

history, averting the spectre of defeat and setting in place the development-
ments which led 19 months later to victory over Imperial Germany on
land and at sea.'[50]

Throughout the war, Hall's insistence on maximum security had
been fully vindicated. The Germans had never realised that for most of
the war Room 40 had been intercepting and decoding their signal traffic. Remarkably their successors would make the same mistake with
Enigma in the Second World War. It is a testament to all the staff at
NID and Room 40 that no one betrayed security.[51]

On 18 January 1919, Captain Hugh Sinclair, who had been one of
Blinker Hall's deputies, relieved him as DNI. Before the end of the
war plans were being drawn up to combine the activities of Room 40
and MI1 (b).

As the war had progressed, MI1 (b) handled cable traffic and Room
40 dealt with wireless messages, which were then passed on to the
Director of Military Intelligence (DMI) or to the DNI. The Foreign
Office only got its intelligence from these sources. This would not
be acceptable in peacetime; a new organisation was required to serve
the Navy, other military and government. On 1 November 1919, the
Government Code & Cipher School (GC & CS) was created; it is now
better known for its code breaking in the Second World War, by that
time being located at Bletchley Park.[52]

The NID was quickly, like much of the sea-going fleet, drastically
reduced after the war. Many of its best people were hived off into
SIS or to GC & CS. In April 1919, Charles Thoroton left the Royal
Marines at his own request. He straight away began work for the
Federation of British Industries in Madrid, a front for a skeleton SIS
organisation on the Iberian Peninsula. In later life he would help his
friend Admiral Hall write his memoirs, which were never published.
In 1923, after the death of Mansfield Cumming, Hugh Sinclair was
appointed Director of SIS. By this time NID had gone into a steady
decline, and by 1924 its establishment numbered only forty-six.[53]

The NID during the decade mid-1920s to mid-'30s became
something of an isolated outpost, although still officially the senior
division of the naval staff. It was a position not sought by ambitious

officers, but more often than not posts were filled by those coming up to retirement.

It is not surprising then that during the Abyssinian crisis of 1936, which brought Britain close to conflict with Italy, the then Deputy Chief of Naval Staff (DCNS, the highest position in the Royal Navy, reporting directly to the First Sea Lord), Admiral William 'Bubbles' James, who had been head of Room 40 in 1917–18, voiced his concerns about the ability of NID to cope.[54] The finely tuned organisation Hall had left in 1919 was a shadow of its former self. Beesly felt there had been a bad deterioration in gathering of 'operational intelligence', and that 'it was little better than it had been when "Blinker" Hall's father had been appointed to the newly created post of Director of Naval Intelligence in 1892'.[55]

Many of the old hands of Room 40 were working at GC & CS. Fortunately for the Navy, Commander Alastair Denniston was its Director and was well aware what was required by NID. Yet how to supply information was a problem with GC & CS largely cut off from the Admiralty.

At the time, Rear-Admiral James Troup was Director of Naval Intelligence (1935–39) and Admiral James, the DCNS, wanted an increase from all sources of information from agents, and their own ships. He wrote to Troup: 'if astute men are put on the work, there is no doubt in my mind that very soon a valuable form of operational intelligence will be built up.' Troup, however, felt constrained, for like all branches of the armed forces, he faced tight financial restraints. Yet he made an inspired choice by appointing in June 1937 Paymaster Lieutenant Commander Norman Denning to implement the reforms. He was a 'born' intelligence officer and as it turned out would bring about the formation of the OIC. He began work that summer with one clerk, Charlie Pace, and only Admiral James's vision as a blueprint. He was given a largely free hand, and could start from scratch rather than trying to reform some existing organisation. He first spent a month at GC & CS working with Denniston and his staff learning the ropes with the naval section. Coming back from Station X, he found out what were the priorities regarding foreign navies for the Admiralty. The three likely protagonists were seen as Italy, Japan and Germany, with the last one standing third as German naval shipbuilding was still restricted by the London Treaty. He then built up a comprehensive card index system.[56] He went on to reorganise the Y stations so that wireless traffic could be given a bigger scrutiny.

The Munich crisis of August–September 1938 brought an instant increase in personnel at Room 39, the home of NID, many of which would stay there throughout the war. This 'running-in' period was so successful that Denning was able to report: 'We had all German units outside Germany and a great number of her larger merchant ships taped the whole time.' It revealed to NID that the German Navy was not prepared for war.[57]

Munich convinced the British government that war with Germany was likely if not inevitable, thus rearmament was accelerated. OIC benefitted from this and plans went ahead for the construction in the Admiralty basement of an underground complex to house the OIC and the war room. Both would need excellent communications and internal distribution teleprinter links were established with Naval Home Command, RAF Coastal, Bomber and Fighter commands, and with GC & CS. The work was just completed when war broke out.[58]

3

THE PHONEY WAR

The first time Ian Fleming entered Room 39 at the Admiralty he would have found that its tall windows faced west on to the gardens of No. 10 Downing Street 'straight opposite, the Foreign Office, St James's Park Lake – Guards Memorial composition to the right of it, and to the left the elegance of Horse Guards, the Treasury and the old Admiralty …' Donald McLachlan thought them rather fragile buildings to house the 'brains of a great war machine'. At that time in 1939 the great parade ground used for Trooping the Colour was a park for the paraphernalia of a barrage balloon section.[1] Within Room 39 there could be up to fifteen people working in the large office at desks jammed in among metal filing cabinets. The government-issue furniture was not designed for comfort and the cream-painted walls made it feel like the newsroom of a daily paper. No doubt the fug of tobacco smoke hung about the place as many, like Fleming, were heavy smokers. Room 38 was next door – the domain of the DNI. Thanks to Admiral Troup, by the time Godfrey was in his new office he had 150 suitable candidates to interview to fill the thirty to forty vacancies in the rapidly expanding NID.[2]

No one dominated the group. The room had no leader, and the Royal Navy officers in the section had given up trying to impose any kind of routine or discipline in what was known among the 'Secret Ladies' and typists as 'the Zoo'.[3]

Yet they all knew their jobs and the work got done. Each desk dealt with a different aspect of intelligence and was given a code number. The department was designated the Naval Intelligence Division 17. Fleming's desk was 17F and he dealt with other intelligence and security organisations. His desk overlooked Horse Guards Parade and was 6ft from the door of Room 38. As Godfrey's personal assistant, people had to get by him to see the DNI.

On 26 July Ian Fleming was appointed a lieutenant in the Royal Naval Volunteer Reserve and could wear two wavy gold rings on the sleeves of his uniform. He would serve in the Special Branch of the NID. At a party held by Shane and Ann O'Neill in September, Ian arrived in his new doeskin blue uniform. One of the women compared him to the man on the Black Magic advertisements and called him a 'chocolate sailor'. To Ian's vexation, the name stuck.[4]

However, within the confines of Room 39 Fleming was anything but a 'chocolate sailor'. McLachlan, his college and NID friend, found: 'His gift was much less for the analysis and weighing of intelligence than for the running of things and for drafting. He was a skilled fixer and vigorous showman, and he seemed to transmit the energy and wide-ranging curiosity of his first chief by whom so much was delegated.' Never, as a colleague put it, did Fleming 'sleep with a problem'.[5]

Soon after taking control of NID, Godfrey had met 'C', the head of the Secret Intelligence Service MI6, Admiral Sir Hugh Sinclair, a former DNI who had been at the helm since 1923. He had taken over from Captain Mansfield Cumming, the original 'C' who started the use of green ink on documents and the famous 'C' signature, which remains in use by the head of the service to this day. Fleming would come to know Maxwell Knight, the head of MI5 who signed his memos with an 'M', well. Brigadier Colin McVean Gubbins, SOE's Director of Operations, who Ian often met, signed the same. Sinclair was known throughout Whitehall as 'Quex', the nickname came from Sir Arthur Pinero's play *The Gay Lord Quex*, first performed in 1900, about 'the wickedest man in London'. Sinclair had a tempestuous marriage, which ended in divorce in 1920.

Like Cumming before him, Sinclair, Godfrey says, was 'a terrific anti-Bolshevik' and very secretive about his movements, for in 1923 Bolshevik and Irish assassins were thought to be numerous on the streets of the city of London. Yet he rode around in a distinctive Lancia Landau, which was like a sofa on wheels.[6] After the 'Zinoviev Letter' of 1924, a conspiracy in which Sinclair played a leading role, a fraudulent letter was published by the *Daily Mail* four days before the general election. It was a document said to have originated from the executive committee of the Communist International (Comintern) in Moscow. It was almost certainly a forgery thought to have been penned by Gregory Zinoviev, the president of the Comintern. Calling on the British communists to infiltrate the Labour Party to bring pressure on the government to ratify a treaty with the Soviet Union, it also urged them to 'agitation-propaganda' in the armed forces. Some sources indicate that the colourful character Sidney Reilly was the author. The *Daily Mail* published it under the headline, 'Civil War Plot by Socialists.'[7] It influenced the downfall of Ramsay MacDonald's Labour government. This severely affected SIS's reputation for being impartial in politics and serving all governments the same.

By the late 1930s SIS had, like many services, been affected by the fiscal repression of the Treasury and by 1939 the service was a shadow of what it had once been.[8]

In October 1939, Sinclair, aged 66, was dying of cancer of the spleen. He was taken into King Edward VII Hospital for officers in Beaumont Place, London. Sinclair was sanguine to the end, sending a message to a friend on 4 November saying: 'First bulletin. Nearly dead.' Later that day he died.[9]

The loss of 'C' to the Neville Chamberlain government caused much anguish. Sinclair's office was one of the most powerful within the government. 'C' was the man who controlled all espionage, counter-espionage and political warfare outside of the British Empire. Indeed, his post was so secret that officially it did not exist. He was the main intelligence advisor to the government and had direct access to the prime minister, foreign secretary and the sovereign at any hour.[10]

The day before he died, Sinclair wrote to Sir Alexander Cadogan, the under-secretary at the Foreign Office, recommending in the event of his death 'the most suitable individual, in every respect, to take my place, is Colonel Stewart Graham Menzies, DSO, MC'. However, despite his endorsement the 'job was no shoo-in'. The head of MI5, Brigadier Oswald 'Jasper' Harker, and Godfrey were under consideration, as was Major Archibald Boyle, Director of Air Intelligence; Winston Churchill, then First Lord of the Admiralty, proposed Captain Gerard Muirhead-Gould. Cadogan let it be known that the foreign secretary would make the decision but the post should be filled 'with the least possible delay'.[11] It still took three weeks to make the decision. Finally, on 28 November at a meeting of the prime minister, the three service ministers and the foreign secretary, it was agreed Menzies should be offered the job.

The dithering over Sinclair's replacement did not help SIS, which had already come in for some criticism from the service chiefs over a lack of intelligence in the first weeks of the war. Menzies defended the service, feeling the complaints were badly timed, and told Guy Liddell of MI5 that he felt too many people were jostling for position, and criticisms were 'being made from every quarter from ignorant people'.[12] The embarrassing 'Venlo Incident' on 9 November, when two SIS officers were enticed to the Dutch–German border and captured, did not help matters.

Walter Schellenberg of the Sicherheitsdienst (SD), the secret service of the SS, found out that a German agent, F479, had been working in the Netherlands for years. He had posed as a political refugee and had built up links to the SIS, suggesting he had links to opposition groups within the Wehrmacht who were planning to topple Hitler. One of these was said to be General Gustav von Wietersheim, who had commanded the 14th Panzer Corps in Poland. Menzies in London checked on Wietersheim's background which had been passed to him as an expert on the German Army and its politics and he found him to be credible although he was not known as a dissident. When Schellenberg was called in, the British had been promised direct talks with a high-ranking representative of the opposition group. He went himself to Holland, taking the identity of Hauptmann Schaemmel, who worked in the Transport Department of the German High Command (Oberkommando der

Wehrmacht, OKW). The real Schaemmel was sent on an extensive journey to the east.[13]

On 21 October Schellenberg, accompanied by another agent, drove to the Dutch border; it was 'a dark rainy day'. Crossing the border, they arrived in Zutphen, where, sat in a Buick, he says (which was in fact a Lincoln Zephyr) was Captain Sigismund Payne Best, who 'spoke excellent German'. They accompanied Best to Arnhem, where they met Major Richard Stevens and Lieutenant Dirk Klop of the Dutch security service. It was one of several meetings, where the British agents assured Schaemmel of support and help toward a new German government controlled by the Army, and that they would certainly welcome the removal of Hitler and his regime.[14] Schellenberg wrote that the British agents asked: 'if it was possible that the leader of our group, or any other German general, could be present at our next meeting, they believed they would be able to present a more binding declaration on the part of His Majesty's Government.'[15]

After this, Best said he told Menzies of his unease, and that the men he met were not gentlemen but rather, he concluded, 'that they were Nazis and probably officers in the SS'.[16]

On 8 November Hitler was in Munich; he was there for two reasons. One was a visit to Unity Valkyrie Mitford, a daughter of Lord Redesdale and an ardent Nazi. At the outbreak of war between Britain and Germany she had attempted suicide with a pearl-handled pistol that had once been given to her by Hitler. She was in hospital in Munich recovering and Hitler went to see her. Eventually he paid her hospital bills and she was given safe passage back to England. However, meningitis caused by cerebral swelling around the bullet still lodged in her head, which was too dangerous to remove, resulted in her death in 1948. The second reason he was in Munich was to visit the Bürgerbräukeller, a beer hall where the Nazis commemorated the Führer's attempted revolution of 1923. There he gave a speech; however, he left early. Twenty minutes later a bomb largely destroyed the building and killed and injured a large number of the party faithful. The next day the Germans announced the assassins were agents of the British Secret Service.[17]

Schellenberg was ordered late that night by Reichsführer Heinrich Himmler to capture the British agents, even if it meant a violation of the Dutch frontier. Referring to the bombing of the Bürgerbräukeller, he indicated that, 'There's no doubt that the British Secret Service is behind it all.' He added that this was a Führer order.[18]

When Best, Stevens and Klop approached the Café Bacchus near the border crossing at Venlo on 9 November expecting to meet a high-ranking German officer, they were seized by an armed group of the SS. Only Klop seems to have resisted and in the gunfight he was wounded. He was taken to a hospital in Düsseldorf, where he died. Schellenberg wrote:

On November 11 I left Dusseldorf [sic] and drove to Berlin. I was dissatisfied with the outcome of the Venlo incident and felt it would have been better if I could have continued the negotiations as I had wished. In Berlin I found the atmosphere extremely tense. The special commission to investigate the attempt on Hitler's life had just returned from Munich. The central office of the security service was like a hornets' nest into which someone had poked a stick.

He went on to conclude that Best and Stevens had nothing to do with the attempt on Hitler's life at the Bürgerbräukeller, it was 'quite ridiculous'.[19]

Meanwhile, Best and Stevens were interrogated at the headquarters of the SD on the Prinz Albrechtstrasse, Berlin. Despite standing orders to give only their names and addresses, both men collaborated with the Germans. They may have felt let down by their political masters as even the prime minister, Neville Chamberlain, gave his personal approval to the SIS discussions with the Germans, even after Best had voiced his concerns.[20] Even so, as Keith Jeffery outlines, Best's and Stevens's 'tradecraft that day was deplorable'. Both were 'carrying some coding material and Best had a list of agents' names and addresses with him'. They even travelled to Venlo in Best's car, a distinctive American Lincoln Zephyr. Maybe because there had been two previous meetings at the same venue, no one thought it necessary to reconnoitre the area ahead of time on 9 November, and there was no back-up plan in case things went badly wrong.[21]

It was against this backdrop that Menzies was appointed 'C', even though Churchill tried to block him on the grounds that the post should have been given to a sailor, who he felt would have a better sense of British Imperial strategy and larger horizons than a soldier.[22]

Thus in the early months of the war NID became the mainstay of British Intelligence. SIS was in turmoil and the Special Operations Executive was not formed until June 1940. It fell to NID to shoulder the burden, with all kinds of people coming to it for various reasons, many of which were beyond its principal role of collecting intelligence about the war at sea. At the same time, the 'Phoney War' was hardly that for the Navy.

Admiral Karl Dönitz had placed most of his small U-boat fleet on patrol by the end of August. This amounted to fifty-six boats, but only twenty were capable of working in the Atlantic. The liner *Athenia* was sunk by one on the first day of the war. Two pocket battleships, *Admiral Graf Spee* and *Deutschland*, were out ranging the Atlantic and Indian oceans. Magnetic mines had been laid in British coastal waters. British merchant ship losses totalled 222 ships in the first three months. The Royal Navy lost the battleship *Royal Oak* in Scapa Flow with a heavy loss of life. It was sunk by *U-47* commanded by Gunther Prien, and was a bitter blow as the anchorage was thought impregnable to submarine attack. The aircraft carrier *Courageous* was sunk off the coast of Ireland by *U-29*. The Germans lost *Admiral Graf Spee* and nine U-boats in the same period. As Godfrey put it, 'the Admiralty had to go to action stations without any "working up" period'.[23]

On 8 September, Fleming was promoted to commander, now with three wavy gold rings on his uniform. The higher rank gave him more confidence to confront seniors at the Admiralty and within the other services. He could even do so with Cabinet ministers he came across in the course of his duties, which was the purpose of the promotion. Donald McLachlan wrote: 'Fleming suffered not at all from very senior officer veneration.' He had no qualms about standing up to senior officers, and even more so than Godfrey, he was willing to 'stand up for the case against any sceptical Vice-Chief of the Naval Staff or Director of plans. This easy confidence made him very effective in defence of the DNI's sideshows …'[24]

With the Battle of the Atlantic yet to reach the intensity it was to obtain, NID started to look at covert schemes. Godfrey instigated some of these:

> I took it upon myself to initiate the posing of a number of clandestine operations aimed at cutting off the supply of Swedish iron ore, blocking the Danube, crippling the Romanian oil refineries (that were supplying Germany), sabotaging barges on the Danube and double agent chicken food. It was difficult to obtain official approval on a high plane for such operations. Senior officers desired the end but hesitated at the means.[25]

This energised Ian's dormant imagination that the Forbes Dennises had fuelled and cultivated so many years before. He began to propose schemes, including forging German banknotes to attack the German economy. It was a project the Nazis would adopt themselves in Operation Andreas and later Operation Bernhard.

He suggested in February that they should try something similar to the Venlo caper but targeting the Abwehr (German military intelligence service) on the Italian–French border near Monte Carlo. They would entice their prey by sowing the seeds that there was 'considerable disaffection among the French Generals of the southern command'. It was leaked to the Germans, in the hope they would act upon it, but they did not.

In July Ian produced a paper on 'Rumour as a weapon', which stated that much more coverage was needed by the media to alert the Germans.[26] Vice Admiral Norman Denning, who worked with Fleming at the time, felt a lot of his ideas 'were just plain crazy' yet 'a lot of his far-fetched ideas had just the glimmer of possibility in them that made you think twice before you threw them in the wastepaper basket'.[27]

One of his more realistic ideas was to watch U-boat movements from the remote Baltic German Frisian islands; it was not new but was inspired by Erskine Childers' 1903 book *The Riddle of the Sands: A*

Record of Secret Service, one of the most influential of all spy stories. Ian recalled visiting the area in 1960:

> The last time I had paid serious attention to these island names – Wangerooge, Spiekeroog, Norderney, Borkum – was when, as a young Lieutenant R.N.V.R, I had studied them endlessly on Admiralty charts and put up a succession of plans whereby I and an equally intrepid wireless operator should be transported to the group by submarine and there dig ourselves in, to report the sailings of U-boats and the movements of the German Fleet.[28]

The idea formed the basis for the plot in his short story *From a View to a Kill*, which appeared in a collection titled *For Your Eyes Only*, where a group of Soviet military intelligence agents bury themselves in an elaborate hideout in the woods near the NATO Supreme Headquarters for Allied Powers in Europe (SHAPE) which was established in April 1951 at Rocquencourt near St Germain in the western suburbs of Paris. From there they ambush NATO motorcycle dispatch riders before Bond takes the place of a dispatch rider, kills the assassin and then locates the hideout. It opened like a 'hinged Easter egg. In a moment the two segments stood apart and the two halves of the rose bush, still alive with bees, were splayed widely open. Now the inside of the metal caisson that supported the earth and the roots of the bush were naked to the sun.' From inside there was a beam of 'pale electric light from the dark aperture between the curved doors. The whine of the motor had stopped. A head and shoulders appeared, and then the rest of the man.' He climbed out, 'crouched, looking sharply around the glade'. In his hand he held a Luger.[29]

It is the only time James Bond rides a motorbike in Fleming's novels, a BSA M20, widely used by the British military during the war and into the 1960s. Bond, when asked by the corporal of the Signal Corps if the bike is OK, replies: 'Goes like a dream. I'd forgotten what fun these damned things are.'[30] *For Your Eyes Only* was published in 1960 and contains five short stories, four of which Fleming wrote in 1958 for a CBS television series that was later cancelled.

Early in the war it became apparent to Godfrey that the Iberian Peninsula would be an important field of operations as it had been in the first war, no doubt under advice from Blinker Hall. Godfrey had Commander Alan Hillgarth appointed assistant to the naval attaché in Paris, which at that time held responsibility for Spain. Hillgarth straight away took up residence in Madrid. Godfrey had first met Hillgarth when *Repulse* was sent to Majorca to take off the British subjects caught up in the fighting of the Spanish Civil War. Hillgarth was British Consul at the time in Palma. By the start of the Second World War he had lived in Spain for years, understood the Spanish and had many good contacts within the military and navy and within the Franco regime. Godfrey would call him a 'super Attaché'.[31] Winston Churchill also knew Hillgarth and called him a good man 'equipped with a profound knowledge of Spanish affairs'.[32]

Hillgarth quickly sent his top Spanish agent, the wealthy Juan March, to London to see Godfrey. He had come up with the idea of buying all the German ships that were interned and laid up in Spanish ports, totalling fifty-nine. He intended to pay the Germans for the ships in pesetas paid into Spanish banks, which could not be drawn on until the end of the war. Once he had control of these ships, Britain could use them and Spain could have the money – a tricky manoeuvre typical of March. However, Hillgarth warned Godfrey not 'to trust him an inch'.[33] Godfrey was impressed by March, even though they had to use an interpreter, and wrote in his diary of their meeting on 23 September:

He explained that he 'had control' of all Spanish ports except on the north and north west coasts (meaning I suppose from Vigo to San Sebastian) and, believing the future of Spain was bound up with Great Britain, he would do all in his power to help us. If we received reports of U-boats taking fuel from a Spanish oiler or in a Spanish port, he asked us not to sabotage the ship or create fires and explosions in the port as we used to do in World War I. Instead would we let him know and he would see that it did not happen again.

The same applied to 'incidents' in Spanish ports which should be minimised rather than exaggerated. He explained that the port authorities were under his control. He said that Franco would never let the German Army into Spain. He wanted the relations of Spain and England to be friendly and tranquil and would do all he could to achieve this end. We kept in touch and he passed me valuable information which was never incorrect.[34]

Godfrey entrusted Ian with the task of liaising with the new Ministry of Economic Warfare and his friends in the city, setting up a Spanish company that would buy the ships with British money. The Iberian Peninsula would figure highly in Ian's work at NID and would provide the foundations for his first Bond book *Casino Royale*, and aid the plots in several others.

As we have seen, part of Ian's work was liaison with other bodies such as MI(R) and Section D, which would later become SOE. His brother, Peter, was already working for MI(R) – the R was for research – and he was studying guerrilla warfare. When the war was looming he had re-joined the Grenadier Guards as a reserve officer and when he completed a month's training with the regiment he was snapped up by MI2, run by the War Office to handle geographical information; Peter was by then a world-renowned travel writer.

Recruiting key NID personnel was also left largely to Ian. One of the oddest, who had more of what might be called the 'Bond' touch, was a 'walk-in' who had offered his services, Merlin Minshall. Lord Beveridge, the Master of Merlin's old college, had advised this approach of popping in to the Admiralty. In 1939, before the war had started, he did get an interview in Room 1001 with Captain Jones, who was far from impressed with what William Beveridge had advised the young man before him to do – who wanted to 'do something in Naval Intelligence?' As he was about to leave, his hopes dashed, Ian Fleming entered the room in the uniform of a lieutenant RNVR. According to Minshall's account, Ian asked Jones to find someone with knowledge of Lake Chad. Merlin piped up that he knew the lake.

He was promptly asked to sit down again, a cup of tea was offered, and then he was asked to explain what he knew. They both heard him out but he had the feeling they thought he was a 'nut case'. He was asked to leave his particulars and then shown the door. Minshall then received a letter from the Admiralty that, should war start, their Lordships would 'probably desire to avail themselves' of his services.[35]

A former Oxford man like Fleming and Bond, Minshall hated education, which 'taught me virtually nothing of the slightest practical use.'[36] *The Times*, in his obituary, called him a 'rumbustious adventurer'.[37] As an amateur racing driver he ran twice in the Monte Carlo Rally, finishing fifth in 1935 driving a Singer 1.5 Le Mans Special starting from Lapland. He became well known on the road races of the European circuit, competing in the Hungarian National Road Race, the Liège–Rome–Liège, a second Monte Carlo Rally, the Mille Miglia Brescia to Rome and back again race and the 24 Hours at Le Mans.

He was asked by the Royal Automobile Club of Italy (RACI) to compete in the 4,000-mile, three-day sports car race, the Mussolini Gold Cup, in 1937. It was run between Rome and Sicily, and although four drivers were killed and half the cars failed to finish, Minshall, in his small Singer, beat all the foreign entrants and most of the Italians to be awarded the Italian Foreign Challenge Trophy. This was presented to him by Benito Mussolini.[38]

Minshall says Mussolini lectured him that Mr Baldwin should stop annoying him about Italy in Abyssinia, but he was delighted to find Merlin spoke fluent Italian. He thanked Il Duce for the cup. Fleming attributed a particular Mussolini characteristic to his villains Blofeld and Le Chiffre, namely that their black eyes were surrounded by very clear whites, giving a 'doll-like effect' and an air of total confidence.[39]

As part of his prize Minshall was taken to a high-class Roman brothel full of 'Contessas', one of which was a 'real honey'. She was British and trying to save enough money to get home. He says he gave her £100 to get home and pay her debts. Months later he received an anonymous registered letter with £100 in it.[40]

Minshall was also a skilled sailor, who had sailed the waterways of Europe from Le Havre to the Black Sea in an old Dutch boat. During the cruise he encountered the beautiful German agent Lisa Kaltenbrunner, whose face glowed when she laughed. She sailed with him while trying to discover his motives and if he was a British spy, during which they had an affair. He later learned that she was an Abwehr agent.[41]

When the war started, Minshall kept pestering NID asking to see Fleming, and eventually his persistence got him in, although Ian was unhappy with his 'fussing' and told him that he would send for him when they had something suitable. Minshall replied by asking how they could possibly manage without him, for example how many people knew the Danube as well as he did? This caught Ian's attention and he asked exactly how well he knew the Danube? 'Like the back of my hand,' replied Minshall, who had sailed the entire length.[42]

Next Fleming introduced him to Godfrey, who was not impressed, especially when he had the impertinence to criticise NID's intelligence on the Danube, and verbally threw him out. But, as Fleming often did, he persisted even against his boss and introduced Minshall to Admiral Roger Bellairs, the Co-ordinator of Intelligence to the War Cabinet (CIWC). Minshall sold Bellairs a plan to block the Danube, on the strength of which he was commissioned into the RNVR and given a crash course on sabotage. He was sent to Bucharest in January 1940 and told to lie low; his cover was vice-consul at the British Embassy. Michael Mason, who was already in Bucharest and using for cover his position as chauffeur in the British Legation, was his back-up.

Together they were to obtain barges to sink at the Iron Gates, a narrow point in the Danube forming the border between Romania and what was then Yugoslavia, to block the river to traffic. They had to bring in British and Australian crewmen to man the barges. Minshall followed them in a high-speed launch, with which he planned to take off the crews once they had scuttled the barges. However, the Romanians got wind of the enterprise and boarded the barges, dismantled the charges and arrested the crews. Minshall escaped in the fast launch, outrunning the pursuing Romanians, and escaped across the border to Trieste. His escape may seem Bond-like; indeed boat chases prevail in the Bond films, but Fleming never used any in his stories. Ian continued to use Minshall in various schemes throughout the war. He finally sent him to Yugoslavia in 1943 as head of a British Naval Mission to Tito's communist partisans.

Minshall later claimed to have never got on very well with Godfrey and recalled the admiral throwing an ink bottle at him, which missed 'but scored a direct hit on a large framed photograph of HMS *Repulse.*' Minshall beat a hasty retreat, and passing through the door he was chased by a loud 'get out'.[43] However, Godfrey gave him an excellent report before the admiral left NID for India, which ended with his handwritten comment that Minshall had shown: 'great zeal and ability. And had achieved some remarkable results by unorthodox methods.'[44]

Minshall later claimed, like several other people, to be the proto-type for James Bond, writing about the Danube mission: 'Now if James Bond had been sent to carry out this really important blocking opera-tion all would have been well. The only casualties would have been a few gorgeous blondes whose virginity certainly and their lives prob-ably would have been sacrificed in a good cause.'[45]

★★★

On 9 April 1940 the Germans invaded Denmark and Norway. Peter Fleming was sent on a reconnaissance mission to Namsos, as he put it because 'nobody had the slightest idea whether Namsos was or was not in German hands …' He was put in command of a small party known as No. 10 Military Mission; he had three other officers and two signals sergeants with radios. They flew from Shetland in a Sunderland flying boat, which landed in a fjord near Namsos. There they found out that no Germans had landed that far north. They took off again and landed at the small port of Namsos, where Peter was the first British soldier to step ashore. That night three destroyers brought in the first wave of Allied troops.[46]

The mission Peter was sent on had little effect on the poorly han-dled Norway campaign. General Carton de Wiart, of Belgian and Irish descent, a heroic charismatic soldier who had lost an eye and won the VC in the First World War, sent Peter back to Britain to find out just what the War Cabinet planned for Norway. He flew back to Scotland, where he stayed overnight. By then reports originating in Stockholm from *The Times* correspondent there said Peter had been killed in an air raid on Namsos. His wife, the actress Celia Johnson, was distraught at the report printed in the *Daily Sketch* with banner headlines 'Author Killed in Norway', although the War Office was quick to issue an offi-cial denial.[47] The *Daily Sketch* was owned by Ian's friend, Lord Kemsley, and Celia blamed her brother-in-law for not stopping the false report.

Evelyn Fleming wrote to Geoffrey Dawson, editor of *The Times*, on 30 April: 'By the mercy of heaven I did not hear the report that he had been killed in action, but my second boy had a ghastly time until he found out it was not true.'[48]

Peter was sent back to Norway for a short spell and survived the evacuation unscathed. Back home, Peter felt the campaign had been hopeless from the start and there was not 'really a great deal to be learnt from it'. He continued to work at MI(R).[49]

In May, Operation Dynamo, the evacuation at Dunkirk, had begun. The country was in flux, when over the Whitsun weekend, a strange letter arrived at the War Office purporting to have been written by a German agent and outlining a plan for an attack on the east coast sea-side town of Southend by parachute troops to take place at 0100 hours on Whit Sunday, 12 May. It seemed genuine and hurried plans were laid to defend the town. Ian and Peter set off to observe the Battle of Southend in a camouflaged staff car. Arriving at the town, they found it in the throes of a bank holiday weekend. Peter later wrote: 'Bands played in Palm Court lounges, courting couples strolled along the front, queues stood outside cinemas.'[50]

That night a company of the Pioneer Corps arrived and dug in on the beach. Ian and Peter went to the roof of a large hotel where there was a large observation post. Peter wrote:

Here, soothed by the muted strains of 'South of the Border' and 'The Lambeth Walk' from the blacked-out ballroom below us, we waited for history to be made. But somehow, as the night wore on, we found it increasingly difficult to take the whole business seriously. In London it had been easy to visualize an airborne attack on Southend in the middle of the night; in Southend, in the middle of the night, it became impossible to do so, and when soon after one o'clock, a report came in that there was no unusual air activity anywhere, the Official Eye-Witnesses sought out their car, put the elderly driver, who was dead drunk, in the back seat and made for London.[51]

A few days later the war was about to start in earnest for Ian Fleming when he flew to France.

4

FIND THE ADMIRAL

There are few parallels in military history of a campaign, between roughly equal powers, being decided so swiftly as the German conquest of Western Europe in a few short weeks in May and June 1940. Within five days of the Germans unleashing Operation Case Yellow on 10 May, the Netherlands had surrendered and the French defences on and behind the River Meuse had fallen apart. By 20 May the British, French and Belgian armies north of the Somme had been cut off from the main French forces. A large proportion of these men would be rescued from the beaches of Dunkirk in Operation Dynamo, however, all their transport and heavy weapons were lost. Fatally weakened, France faced humiliating defeat. Winston Churchill, who had only been prime minister a few weeks, and the Admiralty were becoming increasingly concerned over the fate of the powerful French Fleet.

Admiral François Darlan, who commanded this fleet, was a stocky man with a ruddy complexion and vain, always wearing his hat to cover his bald head. The assistant to the British naval attaché in Paris, Lieutenant Patrick Whinney, thought of him as a man without friends, yet he took the trouble to know everyone on his staff: 'He made sure that no decision of what he thought to be of importance was taken by anyone but himself – a factor which caused many delays. It was something that took us a long time to grasp.'[1]

Whinney places Ian Fleming at the operational HQ of the French Navy at the village of Maintenon 50 miles west of Paris on 10 June.[2] He had been met at Le Bourget airport by Captain the Hon Edward Pleydell-Bouverie, known as 'Ned', who had taken over the post of naval attaché in Paris from the charismatic Captain Cedric Holland, who had the nickname 'Hooky' due to his long nose. Holland had been appointed to command the new aircraft carrier *Ark Royal*. Whinney thought it the oddest time for Pleydell-Bouverie to take up the reins after Hooky Holland had had such a good repartee with the French. 'He took over a success story which was beginning to gallop to total disintegration.'[3]

Pleydell-Bouverie and Fleming at Maintenon made a vigorous approach to the French top brass to try and ascertain what their future plans might be. They got to see Darlan briefly, who passed them onto his staff. All they got from them was that if the Germans reached Paris then the French Naval HQ would move to Tours. Fleming immediately drafted a report on the meeting for the Admiralty, which Whinney sent, before Ian made his way back to London.

On many occasions Whinney and Fleming met in Paris and London, and the former was the main contact for NID in France. He found the director's personal assistant had 'extraordinary versatility' and: 'There was nothing that I ever discovered which he could not do better than most other people.' However, Whinney soon found out he could also be extremely rude, especially to senior officers. Yet on the whole Whinney found him to be 'polite and considerate, perhaps because although [we were] not technically junior to him, we had far less important appointments'.[4]

Back in London, Ian outlined the difficulties Pleydell-Bouverie was operating under. He was still trying to bring about a close relationship with Darlan and his staff. He had only been in the job two months and had already managed to rub the French up the wrong way by questioning their resolve to keep fighting. On catching up with Darlan it became obvious to Ian how serious the rift had become. He then suggested to Godfrey that he should return to France and become the link with Darlan.

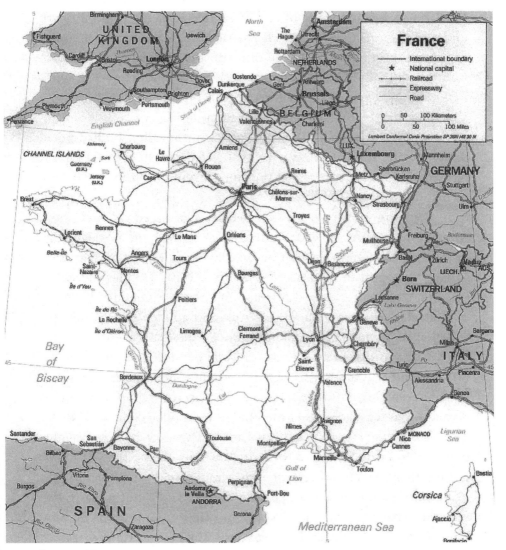

Map of France 1940.

Patrick Beesly, who worked in the communications at NID, indicates that it was Godfrey's idea to send Fleming to France again.[5] Whatever the case might have been, Ian was back in Paris on 13 June and straight away began to help organise moving the different British Intelligence operations out of the city, while France was falling apart under the German onslaught. He managed to obtain a large amount of funds from the Rolls-Royce office in the city, which acted as a front for the SIS. His main contact with the SIS in France was with Peter Smithers, one of his own recruits to NID who would become a lifelong friend. Smithers had been laid up in Haslar Naval Hospital, Portsmouth, in January 1940 suffering from measles; he had been drafted at the start of the war to an auxiliary yacht in the English Channel. He was depressed at the time, having been told that due to his illness he would not serve at sea again, when Ian contacted him, dragging him from his sick bed, and arranged an interview. After a brief meeting he was sent over to Broadway, the SIS HQ near St James's Park. Jimmy Blyth became his handler and he sent him to Paris to report to Commander Wilfred 'Biffy' Dunderdale, who was the exuberant Odessa-born station chief, a Sidney Reilly-type of character who wore handmade suits and gold cufflinks, and was chauffeured around Paris in a bullet-proof Rolls-Royce.

The car was driven by Gresev, a Russian émigré who had fought for the Whites in the Russian Civil War and was a former captain in the Imperial Guard. Biffy and Gresev had been at school before the revolution in Russia. Another member of his motley crew was 'Uncle Tom', Biffy's right-hand man, Tom Greene. Patrick Whinney thought them an odd pair. 'The Irishman, six foot four or five and weighing not less than sixteen stone, with a cavernous mouth, and huge hands, made Biffy look even more like a music-hall dandy. But it was Biffy who commanded.'[6] He got his sobriquet Biffy from his prowess as a boxer in the Navy during the First World War. He was another friend of Fleming's, and later claimed some of his own stories found their way into the Bond stories.[7]

There are obvious comparisons with Auric Goldfinger, 'who was a refugee from Riga'.[8] He too is short, dresses as a dandy, has his strange butler Oddjob and drives a Rolls-Royce Silver Ghost.

Smithers was posted to the SIS office in the rue Charles Floquet near the Eiffel Tower, where he debriefed Dutch tugboat captains. At one point he lived in the Hotel Vouillement, and recalled air raids on the city and taking shelter in the basement. With the Germans closing in on Paris, Smithers moved to the Château le Chene, an SIS safe house in Sologne, in the Loire Valley.[9] Like many of Ian's friends, the name Smithers would appear in the Bond books, in his case in *Goldfinger* his namesake would be Colonel Smithers, the gold expert.[10]

The war correspondent Geoffrey Cox was in Paris shortly before it fell in June 1940, working for the *Daily Express*. He recorded that by the night of Saturday, 8 June 'the guns from the battlefield could be clearly heard in Paris'. On the Sunday, along with other correspondents, he was summoned to the Ministry of Information then operating from the Hotel Continental, where M. Provost, new to the job, wanted to assure them that: 'There is no question of the Government leaving Paris.' Yet in the next breath he told them, 'When it does leave, I will let you know and you will follow my Ministry, attached to me.'[11]

Cox was fond of Paris and the city had been sparkling in those 'last days of May and early June. Dawn came clear, tinted, gentle behind Notre Dame, midday was a blaze of sunshine on the chestnuts along the Champs-Élysées on the red umbrellas on the café terraces; in the evening the sun went down behind the Arc de Triomphe and the soft spring night came slowly over the boulevards.'[12]

Ian described the distinct smell of Paris as 'of coffee, onions, and Corporals'.[13] His creation James Bond he imbued with a dislike of the city, as: 'Since 1945, he had not had a happy day in Paris.'[14] Kingsley Amis, in his book *The James Bond Dossier*, feels Fleming disliked the city because: 'Paris is bad not because it's full of Frenchmen, but because it has pawned its heart to Russians, Romanians, Bulgars, and Germans.'[15]

At 0300 hours on 13 June, Pleydell-Bouverie, Lieutenant S.M. Mackenzie and two Marine colour sergeants clambered into a Citroën with a French driver and set out for the new headquarters at Tours. Patrick Whinney stayed at Maintenon the next morning to send the last messages to London, as files were being burnt out in the grounds of the Château de Maintenon away from the complex of hutted offices that were once home to 400 staff. Trucks moved off with cabinets and personal belongings, heading south for the Loire Valley alongside thousands of refugees. Whinney left early the following morning via back roads to avoid the mass of people leaving Paris for the south.[16]

Miss R. Andrew, an English nurse working at the American Hospital in Paris, set off with five colleagues in a Buick for Chateauroux on Monday, 10 June, to set up an office there. She remembered: 'Millions of Paris inhabitants all had the same idea as us about leaving Paris and the roads were jammed with cars even before we reached the Porte d'Orléans. It was a very hot day and soon everyone's engines began to boil as we edged along in low gear.'[17]

Patrick Whinney's journey was 70 miles shorter than Nurse Andrews' but by then the situation was even worse. He set off in 'glorious' weather and tried to stick to the B roads as he had been advised. He found them 'completely deserted', so much so it was hard to believe 'people were killing each other only a few miles further north'.

Eventually he had no alternative but to join the main route, which he found jammed with all sorts of vehicles, including handcarts, and people on foot. Every vehicle seemed overloaded with people and possessions. Soon he found evidence of the Luftwaffe having strafed the road as there were a few dead bodies on the brown grass verges. It took him ten hours to reach Tours, a distance of barely 50 miles, and by the time he got there he was exhausted. He felt desperately sorry for the people on the roads, some of whom had been travelling for days. He found the plight of the children the worst: 'most of them showed no emotion beyond a dull wide-eyed stare,' yet 'not many of them cried. Perhaps they were past it.'[18] Geoffrey Cox, the *Express* newspaperman, felt the same about the children: the journey to Tours 'was marked for me by dark-eyed tired children, staring from the interior of darkened lorries and of crowded cars as the line of traffic moved a few paces, and then jerked to yet another stop'.[19]

On 14 June, Paris fell. The French Admiralty had set off for Tours the day before, followed by Fleming. The next day Ian relayed a message from London to Darlan urging him to bring his fleet to Britain. Ian had his reply transmitted back to Godfrey. Like a lot of the French high command, Darlan had lost touch with the reality of the highly fluid battle. In the reply there were phrases such as, 'if anything really grave occurs,' and 'For the moment the war at sea will go on as before.'[20] In Tours, Fleming found that the naval attaché's teleprinter line to the Admiralty in London was still working. Patrick Beesly was the teleprinter operator for Godfrey, and he recalled that often the admiral and his PA spoke for long periods, even up to 'half an hour's very confidential conversation'.[21]

It is often cited that Fleming was largely desk-bound at NI and only saw action once on board the destroyer HMS *Fernie* during the Dieppe raid of 1942. Yet this rather ignores France 1940, when Maintenon, Tours and Bordeaux were all bombed during the time Fleming was there. He may also have been caught in the strafing by the Luftwaffe of the refugee columns on the roads he would have travelled.

These roads were familiar to Ian before and after the war. He places Bond in the area twenty years later chasing Goldfinger's Rolls-Royce in an Aston Martin DB III across France. (In the film of the book it is a DB 5.) Landing at Le Touquet, he motors on past Abbeville, following the Rolls with 'an apparatus called the Homer'.[22] With the help of customs officers, who think Bond works for Scotland Yard, he had bugged the Rolls at the (Lydd) Ferryfield, where Goldfinger is shortly to take the Bristol Type 170 Freighter car-carrying aircraft flight across the Channel. Bond and the DB III follow on the next flight.[23] (In the film Southend airport was used and the aircraft was a ATL-98 Carvair.)

On through Rouen, Dreux and Chartres, Goldfinger overnights in Orleans, as does Bond, only 70 miles from Tours to the south-west. Even the weather and the time of year are similar as he motors on the next day toward the Swiss border following his quarry. It is a comfortable journey 'along the Loire', it is 'one of his favourite corners of the world' and: 'In May, with the fruit trees burning white and the soft wide river still big with the winter rains, the valley was green and young and dressed for love.'[24]

Just north of Chartres, Geoffrey Cox and George Miller, a fellow correspondent, stopped in a field for the night, 'from which the hay had recently been cut, took out our sleeping bags, and dined off crusty bread, sardines, cheese and red wine. It was a glorious night, aglow with stars.' At three in the morning they re-joined reality and the slowly moving column of overcrowded vehicles.[25]

On 16 June the government led by Paul Reynaud capitulated, to be replaced by the Vichy government under Marshal Pétain. Godfrey now took advantage of the better contact with Fleming in Tours and was much better informed on the state of French morale. However, he was far from confident that the French Fleet would sail for British ports. He was able to inform the First Sea Lord Albert Victor Alexander and Admiral Sir Dudley Pound, who were about to go to France to try to stiffen French resolve, that he had been advised by Lord Tyrrell, former Ambassador to France, that in his opinion 'Darlan was a twister' and not to be trusted.

Having come under air attack again at Tours, Darlan and his staff set off for Bordeaux. Fleming bundled a wireless operator into a car and set off after the elusive admiral, along the roads of south-west France choked with refugees and military units. It was the last Fleming saw of Darlan as he was soon told to forget the French admiral, which was to his regret as he felt he had got the mark of the man.[26] He was diverted to help with the British evacuation from Bordeaux and its estuary of the Gironde leading to the sea. The town was packed with those desperate to get away. The French and British General Staffs were there, as was the British Ambassador, with a large party, officials of all kinds, dislodged servicemen, refugees and wealthy British nationals. Smithers was there with his SIS people, their wives and mistresses.

Mackenzie and Pleydell-Bouverie only spent a night at Tours before moving straight on to Bordeaux, in a French Admiralty Citroën. They spent the night at the roadside before reaching the southern city on 16 June. There they started to organise the evacuation of British passport holders to Britain, of which there were hundreds besieging the consulate. Mackenzie says Fleming arrived the following day, while on the 18th the destroyer HMS *Berkeley* docked. On board was the First Sea Lord of the Admiralty Alexander and Admiral of the Fleet Pound, their mission a last-ditch attempt to persuade Darlan to bring the French Fleet to Britain, or at least take it beyond the reach of the Germans.[27]

Patrick Whinney's journey to Bordeaux was 'more difficult' than the one to Tours. 'There seemed to be more civilians than ever crawling south-ward, and this time they were nearing the end of their strength. There seemed fewer cars, and lorries, but the human stream was thicker with pedestrians, bicycles, handcarts, anything with wheels.'

Near Poitiers he came across a motorbike towing a handcart on which were sat two young children, the road was cobbled and the vibration had the effect as if the 'children's backsides and the boards on which they were sitting appeared not to be touching at all but rather riding on a cushion of air. As I drew alongside I looked at them, in return they smiled and I think they would have waved if they had not had to hold on with both hands to avoid falling off the back of the cart.'

He had been dreaming about an omelette for a long time on the road. When he arrived in the city, people were having dinner. He found Fleming and Mackenzie at a restaurant near the consulate and their empty plates showed they had eaten. Asked if he had eaten, he confided to them of his desire for an omelette, to which Ian burst into laughter, confessing he had 'just eaten the last omelette in the entire square'. Whinney soon found out Fleming was not joking, which did not improve his mood. However, he was able to tell Fleming and Mackenzie, Darlan was staying in the naval barracks on the outskirts of the city. Ian told him not to lose touch with the French admiral.[28]

One task Ian was given was to make sure a large quantity of aircraft engines and spares found a place on the evacuation ships and did not fall into enemy hands. This tall, well-spoken RNVR officer exuded a confident air amidst the dockside chaos. He duly found space in a ship and supervised the loading; the engines made it safely back to England.

The SIS staff was taken aboard the cruiser HMS *Arethusa* in the Gironde estuary. Formed by the meeting of the rivers Dordogne and Garonne, it is about 50 miles long and 2 to 7 miles wide. However, Smithers was ordered off and told to report to Bordeaux, where Commander Fleming would give him further orders. He found Ian burning papers at the British Consulate and told Smithers he was to act as flag lieutenant for the First Sea Lord Alexander, who was meeting Admiral Darlan for dinner that night.

In the meantime, Fleming and Smithers drove out along the estuary to the anchorage at Le Verdon, past abandoned cars – many Rolls-Royces and Bentleys – crammed with luggage. At the quayside there were hundreds of people milling about trying to get a ship back to England. Ian, aided by Smithers, swiftly took charge, persuading, cajoling or just plain bullying ships' captains to let these people board.

He told one skipper: 'If you don't take these people on board and transport them to England. I can promise you if the Germans don't sink you, the Royal Air Force will.'[29] He paid a local ferryman to take people out to the larger ships with rolls of francs he had taken from the SIS safe in Paris. Ian and Smithers stationed themselves on the quayside, insisting that only two cases per person could be taken on board and checking passports, interrupted from time to time by German aircraft. They worked through the summer afternoon and into the evening until everybody had been taken off.

Patrick Whinney witnessed air raids on the city but they were 'not the heavy bombers so familiar to us later on in the war when they came over to London and the south coast'. They did attack Bordeaux in flights of twos and threes, 'dropping bombs and they machine gunned the city, and there was quite a lot of noise, although one had the feeling that the anti-aircraft fire was not having much effect except, perhaps, as a morale-booster to the guns crews'.[30]

There is no evidence that Fleming or any of the other naval officers there took over an anti-aircraft gun as Bond does when he mans the Bofors gun in *Diamonds are Forever* and shoots down the smugglers' helicopter in Africa. No self-respecting gunner, whether French *poilu* or equally hairy British matelot, would allow some officer to take over his position.[31]

Nurse Andrew and her colleagues who were left at Chateauroux were soon told to go to Bordeaux and return to England or risk internment. There they met an 'adorable young man in Naval Uniform' organising the evacuation. She hoped that he got a medal for his efforts. Later, in a *Sunday Times* article, she identified him as Ian Fleming. She missed at least two ships there, due to sight-seeing trips, but would later return to England from St Jean-de-Luz.[32]

That evening the French and British General Staffs dined at the Chapon Fin Restaurant in Bordeaux. Alexander's attempt to convince Darlan to throw in his lot with Britain or sail his ships to neutral ports failed. It was a sombre affair. Few could engage in the occasion, lost in their own concerns.

Patrick Whinney was probably the last British officer to see Admiral Darlan at Bordeaux, when he delivered a proposal from Admiral Pound to send every French ship he could to the West Indies. He found Darlan at the barracks walking across the parade ground. Darlan did not return Whinney's salute or acknowledge his 'good morning' as normal. 'Instead he looked me up and down as if he had never seen me before, and then grabbed the envelope from my hand. His only acknowledgement was a snapped out "Bien" before he turned and walked away.' The next day Whinney and Mackenzie were ordered to leave Bordeaux for Bayonne, where a substantial number of British refugees had gathered.[33]

Alexander and Smithers returned to England in a Sunderland flying boat, and Ian would go to Portugal. Godfrey was impressed with his PA's performance in France, especially in regard to his actions during Operation Aerial, the code name given to the evacuation of Allied forces and civilians from the ports of western France on 15–25 June, during which a total of 191,870 people were rescued. So much so he was willing to entrust him with another field mission to see Alan Hillgarth, the naval attaché in Madrid, and assess the effect the German victory might have in Spain.

In the Compiègne Forest north of Paris on 22 June 1940 the Nazis stage-managed the surrender terms that France had to accept. Article 8 of the armistice between Germany and France stated the French Navy ships were to be 'demobilised and disarmed under German and Italian control', and all Atlantic bases in the occupied zone were now at the disposal of Germany.[34]

Darlan had assured Churchill 'that whatever happened the French Fleet should never fall into German hands'.[35] However, Churchill and the War Cabinet felt unable to accept the risk. Thus Operations Grasp and Catapult were put into effect to seize or destroy the French ships. On 3 July, the Royal Navy overcame French ships and submarine crews in the harbours of Portsmouth, Plymouth and Alexandria in Egypt. The only casualties were when two British officers, one seaman and a French warrant officer were killed in a fight on the submarine *Surcouf* in Plymouth.

However, the large French Fleet in the Algerian ports of Mers-el-Kébir and Oran posed a far bigger problem. Force H at Gibraltar, under Vice Admiral James Somerville, was given the task of dealing with these ships. Early on the same July morning, his fleet arrived off the Algerian coast consisting of the flagship, the battlecruiser *Hood*, the battleships *Resolution* and *Valiant*, the carrier *Ark Royal*, two cruisers and eleven destroyers. The commander of the carrier and former Paris naval attaché 'Hooky' Holland were seen ashore to give the French commander Admiral Marcel-Bruno Gensoul a six-hour ultimatum: either join the British, go into internment, sail to the French West Indies and disarm, scuttle the ships or be destroyed.

Gensoul thought the British were bluffing and played for time so that his ships could raise steam. The British ships opened fire at 1730. The battlecruiser *Strasbourg,* although sustaining some damage, and five destroyers, broke out and managed to reach Toulon. All the other ships in the two ports were sunk or crippled within minutes. The battleship *Bretagne* exploded and sank, with 977 officers and men killed. The French lost 1,297 men in total.[36]

The ruthless British action against the French Fleet at Mers-el-Kébir boldly underlined Churchill's rhetoric that Britain and her empire would fight on.

5

OPERATION GOLDEN EYE

Quite how Ian Fleming got to Portugal in June 1940 is unclear. To have gone overland would have been extremely unlikely, and as his objective was to get to Madrid if going overland, why go to Portugal? He could have gone by sea, but he would have had to obtain a visa from the Portuguese Consul in Bordeaux. These were freely obtainable, thousands being issued by the consul, Aristides de Sousa Mendes. However, most people travelled by land and the influx was so great that it led to the Spanish closing the border with France, and an increase in tension between Lisbon and Madrid. Sousa Mendes paid for this humanitarian act with his career and the ruin of his family by a furious Dr Antonio De Oliveira Salazar, dictator of Portugal.[1]

Could Ian have taken a flight from Bordeaux? Two weeks before, Sir Samuel Hoare flew south with his wife to take up his post as ambassador in Madrid. His aircraft had refuelled at Bordeaux, where he found the, 'aerodrome was nominally still in use'. His flight was going via Lisbon and would be the last civilian one to leave Bordeaux. He recalled: 'Our arrival created little interest amongst the handful of employees who were still on the aerodrome and it was with a feeling of foreboding that having lunched, we quitted France.' Hoare, a nervous man, was not looking forward to taking up his new post in Madrid.[2]

John Pearson, in his book *The Life of Ian Fleming*, claims that Fleming returned to England by sea first: 'HMS *Arethusa* was waiting off Arcachon to take away the British Ambassador and when she sailed Lieutenant Commander Fleming would sail in her.'[3]

This is maybe more likely as Fleming could then have got a flight to Lisbon; on 4 June BOAC started operating a service from Heston aerodrome, west of London, to the Portuguese capital.

What makes this more certain is that Mackenzie and Whinney say they saw Fleming at the DNI office in London after they had arrived on 26 June. Whinney recalls that Fleming greeted them after they had briefly seen Admiral Godfrey with: 'Hello you monkeys, where have you been? And what have you been up to?'

They had both left Bordeaux on 20 June for Bayonne, where they helped in the continued evacuation of British nationals. There they worked for days getting people away, including King Zog of Albania along with his family and his treasury. Nurse Andrew also finally got away on the SS *Emrick*, which was the same ship that took the king.

On 25 June, Mackenzie and Whinney, their job complete, were taken off by the Canadian destroyer *Fraser*. They were among the last British officers to leave France, which had surrendered the week before. Unfortunately their adventures did not end there. On the return voyage, in poor visibility and rough seas, *Fraser* was cut in two by the cruiser *Calcutta*, which hit the destroyer just forward of the bridge. *Restigouche*, another Canadian ship, rescued most of the passengers. Whinney recalls leaping across from one destroyer to the other: 'it seemed a longish drop, and then capable hands steadied me on deck.' *Fraser* lost forty-five people in the collision and *Calcutta* nineteen.[4]

In Lisbon the only flight Ian could get to Madrid was with Lufthansa, who at first refused him as an enemy alien. Never noted for taking no for an answer, Ian persuaded and bullied them into taking him, pointing out that as they were flying from a foreign country, as a commercial airline they were duty-bound to take him. If not, the Portuguese authorities would surely be interested. Thus, late in June he arrived in Madrid for his vital assignment with Hillgarth. In the Spanish capital events had taken a turn for the worse for Britain. The Franco regime had changed the war status of Spain from 'neutrality' to an undefined 'non-belligerence', which showed a clear sympathy for the Axis. On 10 June, Mussolini's Italy had entered the war and many expected Spain to follow suit.

In June 1940, Alan Hillgarth was 41 years old, nearly ten years older than Fleming, a handsome man with an olive complexion and dark flashing eyes. Aged 12, he had been sent to Osborne College on the Isle of Wight in preparation to join the Royal Navy, where he had been nicknamed 'the little dago'. He served through the First World War, mainly in the Mediterranean. It was in the Navy that he started writing, his first story being published in *Sketch* magazine in July 1918.[5] In 1922, after eight years' service, Alan was placed on the retired list at his own request.[6] He did not have the burning ambition to stay in the Navy. In 1923 he commuted his annual pension of £97 for a one-off sum of £1,370.[7] He then took up his pen to earn a living as a writer and travelled a lot.

Two years after leaving the Navy he changed his given name of George Hugh Jocelyn Evans to Alan Hillgarth, having first used it as a nom de plume in his writing. The change of name was announced in *The Times* on 3 September 1926.[8]

In 1930 Hillgarth married the divorcee Mary Hope-Morley and they moved to Majorca. None of his adventure novels sold particularly well. He did sell the film rights of *The Black Mountain* to an American company for $5,000 but it was never made.[9] In 1932 he was appointed acting 'vice consul' in Palma by the British government. Winston Churchill and his wife Clemmie stayed with the Hillgarths in 1935 while visiting the island.

Godfrey and Alan met in 1938 when *Repulse* visited Majorca. They found they had much in common, having both served in the Gallipoli campaign as junior officers. Godfrey had a mission to visit the British Legation near Barcelona. This was during the height of the Spanish Civil War and he was worried his ship might get caught up in Italian air raids. However, Hillgarth, through his contacts within the Spanish Command and Italian Air Force, obtained an agreement that no raids would be conducted in the area during *Repulse*'s visit. Godfrey was impressed and called it an outstanding feat 'in practical diplomacy'.[10] In August 1939, instigated by Godfrey, Hillgarth took up the post of naval attaché in Madrid and was recalled to the Navy's active list.

The enemy Alan Hillgarth faced in Spain in the early months of the war was powerful and well established. The shrewd head of Abwehr, Admiral Wilhelm Canaris, knew Spain well, having served there in the First World War, and since 1937 had built up several stations on the Iberian Peninsula. Running a large number of agents and contacts, the Abwehr enjoyed another advantage of being able to work closely with the Spanish Secret Service, the Sirene, run by General Martinez Campos, another old friend of Canaris.

Ian Fleming stayed with the Hillgarths in Madrid. He and Alan then went by road to Gibraltar, taking Mary along with them to give the outing the cover of a sightseeing trip, although they flew a White Ensign from the car's aerial. Mary was not impressed with Ian as an NI officer, as he left his wallet behind at a restaurant, but she found him amusing.[11]

Their main aim from the trip was to lay the foundations of a stay-behind sabotage and intelligence-gathering operation within the Iberian Peninsula, in case the Germans invaded, and also to establish an NI office in Gibraltar. On the way they met Colonel William Donovan, the United States intelligence chief, who was on a fact-finding visit to Europe. They briefed him on the vital efforts being made to keep Spain neutral. From Gibraltar Ian went on to Tangier to create a haven there in the event the Rock should fall.[12]

Back at his desk in London by August, Ian began work on the stay-behind operation for Spain and Gibraltar should the Germans move in. So, where did the name Golden Eye come from? Fleming would later name his Jamaican home Goldeneye, after all. It seems likely that at the time he was reading the Carson McCuller novel *Reflections in a Golden Eye*. Maybe the name, in some way, reminded him of Spain. The novel was not published until 1941 by Houghton & Mifflin but was serialised in the October–November issue of *Harper's Bazaar* magazine and likely advertised in the August–September issue.[13]

Soon after returning, Fleming wrote to Hillgarth, thanking him and Mary for their hospitality and kindness to him and praising Alan's excellent work as naval attaché in Madrid. He added that NI was fortunate to have such a strong team 'in our last European strong hold', resulting in the 'great contribution you are making to winning the war'. Later in the same letter he turned to Golden Eye:[14]

4) You will by now have a signal about receiving Golden Eye messages. Mason Macfarlane [Lt-General Noel Mason-Macfarlane Governor of Gibraltar] has no objection, and C.N.S [Commander Naval Station] is about to give his decision, which I have no doubt will be favourable.

He concluded with Portugal:

7) I discussed the inclusion of Portugal in Golden Eye on my way through Lisbon, and got the Naval Attaché's reaction on a very general plane. This has been put up to the Planners, and I have no doubt that the answer will be 'yes' and that Owen will be instructed to go down to Gibraltar to report to the delegation.[15]

There was a lot involved in the planning of Golden Eye at a time when Ian had many calls on his time. For a start, the operation had to be sub-divided into two plans: Operation Sprinkler to assist the Spanish if they resisted a German invasion and Operation Sconce if the Spanish co-operated with the Germans. Both would mean that Section H of the newly formed SOE would deploy sabotage teams using Spanish guerrillas to hit transport links and fuel stores. Selected members of these teams started training in the highlands of Scotland at a converted farmhouse in Camusdarach near Inverness in December 1940. One report commented that: 'The most striking thing about the Spanish troops is their pride in being members of the British Army, and also their gratitude for the work that has been done in this country on their behalf.'[16]

Ian was no doubt glad to head for Spain again in February 1941 to review Golden Eye on the ground. He would be happy to get away from his desk, and the bickering between the SIS and SOE over the operation, but also to get away from the Luftwaffe bombs. In the Blitz he managed to survive three buildings that were badly damaged. One was the Carlton Hotel, where he stayed because the skylights at his flat at 22 Ebury Street could not easily be blacked out so he had to find temporary accommodation. Here his third-floor room was destroyed by a bomb. Ian helped rescue a waiter and maid who had been buried under the wreckage. Later he went to sleep with the other residents in the grill room. He was woken there by what he thought was running water, only to find an old man relieving himself on the carpet. Later he found out that the old man was an eminent bishop.[17]

On 16 February Ian flew out to Lisbon and then to Madrid, where he was issued with a courier's passport from the embassy dated the same day. It was issued in order to ease his travel between the Rock and Madrid. He was glad to travel in civilian clothing and wore a dark blue suit with an Etonian tie. He carried a commando fighting knife, which he bought from Wilkinsons and carried on his foreign assignments. It was engraved with his name and rank on the blade. His fascination with gadgets extended to a fountain pen that could be fitted with a cyanide or tear gas cartridge, which he carried as well. He was fully prepared to explore his fantasies of life as a secret agent.[18]

Fleming equips his hero Bond with a Swaine Adeney 'slim, expensive-looking attaché case', to take to Istanbul in *From Russia with Love*, full of secret agent goodies. It contains '50 rounds of .25 ammunition' for his Beretta, while his Palmolive shaving cream tube houses the silencer. The case also contains two flat throwing knives by Wilkinson. In the handle is a cyanide death pill, which Bond promptly throws away, and the lid contains 'fifty gold sovereigns'. Bond manages to get past customs, wondering what they might think if they weighed his case before he boarded the BEA Flight 130 to Rome, and on via Athens to Istanbul. However, 'the bag was a convenient way to carry the tools of his trade, which otherwise would have to be concealed about his body'.[19]

Arriving in Gibraltar, Ian saw first-hand the amount of activity going on in the colony and the work that had been done since his last visit. Before the war there had been no land-based aircraft able to operate from the colony, only three Swordfish float planes. A runway had now been constructed, which though not full length, would take

Wellingtons carrying light loads. The decision had been taken not to antagonise Spain, so that it was not until October 1941 that the runway was realigned and extended out into the bay for nearly half a mile on reclaimed land, all of which would have been keenly observed by German agents from the balconies of the Hotel Reina Cristina in Algeciras. The runway would have a public road crossing it, which is still a feature today. In 1940 the decision was made to locate as many installations and support facilities underground as possible in order to expand on Gibraltar's limited space.

Accommodation, hospitals, storage caves, water and sanitary arrangements were built into a vast network of tunnels and chambers running the length of the Rock. In all there would be 34 miles of tunnels, most of which were finished by 1943. The work was carried out by four companies of Royal Engineers and a Canadian tunnelling firm that had perfected a diamond drill blast method, a new drilling technique that saved a lot of manual labour.[20]

This clearly had an influence on Fleming's later writing. In Dr No, Bond and Honeychile Rider are imprisoned by Dr Julius No in a warren of rooms built into the 'side of the mountain' on Crab Key, the island that ended in a 'cliff face'. The walls of the corridors were moisture free, and 'the air was cool and pure with a strongest breeze coming towards them. A lot of money and good engineering had gone into the job.'[21]

At Gibraltar, Ian set up a Golden Eye liaison office with its own cipher link. It was to consist of a team of ten naval personnel led by a commander, and including demolition officers and a petty officer telegraphist.[22] However, if Spain succumbed to German entreaties to join the war or was invaded, it was unlikely Britain would be able to hold Gibraltar. To be able to continue monitoring Allied shipping in the Mediterranean and the Atlantic another back-up office was set up in Tangier and commanded by Henry Greenleaves.

On 14 June 1940 Spain had occupied the international zone of Tangier on the pretext of guaranteeing its neutrality. This, however, was a ploy as Franco dreamed of annexing the whole of Morocco. At the time, the city of Tangier was a hotbed of agents from both sides. The Abwehr had established offices there. It was only two and a half hours by boat across the straits to Spain, seven hours by road from Casablanca and three hours on a flight from Lisbon.

The old town with its Grand Socco market square was called the Medina, and was made up of narrow streets that no traffic could enter. The red light district of Zoco-Chico was full of bars and brothels where all tastes in alcohol, drugs and sex were catered for. The Café de Paris was opened in 1920 by Madame Leotine, who was the first woman to run such an establishment in Tangier, and it soon became a meeting place for spies. Paul Bowles, the American writer who lived in the town for many years, wrote: 'During the war it was thought every fourth person was a spy, smuggler, or refugee.' He preferred the Café Hafa, where you could get a coffee at five in the morning and it stayed open all night.[23]

Only a year later, the film *Casablanca* premiered, based on the Murray Burnett and Joan Alison's unproduced play called *Everybody Comes to Rick's*. It was in some ways a fair depiction of what was going on in Tangier at the time. One line in particular rang true. 'That everybody in Casablanca [Tangier] has problems.'[24]

Ian Fleming enjoyed a night on the town with Henry Greenleaves there and the heady atmosphere for him was like a tonic. The mysterious Mr Greenleaves does emerge in the Admiralty files in his report to Commander G.H. Birley at Gibraltar dated 17 April 1941 on his work in Tangier, which Birley passed on to Godfrey. In it Birley summed up: 'Finally I wish to report that I am more than satisfied with Mr Greenleaves' activities; he mixes well; is a popular member of the community and has enough private means to entertain judiciously.'[25] The drinking antics of Fleming and Greenleaves would become famous in NID; is this a Felix Leiter-type character who like Bond was fond of his hard liquor? 'Better have one last Bourbon and branch-water,' he tells Bond before he heads for Las Vegas in *Diamonds are Forever*, when they have already consumed a huge quantity.[26]

Fleming's work would seem to have brought tangible results, which must have been a fillip for him, for even in the short time he was there he learned that General Erwin Rommel had arrived in Tripoli, Libya, to command the newly formed Afrika Korps.

The British Consul to Tangier, the straight-laced former Guards-man Major Alvary Trench-Gascoigne, had been in the post for less than a year. He is likely not to have been too impressed with his new attaché, or the visiting NID officer, for carousing around the town. After all, he already had enough on his plate. Despite his protests, Franco had allowed the German Consulate, closed since 1914, to reopen. The consulate became a large legation on the site of the Mendoub's palace that was to run a serious espionage centre for the next three years.[27] In the report Fleming sent to Godfrey he noted: 'Although H.M. Consul-General [Trench-Gascoigne] and Greenleaves are on friendly terms, the former still cannot, I think, rid himself of the feeling that Greenleaves is an interloper.' This state of affairs was not helped by 'the fact that Greenleaves and the SIS do not get on well together whereas H.M. Consul-General has implicit faith in SIS'.[28] In an earlier report by Greenleaves to Birley he had noted in regard to SIS: 'On your instructions, I shall have no further contact with this Department.'[29]

Part of Ian's remit from Godfrey was to meet Colonel William Donovan at Gibraltar. Donovan was reaching the end of his second journey to Europe on behalf of the US government, where he had investigated the economic, political and military situation in the Mediterranean and Middle East. Colonel Vivian Dykes, Churchill's personal representative, escorted him.[30]

Donovan was a giant of a man, 50 years of age in 1940 and of Irish descent. His sobriquet was 'Wild Bill', and he had received a chestful of medals when he commanded the 1st Battalion, 165th Regiment, which was part of the New York's 69th (Fighting Irish) Division in the First World War. His men had given him the nickname due to his impressive feats of endurance. He had met Admiral Godfrey in 1940 while on his first mission to Europe to find out if Britain would fight on as Churchill had promised. He returned from the mission convinced it would. He advised the President that the US should do everything possible to aid Britain, including full collaboration in intelligence.[31]

On the second journey, Donovan left the USA on 6 December and would not return until March 1941. He visited many countries around the Mediterranean basin and spoke with all sorts of people, from common soldiers to dictators.

On 24 February, Donovan landed in Gibraltar harbour on board an RAF Sunderland flying boat, which had dealt with a 40mph headwind and touched down with only fifteen minutes of fuel left. They stayed at Government House that night. As Donovan had a problem with his eye, resulting in a minor operation, he missed the dinner Dykes took with Hillgarth and Fleming, the Governor and several other guests.[32]

The next day the party set off for Madrid at 0710 by road. Dykes recorded in his diary for Thursday, 25 February 1941: 'I sat with Ian Fleming much of the way. He is the brother of Peter Fleming and was on Reuters staff before the war. He told me some interesting experiences as a Reuters man and was inclined to knock it [alcohol] back too much.'[33]

In Madrid, Hillgarth and Fleming held final discussions on Golden Eye before Ian returned to London. There was likely a rift between the two men, who did not agree on the best way of going forward with it. Hillgarth was beginning to sense that there were too many people involved, and was concerned about the wisdom of sending so many agents from the SOE, then known as SO2, from the sabotage section of SIS, into the country, where they were colluding with the left in Spain. He referred to this as 'dangerous, amateurish activities'.[34] Fleming also had reservations, confiding to Dykes that he believed SIS and SO2 were on course for a 'crash-out'.[35]

In April, Ian wrote a report on: 'Divisions of interests between SIS & SO2 (SOE).' He observed that since the creation of SO2 'as a separate entity, charged with sabotage in enemy countries, SO2 and SIS have been in competition'. In Spain he felt the attempts by SO2 to form a 'sabotage organisation' had left the naval attaché trying to direct these operations 'compromised to a certain degree'.[36]

Yet in January only a few weeks before, Hillgarth had been in London and met with Hugh Dalton, the Minister of Economic Warfare and head of SOE, who told the prime minister that Hillgarth 'has consented to supervise the whole of our activities in Spain'.[37] Godfrey was not happy with his star attaché being compromised and wrote to the chiefs of staff in April that 'intelligence is of primary importance' and SIS should be given precedence and have the right of 'veto' over SO2 projects.[38]

Hillgarth tried to smooth things over with Godfrey, and even tried to persuade Hoare, the British Consul in Madrid, who was dead set against any cloak and dagger business, that SO2 [SOE] could do important work in preparation for a German invasion 'provided they were rigidly controlled'.[39] He later wrote a report on 'The role of the Naval Attaché', as he felt he had had to create a sort of 'substitute SIS in Spain'. He explained that this would not cause trouble because: 'a) my reports were to both DNI and CSS and b) my relations with SIS in Madrid were first class.'[40] He went on further to explain:

> When SOE was formed as a separate entity from SIS there was inevitably rivalry between them. Though their functions were different, there were unavoidable instances of trespass.
>
> You cannot carry out clandestine operations without intelligence to guide you, and you cannot help acquiring intelligence in the course of your proceedings.
>
> The natural desire of SOE to operate in the Iberian Peninsula and Spanish Morocco met, however, an even stronger opposition from the Foreign Office and the Ambassadors in Spain and Portugal who were all, very naturally, fearful of some stupid explosion or an ignominious capture of British agents, with consequent harm to our general policy. In this fear they were justified, although my Ambassador recognised that SOE could do important work in the preparations against a possible German invasion of the peninsula, provided they were rightly controlled. A compromise was eventually reached by which SOE were allowed to operate in the peninsula in a precautionary way only, and I was chosen to control them. That is to say, they could initiate nothing without my approval and the progress of what was approved had to be fully disclosed to me every day.
>
> On the whole this worked very well, but it was an unenviable task for the controller, I was continually berated by the Ambassador and by the Foreign Office whenever I went to London for allowing anything at all, while the chief of SOE on the other side was continually at me to allow more. Meanwhile the DNI was always fearful that I

would slip from controlling into directing and get involved and compromised. So I was under fire from three sides.[41]

Two incidents with SIS caused alarm within the British Embassy Madrid and created more work for Hillgarth. The first centred on Paul Lewis Claire, a French naval officer, who transferred to the Royal Navy after France fell. He was taken on by SIS O Section to land agents in France by sea. On 23 July he was in the Vichy Embassy in Madrid revealing SIS secrets to the naval attaché. This news reached Hoare, who requested immediate instructions from SIS as Claire was expected at the British Embassy the next day to pick up his passport. Frank Slocum at SIS advised Hillgarth should take 'what steps he can to intercept Claire'. He also suggested that SOE might 'liquidate Claire' and even thought about kidnapping Claire's wife in an attempt to bring him to heel. Colonel Stewart Menzies 'C' of SIS was in favour of capture.

Leonard Hamilton Stokes, head of SIS Madrid section, and Hillgarth lured Claire to the embassy, where he was beaten up and drugged with morphine. He was then bundled into a car and they set off for Gibraltar, with instructions that under no circumstances should he be allowed to escape.

On the long journey south, Claire began to regain consciousness and called for help in a Spanish village. To keep him quiet, he was hit over the head with a pistol, but the blow proved too hard and he died. The message from the SIS agent in Gibraltar read that the 'consignment arrived in this town completely destroyed owing to over attention in transit' and would be disposed of.[42] Hoare claimed in Madrid 'once again we here have had to save SIS from catastrophe', rather ignoring that Hamilton Stokes was an SIS officer.[43]

However, Claire was hardly dispatched with the calm skill of 007 when the need had arisen, such as when Bond deals with the Mexican Bandit at the start of *Goldfinger*, and then 'looked down at the weapon that had done it. The cutting edge of his right hand was red and swollen.' He keeps exercising the hand on a plane so that it will heal 'quickly' as: 'One couldn't tell how soon the weapon would be needed again.'[44]

There were protests from the Spanish Foreign Ministry after Vichy France broadcast on the radio about the affair. Two days later, the London *Daily Telegraph* hit back with the headline: 'Nazis Invent Kidnapping.'[45] Later, Fleming informed the Red Cross that Claire was 'missing believed drowned' while on board the SS *Empire Hurst*, which had been sunk by enemy aircraft on 11 August 1941. After the war, to protect SIS, Claire's widow was paid a pension.[46]

The second incident to cause alarm was that of Lieutenant Colonel Dudley Wrangel Clarke. In this case, Hillgarth had to retrieve him out of a Spanish jail after he had been arrested in drag.

Clarke was the head of the deception unit in Cairo at GHQ Middle East. He travelled to Lisbon, then Madrid, his cover being a war correspondent for *The Times*. He was actually there to develop contacts to help his department with the assistance of SIS. He saw Hamilton Stokes at the embassy on 17 October 1941 and the next day he was arrested by the Spanish Police in a main street dressed as a woman, brassiere and all. He told the police he was a novelist trying to get under the skin of a female character. Then he told Hillgarth that he was taking the garments to a lady friend in Gibraltar, despite the fact that the clothes all fitted him, including the high-heel shoes. Later he maintained it was a ploy to see if his cover could hold with the Spanish and Germans.[47]

Hillgarth sent photographs to the prime minister's office with a light-hearted note for the staff: 'Herewith some photographs of Mr Dudley Wrangel Clarke as he was arrested and after he was allowed to change. I promised them to the prime minister and thought you might like to see them too.'[48]

When the risk of German invasion in the spring of 1941 seemed likely, Hillgarth visited Gibraltar to check all was in order. He found to his fury that when the mission moved to Spain, Brigadier Bill Torr, the military attaché, would command it. He wrote to Godfrey in anger: 'I am not quite clear what I'm to be or do – either just a lackey to the Ambassador and separated from the mission or a sort of glorified interpreter … Please take me away out of it to another job where I can be of some use.'[49] Godfrey quickly intervened to promote Hillgarth to the dormant rank of commodore and designated him as the Chief

British Liaison Officer. Godfrey wrote to him that he had spoken to the prime minister about Golden Eye and that the operation was still under review. He assured him that he had put forward proposals that were in 'accordance with your wishes and in accordance with the recommendations which Fleming brought back from Spain and of which I know you are aware'.[50]

Godfrey thought that Hillgarth had written his letter 'rather hastily' and assured Hillgarth that he had his 'best interests in mind and that I appreciate your services in Spain sufficiently to make every effort to protect your future status against incursions from whatever quarter'.[51]

Later that year Hillgarth wrote a report on Golden Eye to argue that the 'fact that no invasion has yet taken place does not justify any relaxation. I feel however that the original plan from a naval point of view was unnecessarily ambitious.'[52]

It was, of course, Fleming's original plan, but Admiral Godfrey was happy with his work. On his return to London, Ian was tight-lipped about the trip, though he did tell Maud Russell, who worked in NI, that 'he had enjoyed the spring almond blossom in Seville'.

In a letter to Hillgarth, he commended him: 'It is lucky that we have such a team in our last European stronghold and results have already shown the great contribution you are all making towards winning the war.' He also promised Hillgarth some Henry Clay cigars, which he begged him to smoke himself 'and not give them to [his] rascally friends'.[53]

6

OPERATION RUTHLESS

The Britain Ian Fleming returned to in August 1940, after his first wartime trip to the Iberian Peninsula and Morocco, faced the imminent prospect of invasion. The Battle of Britain raging above the skies of southern England was reaching its height. After gaining air superiority over the Channel, the Luftwaffe had upped their game and on 12 August had struck hard blows at the RAF airfields and radar stations. For a week they launched heavy raids, on the 15th alone flying 1,786 sorties before cloudy weather intervened.[1]

Across the Channel, hundreds of barges and a motley collection of steamers and launches were gathering to transport the Wehrmacht to the south coast of England. Winston Churchill, only a few weeks in office, made rousing speeches to inspire the nation and to put backbone into the appeasers, including 'This was their finest hour' on 18 June in the House of Commons.

Yet how real was the threat? Even in the best of conditions, the ramshackle invasion fleet would cross the Channel slower than Caesar's legions 2,000 years before. The Kriegsmarine expected to lose 10 per cent of their lift capacity due to accidents before the Royal Navy and RAF put in an appearance. And on the German side there were 'irrevocable differences' between the army and navy.[2] Ian's brother,

Peter, wrote in his 1957 book *Invasion 1940* that, 'Operation Sealion, as planned and mounted was doomed to failure and, had it been launched could only have ended in disaster.'[3]

At this time the code breakers at Bletchley Park were concerned at their failure to break the German naval codes. It had already been perceived, that as in the First World War, the U-boat threat was Britain's greatest danger. Winston Churchill wrote: 'The only thing that ever really frightened me during the war was the U-boat peril.'[4]

The cryptologists at Bletchley Park had already broken German Army and Abwehr Enigma messages. But the Kriegsmarine three-rotor encoding machine was proving a tougher nut to crack. Admiral Godfrey sent Fleming, his troubleshooter, to see Dilly Knox at Bletchley Park, a place he visited often, who told him that a German Navy codebook would be of great assistance. So he came up with a plan to capture a German vessel that would be carrying the book. He soon identified that the Germans were running an air-rescue boat out of Denmark that would pick up air crews that had ditched in the sea after a raid.

If a rescue boat could be lured to pick up a crew of a downed bomber, which would be British in disguise, the crew might be overpowered and the codebook taken. Fleming outlined his idea in a note to Godfrey:

D.N.I.

I suggest we obtain the loot by the following means.

1 Obtain from air ministry an airworthy German bomber.

2 Pick a tough crew of five, including a pilot, w/t operator and word-perfect German speaker. Dress in German Air Force uniforms; add blood and bandages to suit.

3 Crash plane in the Channel after making s.o.s. to rescue services in P/L.

4 Once aboard rescue boat, shoot German crew, dump overboard, bring rescue boat back to English port.

In order to increase the chances of capturing an R. or M. With its richer booty, the crash might be staged in mid-Channel. The Germans would presumably employ one of this type for the longer and more hazardous journey.

F. 12.9.40[5]

A Heinkel He 111 bomber was available; the aircraft had been captured in an airworthy condition from the bomber unit Kampfgeschwader 26. In early February it had made a forced landing near North Berwick after tangling with a Spitfire over the Firth of Forth. It was then assigned to the RAF and flown by the Air Fighting Development Unit, although Group Captain H.J. Wilson pointed out crashing this type of aircraft in the Channel would result in the collapse of the bomber's perspex nose and the crew would likely drown before they could get out. However, he reluctantly agreed to the operation after the Heinkel's nose was reinforced.

Fleming volunteered to be one of the crew with his excellent German but Admiral Godfrey banned him from taking part as his possible capture was too great a risk. Rear Admiral Jock Clayton, head of the OIC, supported the scheme but wanted to see a more detailed plan. Ian set to work on the details.

The Heinkel, Werk No. 6853, would take off just after dawn following German aircraft returning to base after a raid. When it spotted a German rescue vessel it would cut one engine and produce smoke by injecting oil into the exhaust, send an SOS and ditch into the sea. The operation was scheduled for the early part of October as German codes were changed at the start of each month. Fleming and his team went to Dover to await the next suitable bombing raid, but aerial reconnaissance and wireless monitoring failed to locate any German rescue vessels and they were stood down. Operation Ruthless was shelved on 16 October, with a recommendation that it should be tried again from Portsmouth, and that: 'Lieutenant Commander Fleming returns to Admiralty 1800 today Wednesday.'[6] Frank Birch, head of the naval section at GCHQ, wrote in a letter four days later that Alan Turing and Peter Twinn were 'all of a stew about the cancellation of Ruthless'.[7]

However, the bones of Operation Ruthless would resurface in the Bond book *Thunderball* published in 1961, as Plan Omega hatched by SPECTRE, the Special Executive for Counter Intelligence, Terrorism, Revenge, and Extortion. Its founder and chairman, Ernst Stavro Blofeld, was the arch villain. Born in Gdynia, Poland, of Polish/Greek parents, he was overweight, asexual and power-obsessed. As with most Bond villains, he has a physical peculiarity, his Mussolini-like eyes with long 'silken black eyelashes' and the gaze of the 'soft doll's eyes was totally relaxed and rarely held any expression stronger than a mild curiosity in the object of their focus'.[8] He makes a fortune in the Second World War selling secrets to both sides, starting with the Abwehr, and he will only accept payment in US dollars. He is lucky to have started before the Germans put Operations Andreas and later Bernhard, the forgery of banknotes, into effect, and paying their agents and supplying their operatives with them. Millions in pounds and US dollars were produced. Perhaps the most famous case was the German agent, the Albanian Turk Elyesa Bazna, code-named Cicero, who was paid in forged currency for rolls of film he took of top secret documents when he was the valet to the British Ambassador in Ankara. He was paid a total of £300,000, all of which was worthless. After the war he tried to sue the West German government for compensation but was unsuccessful.[9]

Fleming must have had a soft spot for Blofeld as he gave him his own birthday, 28 May 1908.[10] However, while Blofeld is pulling the strings, in *Thunderball* it is his subordinate – Emilio Largo, former member of the Italian naval commandos, the famed Decima Flottiglia MAS (X MAS) – that Bond must face. A keen swimmer and diver himself, Ian was intrigued by the exploits of X MAS, and has Bond refer to them in *Thunderball*, when he tells Felix Leiter of the CIA that the *Olterra* affair was 'one of the blackest marks against Intelligence during the whole war'.[11] The *Olterra* was a wrecked ship that X MAS used as cover to attack ships anchored at Gibraltar. X MAS will be covered in detail in the chapter on Gibraltar.

The SPECTRE plan is to hijack a Vindicator bomber carrying two nuclear bombs, so they can hold the world to ransom. Largo uses his luxury motor yacht, *Disco Volante*, which has its own below-the-water-line compartment, to recover and move the bombs.[12]

Giuseppe Petacchi of the Italian Air Force is another character that comes out of the Second World War. He is used to hijack a Vindicator bomber flying from Boscombe Down airfield while he is a NATO observer. The Vindicator is a figment of Fleming's imagination and an Avro Vulcan is used in the 1965 film. The 34-year-old Petacchi, we are told, had flown a Focke-Wulf 200 Condor over the Adriatic in 1943, 'one of the few hand-picked Italian airmen who had been allowed to handle these German planes'. On his final flight he shoots the other crew members and brings the aircraft to Bari and to the Allies complete with a 'pressure mine', for which he is paid £10,000.[13] German pressure mines were developed in 1943, but not used until the night of 6–7 June 1944 in the Normandy invasion area. By the end of the war the Germans very nearly had ready to use a mine that could not be swept.[14]

Petacchi, having been a turncoat already, and having had 'all his life a passion for owning things', has seen a Maserati 3500 GT bodied by Ghia at the Milan Motor Show that he must have, and thus is easy for SPECTRE to recruit.[15] He would be paid a million dollars; he poisons the crew with cyanide gas introduced into the pressurised cabin while he puts on an oxygen mask. Once they are all dead he closes the cyanide canister but keeps his own mask on, never quite believing the tests he makes to verify the air is clear and: 'The giant plane whispered on into the night.'[16]

He brings the plane down into a perfect landing on to the sea. 'The belly of the plane gave a jolt' as the back broke. She sinks slowly and 'there was a hiss of steam from the submerging jets'. He climbs out onto the wing; a boat comes out to meet him and he is quickly dispatched with a stiletto 'through the roof of the mouth, into the brain'.[17] So much for the million dollars.

On a 'hunch' that the plane has gone down somewhere in the Bermuda Bahamas area, M sends Bond to Nassau to start searching.[18] At this stage we might ask who was James Bond, was he based on any individual? Many people have been put forward as models. We can be fairly certain what Ian Fleming felt he looked like, as in *Casino Royale* his doomed girlfriend, Vesper Lynd, says to Rene Mathis of the French Deuxième Bureau that Bond 'is very good looking. He reminds me of

Hoagy Carmichael.'[19] While in *Moonraker*, Gala Brand observes he was: 'Rather like Hoagy Carmichael in a way. The black hair falling down over the right eyebrow. Much the same bones.' Yet there was a cruel streak about him.[20]

Hoagy Carmichael was an American singer, songwriter and actor, hugely popular over three decades from the 1930s to the '50s. His music was influenced by jazz and he came out of the Tin Pan Alley area of New York. He wrote *Georgia on my Mind*, and in 1951 won the Academy Award for Best Original song with *In the Cool, Cool, of the Evening*. He appeared in fourteen films and wrote two autobiographies. As far as Bond is concerned, he would seem a little old, being 54 in 1953. Whereas Bond, considering his *Times* obituary in *You Only Live Twice*, would have been barely 30.[21] Of course, Fleming was likely to have had a younger image of Carmichael in mind, although there is something in his 1947 photograph that hints at a hardness.

You do not have to look very far to find another character in our story with a passing physical resemblance to Hoagy Carmichael, who given his life in some ways makes a better Bond model altogether. This is Lieutenant Commander Lionel Kenneth Crabb, known as 'Buster' although he hated the nickname, one of the most famous Royal Navy frogmen of the Second World War and beyond. He too has the shock of dark hair, although in fact his hair was red, and the high forehead, but there is more humour around the eyes. He was renowned for taking on the Italians of X MAS in the waters around Gibraltar, when commanding, the oddly named 'Gibraltar Underwater Working Party' in Operation Tadpole, which we will come across later.

After the war Crabb worked in Palestine combating Jewish divers' attempts to mine ships, and in 1947 he was demobbed. He took on several civilian diving jobs before returning to the Navy.

In 1950 he was involved in attempts to rescue submariners aboard *Truculent*, which had sunk in the Thames estuary after a collision with a ship. The following year the submarine *Affray* went missing after leaving Portsmouth heading south to take part in Exercise Spring Train. She was due to land some Royal Marines of the Special Boat Section on an isolated Cornish beach. All contact was lost with *Affray*, which was eventually found on the bottom near Alderney. Divers, including

Crabb, were sent down but could find no firm evidence of why she had sunk. Seventy-five men remain entombed within her to this day. In 1955, accompanied by another diver, Crabb investigated the hull of the advanced Soviet cruiser *Sverdlov*, which was jokingly referred to as 'looking at the Russian's bottom'.[22] That year Crabb had to retire due to his age. Yet almost immediately he was recruited by MI6 for further clandestine diving jobs, albeit a life of heavy smoking and drinking had taken its toll. Crabb would have likely smoked Senior Service or Player's Navy Cut, not the specially made Balkan and Turkish blend Morland of Grosvenor Street that Bond smoked. Crabb was a beer drinker; no vodka Martinis for him, shaken or stirred.

Bond's testing of the hull of the *Disco Volante*, with a Geiger counter for nuclear bombs, in *Thunderball* was influenced by Commander Crabb's ill-fated mission to examine the Soviet cruiser *Ordzhonikidze*.[23] The warship and escorting destroyers had brought the Soviet leaders Nikita Khrushchev and Nikolai Bulganin on a goodwill visit to Britain. The cruiser had docked in Portsmouth.

MI5 bugged Khrushchev's rooms in Claridge's Hotel but learned nothing; Peter Wright wrote that he listened to 'Khrushchev for hours'. But all they learned was about the Soviet leader's attire, which he discussed endlessly with his valet: 'He was an extraordinarily vain man. He stood in front of the mirror preening himself for hours at a time, and fussing with the parting of his hair.'[24]

MI6 ran the operation against *Ordzhonikidze*, keeping MI5 largely in the dark. They wanted to know the size and location of her propellers so that the Admiralty might learn why she was so fast. The year before, an X-Craft midget submarine had been used to release a diver close inshore, to examine her in a Soviet port. They had got close but security around the ship was too tight and the mission was called off.

On Tuesday, 17 April Crabb booked into the Sallyport Hotel Portsmouth, accompanied by a 'fair-haired man of about forty known as Mr Smith ...'[25] The next day, Crabb met some of his old friends from HMS *Vernon*, the shore establishment for the mine and torpedo schools. On the 19th, Crabb dived into Portsmouth harbour and was never seen again. He would have been wearing oxygen breathing gear so that no bubbles would be seen. However, this equipment at the time was not considered safe below 30ft, and he would have had to dive considerably deeper. It is likely he 'contracted oxygen poisoning'. Also, he should not have been diving alone.[26]

The Soviets reported that a frogman had been seen floating between the Soviet destroyers at 0730 on the morning of 19 April. MI6 and NI tried to cover things up, releasing a statement that Crabb had been lost while taking part in secret trials of underwater apparatus in Stokes Bay on the Solent. Smith had returned to the Sallyport Hotel, paid the bill and took away Crabb's belongings.[27] The press were soon on to the story but found four pages from the hotel register had been removed. According to Peter Wright, Malcolm Cummings of MI5 'telephoned the CID in Portsmouth and arranged for the hotel register to be sanitized'.[28]

The Commander Crabb incident was debated in the House of Commons on 14 May. Hugh Gaitskell, leader of the opposition, paid tribute to him: 'Whatever may be the circumstances in which he met his death all of us will agree that this country would be poorer if it were not for men like Commander Crabb.'[29] The incident was another nail in the coffin of the ill-fated Anthony Eden premiership, and the head of MI6, Major General John Sinclair, known as 'Sinbad', was sacked.

There have been some claims that Crabb was captured by the Soviets and might have died on board *Ordzhonikidze* under interrogation, others that he was taken back to the Soviet Union and lived there. Tim Binding's 2005 novel *Man Overboard* takes up this idea. Not unlike Bond at the end of *You Only Live Twice* finding his way to the Soviet Union, and then being brainwashed by the KGB in *The Man with the Golden Gun*. He tells M: 'They gave me VIP treatment. Top brain specialists and everything.'[30] Bond then promptly tries to kill M with a cyanide pistol.

Fleming carried a pen capable of using poisons on several of his Second World War missions, although whether it was ever filled is not known. There are examples of the KGB using poison sprays in assassinations. The KGB agent Bohdan Stashynsky killed Ukrainian nationalist leaders Lev Rebet in 1957 and Stepan Bandera in 1959 using a poison spray gun. The weapon fired a jet of poison gas from a crushed cyanide capsule, which brought on a heart attack and so made it appear that the men died of natural causes.[31]

Another twist in the story was that the ill-fated prime minister Anthony Eden, close to a nervous breakdown after the Suez crisis in November 1956, took a complete rest on the advice of his doctors, at, of all places, Ian Fleming's house Goldeneye on Jamaica. He was mercilessly lampooned in the press for doing so. A competition in the *Daily Mail* featured how best to solve the Suez crisis, with the first prize being a three-week holiday for two in Jamaica. Ian was delighted to have such paying guests as it brought him huge publicity.[32]

There are many other characters that claim they influenced Fleming in his creation of James Bond, some of whom we will come across later, but the main input to 007 was probably the author himself. Len Deighton's spy with no name, although he is named Harry Palmer in the films starting with the *Ipcress File*, clearly has several of the author's characteristics. He too lives in a bedsit, as Deighton did when he wrote the first book, wears heavy glasses and is a good cook.[33]

John le Carré went even further when talking about his characters: 'All fictional characters are amalgams. All spring from much deeper wells than their apparent counterparts in real life. All in the end, like the poor suspects in my files, are remoulded in the writer's imagination until they are probably closer to his own nature than to anyone elses.'[34]

As John Pearson says, Bond had many of Fleming's traits: he smokes the 'same number of cigarettes as Fleming did. He wears the same clothes. He likes the same cars, is the same height and has the same love of scrambled eggs.'[35]

THE HESS AFFAIR, MAY 1941

For months in 1940 the Fleming family had agonised over the fate of Evelyn's youngest son and Ian's brother, Michael. News came through three months after Dunkirk that he had been wounded and taken prisoner. A father of four, he had set off for France as captain and adjutant of the 4th Battalion Oxfordshire and Buckinghamshire Light Infantry, a territorial unit.

The 4th Battalion suffered heavy casualties on the retreat to Dunkirk, one of which was Michael, wounded by a shell splinter in the left thigh. Before this he was mentioned in dispatches three times. The battalion war diary of 28 May 1940 paid tribute to him:

> Throughout the whole battle the men, though very tired and hungry, kept extremely cheerful and were greatly helped by the adjutant, Captain Fleming, who completely unmoved by any form of fire, came riding on his motor-cycle over the rubble of demolished houses looking as though he were out for a Sunday afternoon ride and distributing cigarettes or other luxuries he had discovered.[1]

Shortly after this, Michael was wounded and was left behind with other serious cases and captured. He was treated at the PoW hospital near

Zuydcoote. Unable to walk, he was sent to the British PoW hospital at Lille. His wound would not heal and gangrene set in. The leg was amputated but too late; he died on 1 October.

It was not until November that Letitia, his wife, known as Tish, received the heartbreaking news that he had died of his wounds. Tish, with four small children, three boys and a girl, went to live at Merrimoles with Celia, their aunt, who was Celia Johnson, the actress and wife of Peter Fleming. Peter, given his wartime commitments, did as much as he could for them and took responsibility for their welfare.[2]

Ian was stunned by the death of his bright brother, Michael, but like many people he could not dwell on it. The demands of NI were swallowing most of his time. And for Londoners at the time in the midst of the Blitz, death was a daily trial to overcome.

The increasing workload Ian was given included a widening role as peacemaker between the various intelligence agencies. The birth of the SOE in July 1940 had been fraught with difficulties. It was set up under Hugh Dalton, the Minister for Economic Warfare. Gladwyn Jebb was the chief executive officer, who promptly took over SIS's section IX that did most of the sabotage and propaganda work, and the MI(R) branch at the War Office with a similar remit for propaganda. The transfer was completed before SIS had formally been notified. Stewart Menzies, head of SIS, complained about this, although he told Jebb he welcomed the change, not wanting 'to retain responsibility for sabotage and subversion activities'.[3] Jebb was well aware of the need for 'friendly co-operation of "C" if special operations were to function efficiently ...'[4]

Admiral Godfrey submitted a report on the clash between SIS and SOE, and of the importance of the former to Naval Intelligence, which was likely compiled with Ian Fleming:

The collection of Naval Intelligence is still in a large measure dependent on S.I.S and I am, therefore, closely interested in the security of S.I.S agents and of their communications, and in the expansion of the organisation as a whole.

2 Since the establishment of S.O.2 [SOE] as a separate entity, charged with sabotage in enemy countries, S.O.2 and the S.I.S have been in

keen competition. I am aware of the competition in questions of transport, recruitment, communications, equipment and the 'use of cover' all over the world. The following are some examples:–

(a) Spain

The position of the S.I.S in this most difficult country is becoming daily more precarious in the face of attempts by S.O.2 to create a 'sabotage organisation' in the Peninsula, with untrained personnel. Spanish suspicions have been aroused by certain S.O.2 intrigues with the Left, and endeavours which the Naval Attaché has made to direct S.O.2 activities have led to him being compromised to a certain degree. The A.N.A Europe, Commander Furse, is also under suspicion and the Ambassador has been forced to adopt a very strong line with S.O. (E) for fear that his own work might be jeopardised.

(b) Portugal

Episodes have occurred, resulting from the use of Portugal as a base for S.O.2 operations in the Peninsula, which have made an Intelligence service much more difficult to maintain.[5]

It came to a head in Portugal in February 1942 when the Policia de Vigilancia Defesa do Estado (PVDE, Portuguese Secret Police) suggested that SOE were orchestrating anti-government unrest via the Communists. This came about during the 'Wolfram Wars'. Portugal and Spain were two of the main producers of highly prized tungsten used to harden steel; giving shells enhanced armour-piercing qualities coveted by both the Allies and Axis powers. Destabilising government was a line none of the warring parties were to cross. Antonio de Oliveira Salazar the Portuguese dictator summoned the British Ambassador Sir Ronald Campbell to his office behind the Palace of São Bento. There he expressed his concerns, pointing out Operation Panicle, a sabotage scheme similar to Operation Golden Eye but for Portugal, he had found out, went much further than what had been agreed. He then announced much to Campbell's shock that he wanted SOE to be dismantled in Portugal. In the days after the meeting the PVDE conducted a series of arrests and interrogations against British interests, and some 300 people were picked up. In fact the PVDE had been tipped off by the Germans; however, SOE had taken a serious risk in having known communists working for them.[6]

Godfrey also highlighted problems in Sweden. SOE activities there had made relations with the authorities 'difficult'. In Norway their operations were on such a scale that they endangered 'the permanent Intelligence Centres which had been established and which are planned for the future'.

He went on to point out that SOE projects 'again and again' were adversely affecting 'the more permanent S.I.S work'. He believed the SIS should be given priority over any SOE schemes, although he felt SOE should have the right of appeal 'to the three Directors of Intelligence or through to the Chiefs of Staff'.

Godfrey concluded his observations with: 'I believe that this is not only desirable for the reasons I have stated, but particularly in order to remove the possibility of the S.I.S excusing failure to produce Intelligence on the grounds that their efforts are nullified, in particular instances, by the activities of S.O.2.'[7]

Although Fleming wrote many letters highlighting the shortcomings of SIS, he was far more sympathetic than his irascible boss. With the support of Admiral Sir Dudley Pound, Godfrey outlined an idea for a separate naval secret service, which in time would absorb SIS. But Churchill instead ordered an inquiry into SIS, and its findings were that the service performed much better than was thought. Perhaps Churchill was also influenced by his own scheme in 1915, along similar lines, which he had found to be unworkable.

After the inquiry, Fleming came to the support of SIS and 'C'; was it at the back of his mind he was saving the service for his hero James Bond, although by then unnamed? He would, of course, make him a Navy man and installing M, a former admiral, as the director was a nod to NI.

Of the inquiry, Fleming wrote an assessment for Godfrey: 'I am sorry to say that I think this report very reasonable. As to the individuals concerned, the points made also seem just, but any reorganisation which might be necessary there is a grave danger, as with all reorganisations of "letting the baby out with the bath water".'

He went on to say that introducing new people into SIS would be 'better than chopping off hoary but experienced heads'. He finished by indicating that the high flyers of SIS might do well to have 'young staff officers cum-secretaries attached to them. It would probably be a good thing if "C" himself had such an individual.' Was Fleming here angling for a new job? However, Godfrey was not about to let him go.[8]

Patrick Beesly thought Godfrey looked on Fleming as the son he had never had. Godfrey remarked after the war: 'Ian should have been the DNI and I his naval adviser.'[9]

Unlike 007, the inspiration for M is much easier to identify, with so many similarities to Ian's boss at NID, Admiral John Godfrey. Both were crusty and bad-tempered, and the allusion to Godfrey is made clear in On Her Majesty's Secret Service with the reference to the battle-cruiser Repulse, the ship Godfrey had commanded in the Mediterranean during the 1930s. M is identified in The Man with the Golden Gun as Admiral Sir Miles Messervy.[10] Bond uses 'the clapper of the brass ship's bell of some former HMS Repulse' to gain admittance to 'M's house' and that 'Repulse had been his last sea-going command'. Chief Petty Officer Hammond still looks after the admiral, as he had in the service. Admiral Sir Miles 'M' Messervy is a bachelor, unlike Godfrey who was married. Repulse was sunk off Malaya with the battleship Prince of Wales by Japanese naval aircraft on 10 December 1941.[11]

There are other possible influences on the character of M in the Bond books. One was Brigadier Colin McVean Gubbins, code-named 'M' in SOE. Born in Japan in 1896, the son of a diplomat, his father, although English, had Irish roots and his mother was a Highland Scot, which is where he grew up. He was commissioned into the Royal Artillery at the start of the First World War. He gained a Military Cross on the Somme. Later in the war he suffered the effects of mustard gas poisoning but recovered, only finally to be sent home in 1918 ill with trench fever. He continued as a regular in the Army, serving in northern Russia, Ireland and India. In 1939 he was placed in the War Office section General Staff research group, studying guerrilla warfare and writing several pamphlets on the subject. He was in Warsaw at the start of the war and saw action in Norway in 1940. When SOE was set up in July 1940, he was appointed Director of Operations and Training, code-named 'M'. In 1943 he became head of SOE. Ian Fleming got to know him well through their private meetings to iron out difficulties that arose between SOE and NI.[12]

There is another, not so obvious, influence on the fictional M, Maxwell Knight the MI5 spymaster. Godfrey and Knight disliked each other. Knight ran his own section, B5(b), its remit to infiltrate subversive organisations, from his offices in Hood House, Dolphin Square, largely with autonomy. In 1939, MI5, greatly expanded, had moved from Thames House to Wormwood Scrubs, so rapidly that unemptied chamberpots were found in some cells and there were still prisoners in some of the cell blocks. They were soon on the move again after the Scrubs was damaged by incendiary bombs in 1940, this time to Blenheim Palace. The staff referred to the move as 'from prison to palace'.[13] Not that MI5 was any better run than the other intelligence services. Derek Tangye worked as a press officer for MI5 and felt most people worked in 'isolation with little support'. There was too much 'secrecy within secrecy', and he found it difficult to fathom many colleagues, specifically 'whether he was hiding information from me or whether he felt at a disadvantage because I had shown I knew more than he did'.[14]

Anthony Masters cites in his biography of Knight that it was Fleming and Knight who cooked up the idea to lure a Nazi leader to Britain, as Godfrey would never have sanctioned such a risky enterprise.[15] This appears highly unlikely, yet there is some circumstantial evidence that suggests Fleming was involved in a deception heist. The initial spark for him may have been ignited by the publication of his brother Peter's book *The Flying Visit*.

In March 1940 Peter had to spend a week in bed with German measles, of all things. He was almost never ill but maybe the irony of his situation inspired him, for in that time he wrote a novella of 20,000 words, *The Flying Visit*, which was published by Jonathan Cape in July. In it Hitler flies over Britain to gloat over the damage the Luftwaffe is inflicting. However, his aircraft is sabotaged by a time bomb. He is the only survivor and lands by parachute in the Chilterns.[16] After various adventures, including winning a village hall fancy dress competition where he makes a speech, and is cheered to the rafters, the villagers are convinced he is an Englishman impersonating Hitler. He is captured by the British but they have no idea what to do with him, convinced the Germans will have a lookalike ready to take over. The

Cabinet decide to send him back in an RAF bomber and he is para-
chuted down into 'a wide shallow bog in Eastern Germany'.[17]

It is a comic tongue-in-cheek book, albeit with a thread of con-
tempt for the principal character running through it. What is more
remarkable is that less than a year after publication of *The Flying Visit*,
the Deputy Führer Rudolf Hess arrived in Scotland after parachuting
from an Me 110 fighter-bomber.

Who was Rudolf Hess? He was born in Alexandria, Egypt, in 1894,
his father was a prosperous merchant and he was destined to join the
family firm. Aged 14, he was sent to Germany to a boarding school at
Bad Godesberg on the Rhine. A good student, he did well in maths
and science and was fond of classical music. He later studied at a commercial college in Switzerland, yet he had no wish to join the family
business and was saved from this fate by the outbreak of the First
World War. He joined the army as a volunteer and rose through the
ranks to officer before transferring to the Air Force. He was shocked
by Germany's defeat. After the war he studied Political Economy at
Munich University. It was in the city he first heard Adolf Hitler speak
in 1920, at a meeting of the National Socialist German Workers' Party,
the Nazis, about restoring German honour. He became a devout fol-
lower of Hitler, helped him write his memoirs, became his secretary,
and when Hitler gained power in 1933 became his deputy.

Geoffrey Shakespeare, a junior British minister in 1933, was in
Germany and met Hess. Over several years he got to know him well.
He found him a rather simple soul, infatuated with Hitler. He had little
'knowledge of government', but had the notion that 'England and
Germany between them could govern the world. I do not think he
liked England, but he admired the English in many ways.'[18]

There is some ambiguity whether Clydesdale Marquess of Douglas,
Douglas-Hamilton, eldest son of the Duke of Hamilton, met Hess at
the Berlin Olympics in 1936, but they were both present at a dinner
given by Hitler. It hardly seems possible that two accomplished avia-
tors – in 1933 Clydesdale was the chief pilot for the first ever flight
over Mount Everest – did not meet. Lord Malcolm Douglas-Hamilton,
Clydesdale's younger brother, met Hess at the same party, as did MP
Henry Channon, who wrote in his diary that he and Clydesdale had

been invited to lunch by Hess; he declined but Clydesdale accepted. When Hess arrived in Britain looking for Clydesdale, he denied he had ever met Hess in 1936, most likely to try and dispel the implication that he was a Nazi sympathiser.[19]

Whether the two men ever met is not that important for they shared a close friend, Albrecht Haushofer, an academic geographer, who was the son of General, later Professor, Karl Haushofer and his half-Jewish wife, Martha. Hess protected Haushofer and his brother from the consequences of their Jewish blood. In return, Haushofer reluctantly served Hess as a roving expert on foreign affairs; he was seen as an expert on British politics and personalities. Well aware of the evil nature of the Nazis, he was a double agent working for groups opposed to Hitler.

In June 1940, Hess conceived the idea of a peace mission to Britain. He later told his captors in Britain that in August he had asked Haushofer about approaching people of influence in Britain who were interested in peace. He then instructed him to find such people. He knew that Hitler wanted a compromise with England and when his peace offer was rejected, Hess came to the conclusion, as he told Sir John Simon, Lord Simon, one of those chosen by Churchill to interview Hess, that: 'if I were over there in England, she could use this as grounds for negotiation without losing prestige.'[20]

At the time the impression in German circles had been that power in Britain was anything but settled. Joseph Goebbels, the Nazi Minister of Propaganda, wrote in his diary that there were two parties vying for power: 'One thoroughgoing war party and one peace party. They wrestle for the upper hand.'[21] There was some justification for this albeit misguided view. On 22 May 1940, the Emergency Powers (Defence) Act had been strengthened in Britain to increase the scope of internment without trial of anyone showing sympathy to the enemy. There was no appeal against the 18b Regulation. Within days Oswald Mosley and most of the leadership of the British Union of Fascists (BUF) had been rounded up, along with the pro-fascist Right Club.

Joan Miller, an MI5 agent, had infiltrated the Right Club for Maxwell Knight's B5 (b) to check on the activities of Captain Archibald Ramsay, Conservative MP for Peebles and Southern Midlothian. She uncovered a considerable espionage operation, which was altogether a more serious matter than the BUF activities. Over many months, a spy ring run by Ramsay was uncovered that was planning an attempt to bring down the government. Tyler Kent, a cipher clerk working at the United States Embassy in London, got involved with Anna Wolkoff, the daughter of a White Russian admiral, who had extreme anti-Semitic and pro-German views, and was a member of the Right Club.

Kent kept copies of the messages he had seen, and began showing them to members of the group, including highly secret correspondence between Churchill and Roosevelt. In one instance, a message referred to fifty old US destroyers that were given to Britain in exchange for the use of Caribbean bases. This would 'have strengthened the hand of American isolationists whose influence Churchill was struggling to diminish'.[22]

The leaders of the Right Club had a contact with the military attaché of the Italian Embassy. On 23 May, details of the arrangements for the old destroyers were transmitted by the German Embassy in Rome to Berlin. However, the Italian diplomatic telegrams decrypted by British code breakers revealed almost all US Embassy dispatches to President Roosevelt were being passed to Rome. The US Embassy was alerted on 18 May and all the group's members arrested. Kent was sentenced to seven years in prison; however, in 1945 he was deported to the USA and released. Wolkoff was sentenced to ten years but released in 1947. Ramsay was interned until the end of the war, the only MP to be so under 18b.

The Link, founded in 1937, was another pro-German organisation that by 1939 had thirty-five branches and 4,000 members. It produced its own publication, the *Anglo-German Review*. A propaganda platform for Goebbels, the organisation was run by its founder, Admiral Sir Barry Domvile, a former DNI 1927–30 and President of the Royal Naval College, Greenwich 1932–34.

Ian Fleming, it has been suggested, went to Maxwell Knight and studied the file on Domvile. The two of them then cooked up an idea that through the Link they might lure a Nazi leader to Britain. They would indicate that the organisation had merely been driven underground but was still strong enough to 'overthrow the Churchill Government'. Again, there is no concrete evidence for this.[23] However, it was true that many of the more prominent and powerful British Nazi sympathisers remained free, such as the Duke of Buccleuch and Queensberry, and the Marquess of Tavistock, heir to the Duke of Bedford. Fleming could never have sold the idea to Godfrey, but Knight was not averse to the risk involved; the isolation of his department in Dolphin Square was an advantage to keeping it secret from the other agencies.

As France fell to the Nazis, the former King Edward VIII, who had abdicated because of his determination to marry Mrs Wallis Simpson, a divorcee, fled south from the Villa La Croe on Cap d'Antibes, where they had been staying. On 23 June they were in Madrid and had met the British Ambassador, Sir Samuel Hoare. The then Duke of Windsor had been vocal in his admiration for the Nazis, while Hoare was looked on as an 'appeaser' and while serving in the Chamberlain government had been openly critical of Churchill. When Churchill came to power he had dismissed Hoare, but was well aware of his diplomatic skills and sent him to Spain as ambassador with the task to keep Francisco Franco from joining the Axis. The German propaganda machine went into overdrive spreading rumours that Hoare and the Duke of Windsor were conspiring for a negotiated peace.

Haushofer at first did not rise to this bait but rather tried to arrange a meeting in Portugal with Clydesdale, who had by now succeeded his father to become the 14th Duke of Hamilton. However, his letter was intercepted, and soon revealed the cover address was for an Abwehr station in Portugal.[24] Although it did prompt an MI5 investigation into Hamilton's loyalty, there was some discussion about sending the Duke, a serving RAF officer, to Lisbon. But this was finally dropped by Major T.A. 'Tar' Robertson of section B1a, which ran double agents, on the grounds there had been too long a delay in answering the letter and the opportunity had passed.[25]

In the winter of 1940–41, Haushofer was able to start a dialogue through a former pupil of his, Herbert Stammer, who was a legation secretary in the German Embassy in Madrid, with Sir Samuel Hoare, through the Swedish Embassy. However, the precondition to any talks was a change in both British and German governments. Franz von Papen, German Ambassador to Turkey, had expressed the view both Hitler and Churchill should be replaced, and his counterpart,

Sir Hughe Knatchbull-Hugessen in Ankara, reported this to Anthony Eden.[26] He also wrote in his own memoirs that von Papen saw the war as damaging 'to German and British interests' and late in 1939 he approached Knatchbull-Hugessen through a neutral friend with 'proposals that involved the removal of Herr Hitler and the installation of a less violent regime'.[27]

Hess would not have been in favour of any attempt to remove his idol Adolf Hitler from power. He was unaware that his chief envoy Haushofer, with his approaches through Spain and other countries, was playing a double game.

Meanwhile, Hoare had been informed by Eden in February 1941 that all German peace approaches should be met with 'absolute silence' and that if 'these approaches sometimes afford useful information, you should continue to report fully any indication of German inclinations to negotiate you may receive'.[28]

In March, Prince Max zu Hohenlohe arrived in Madrid and asked to speak to Hoare, who granted the request, ignoring the Foreign Office instructions. The Hohenlohe family had close ties with Spain and Max was a friend of Himmler and Goering. He had been a mediator between Germany and Britain before the war and continued the role during the war. Hoare saw Hohenlohe in the flat of the British military attaché, Brigadier Bill Torr, who was present. There was nothing new in Hohenlohe's message, which was that Hitler wanted to be reasonable and the war was a calamity for both countries. Hoare countered that Britain was not prepared to see Germany dominate Europe. He later explained to Sir Alexander Cadogan of the Foreign Office that in the ordinary course of events he would have reported the request but as Hohenlohe was shortly to leave Madrid, 'it was a case of seeing him yesterday or not at all'.[29]

As such the meeting is not all that important, other than to demonstrate that Hillgarth and Torr knew what was going on, and Hillgarth had direct links to NID and Fleming. Days before Hess flew to Britain, Hillgarth was at a house party at Chequers with his friend Winston Churchill. Jock Colville, Churchill's private secretary, that day wrote in his diary that Hillgarth was 'a fervent disciple of Sam Hoare'.[30] Only the month before Hoare in Spain had been voicing his concerns over the imminent collapse of Churchill's government and his own recall to form a new government to end the war, all of which was easily reported back to the German and Italian embassies. Here surely was the Hoare, Hillgarth and Fleming triangle in operation, conducting a deliberate campaign of disinformation and hoping someone would rise to the bait. This is much more likely to have been the way Ian Fleming was involved with the Hess affair.[31]

There were some reports emanating from France that Hess flew to Spain in April to meet with Hoare but he doubted this, as the German Ambassador was in Barcelona at the time. There were no reports of Hess in Barcelona either, and if he was there Hoare felt it had been kept 'remarkably secret'.[32]

It is equally likely that Stewart Menzies, 'C' of the SIS, also worked at disinformation to lure Hess to Britain, not only through Hoare in Madrid, but also through British ambassadors in Berne and Stockholm. Sir William Wiseman, head of MI6 in the United States during the First World War, was in San Francisco in late 1940; he was not trusted by Menzies. He was overheard in a hotel room bugged by the FBI meeting the suspected German spy Princess Stephanie von Hohenlohe, a relative by marriage of Prince Max von Hohenlohe. He told her he represented a group of Englishmen who wanted peace with Germany and asked her to report this to her superiors. The next day, Wiseman met with Captain Fritz Wiedemann, who worked for Hess. Again the FBI listened in to hear Wiseman say he represented a powerful political group led by Lord Halifax but doubted even they could trust Hitler, which led to a discussion on the restoration of the German monarchy.[33] When Wiseman's remarks were reported to the British they disowned him.

John Cecil Masterman's Twenty Committee, known as the XX or Double Cross Committee and part of MI5, also fed the Germans a picture of British demoralisation under the bombing, the peace party's powerful opposition to Churchill and even the names of its members.[34]

Was Hess also lured to Britain through his fascination with the occult? In the spring of 1941 Hess, knowing Hitler planned to invade the Soviet Union and, fearing a war on two fronts, asked his 'astrological advisor' Ernst Schulte-Strathaus when might be a good day for a journey in the interests of peace. Schulte-Strathaus predicated 10 May based on the unusual constellation of six planets in the sign of Taurus coinciding that night with a full moon. He got a second opinion when he asked the Munich astrologer Maria Nagengist the same question and she came up with the same answer: 10 May.

The enchantment Hess had with astrology and the occult was well known at the time. Maxwell Knight had links to that world and was the man who likely came up with the idea of approaching Aleister Crowley. He had been introduced to the 'Great Beast', as Crowley was known, by Dennis Wheatley, the occult and thriller writer, in the mid-1930s. They had both attended some of Crowley's occult meetings, allegedly to conduct research for Wheatley's books.[35] Knight got cold feet over using Crowley in the Hess deception as he was too well known in the occult world. However, Fleming was taken with the idea and used another astrologer via Switzerland to infiltrate the occult circles Hess was known to use, producing another horoscope that predicted a strong 'peace party' in Britain was ready to bring down Churchill's war government.[36]

Much of the lure of astrology is conjecture; however, once Hess had arrived Fleming did approach Crowley for help with the interrogation. Knight was against this but Fleming found out Crowley was living near Torquay on his own; the ugly old man with pock-marked face and pointed ears amused himself by writing patriotic poetry to aid the war effort. Fleming took the idea to Godfrey, while Crowley wrote to the DNI offering his services:

Sir:
   If it is true Herr Hess is much influenced by astrology and Magick, my services might be of use to the Department in case he should not be willing to do what you wish. I have the honour to be, Sir.

Your obedient servant
Aleister Crowley[37]

There is further evidence of Fleming's involvement in the Hess affair through a Foreign Office note sent to the DNI dated 28/5/41. It is stamped 'Most Secret' and 'By Hand, not to pass through any Registry.'

It contains the transcript of an interview with Hess on 22 May. There are a lot of Admiralty people selected to read it, from the First Sea Lord to various other admirals. Across the first page there is a hand-written note by Fleming: 'DNI-PA I'd like to talk to you about this.' Here is Fleming talking to Godfrey. The transcript from a naval point of view concerns Hess talking about German submarine construction and use. However, we do not know what Fleming wanted to talk to Godfrey about, it might have been the Crowley offer.[38] Whatever it was, Fleming kept Crowley's note. Pearson, Fleming's biographer, wrote that: 'there was much hilarity in the department at the idea of the Great Beast 666 doing his bit for Britain'.[39]

More than a decade later, after Crowley's death, he became the inspiration for Bond's first villain Le Chiffre in *Casino Royale*. As he arrives opposite Bond at the baccarat table he takes his seat 'with the economy of movement of a big fish'.[40] In Chapter 11, Moment of Truth, with Bond and Le Chiffre ready to do battle across the green baize of the table within the negresco baroque of Casino Royale, Fleming gives full vitriol to his description of his first villain. He has a doll-like gaze, thick hands with stubby fingers; he is a drug addict inhaling Benzedrine at the table through this performance. Bond had held his gaze. He is white-faced, he has short reddish-brown hair and an 'unsmiling wet red mouth'. He is a huge man dressed in a tent-like black dinner jacket, and Fleming likens him to a 'black fleeced Minotaur rising out of a green grass field'.[41]

Le Chiffre becomes a blueprint for most of the Bond villains. Almost all are grotesque in one way or another. Several have huge bodies, be they over 6ft like Le Chiffre or short and squat like Auric Goldfinger, who is 5ft tall; most weigh in at 18 to 20 stone. Across the board, they are pretty much all megalomaniacs obsessed with power and world domination. There are exceptions to the rule but only two might be termed good-looking: Emilio Largo, the Italian of *Thunderball*, who may be loosely based on the dashing nobleman Prince Junio Valerio Borghese, who led the famed Decima MAS naval unit; and Red Grant, the IRA man working for SMERSH in *From Russia with Love*. Both of these are merely lieutenants to arch villains.

Crowley was born in 1875 into a Christian fundamentalist family of the Plymouth Brethren, a non-conformist evangelical movement. His father spent some time as a travelling preacher but died of tongue cancer when Aleister was 11, he called him 'my hero and friend'. Inheriting a third of his father's wealth did him no favours, his mother labelled him 'the beast'.[42] Crowley spent the First World War in the United States, where he campaigned for the German war effort against Britain, claiming Irish ancestry and working for Ireland's independence. Later it was revealed he was a double agent and had infiltrated the pro-German movement to assist British Intelligence. After the war he set up the Thelema community in Cefalu, Sicily, in an old villa, based on the concept 'Do what thou wilt shall be the whole law'. It soon degenerated into drug addiction and orgies. Within two years he was in Paris, a drug addict trying to kick the habit and by the Second World War he was looked on as a joke. However, in the summer of 1940 he was approached by Louis de Wohl, the Hungarian astrologer, who was serving in the British Army and attached to the Department of Psychological Warfare, recruited Crowley for Operation Mistletoe.[43]

Cecil Williamson, another high-profile occultist, conceived the idea. He sold it to MI6, who had hired him in 1936 to investigate the Nazi occult movement, for which he compiled a list of 2,000 members. Operation Mistletoe was a fake propaganda exercise conducted in the Ashdown Forest, Sussex, with forty Canadian soldiers dressed in suitable robes dancing around effigies of Nazi leaders being burnt on satanic thrones. The object was to convince German occultists that a British coven of warlocks and witches were working against them. Williamson later worked on Operation Fortitude, the deception plan to convince the Germans the D-Day landings would take place in Pas de Calais and not Normandy.[44]

Several people say that Ian Fleming witnessed one of the Black Masses in the Ashdown Forest. One was Amado, who claimed to be Crowley's illegitimate son. Most Crowley scholars have dismissed his claim.[45] It is likely Ian was not all that interested in the occult as a subject but like a sponge he liked to soak up the bizarre and unusual. He went as far as to say so about astrology in his book *Thrilling Cities*, based on a series of travel articles he wrote for *The Times*. Having his horoscope read held little interest but he was 'intrigued by fortune telling and all matters with extra-sensory perception'. He was not greatly impressed by a 'soothsayer' he met in Tokyo for he was 'far too happy and well-fed for a man who should be in communion with the spirits of darkness ...'[46]

In *Live and Let Die* Fleming relies on Patrick Leigh Fermor's book *The Traveller's Tree* for an explanation of the 'voodoo pantheon', covering four pages in Chapter 3, A Visiting Card.[47] In 1948, 'Paddy' Fermor, the travel writer and wartime intelligence officer, spent a day at Goldeneye, Fleming's modest house on Jamaica, with his wife, Joan. Ann Rothermere, who would later become Ian's wife, was also there. At the time Fermor was conducting a study into voodoo that had 'utterly absorbed' him.[48] No doubt some of this rubbed off on to Ian to be stored away. Fermor was a wartime hero involved in the abduction of the German General Heinrich Kreipe on Crete in 1944. The incident was made famous by W. Stanley Moss's book *Ill Met by Moonlight*, in which Moss and Fermor helped Cretan SOE agents with the operation.

Fleming was taken with sadomasochistic pornography and began collecting it in his youth. His girlfriends bore witness to his preoccupation with sex. Mary Pakenham felt he was obsessed by it and often tried to 'show her obscene pictures'. Another found while waiting for him to complete some task in his flat that he would tell her to entertain herself with his pornographic books, which she found boring, with women 'dressed up as schoolmistresses in lace collars, standing over manacled men with a whip'.[49]

Sadism is a factor with most of the Bond arch villains. Le Chiffre in *Casino Royale* tortures Bond with a carpet beater and a carving knife.[50] Bond, bound to a chair naked, is defenceless. Le Chiffre then begins to apply both instruments to his testicles while speaking to him in a fatherly manner, telling him 'the game of Red Indians is over'. (Red Indians is a name Fleming gave to the Commandos of 30AU.) He must join the grown-ups, which he had 'already found a painful experience'.[51]

The torture of Bond in *Casino Royale* also came out of the Second World War, as Ian explained in an article about thriller writing, though first he recounts he was bullied at school, where he also lost his virginity to a local prostitute, 'like so many of us used to do in the old days'. He added that he had 'never been tempted to foist these and other harrowing personal experiences on the public'. Yet perhaps this might explain his sadistic tendencies; like many people abused in early life, they abuse others. Ian was able to channel this into his fiction. With the torture scene Fleming said he censored this and it was 'a greatly watered down version of a French-Moroccan torture known as *passer à la mandoline*, which was practised on several of our agents during the war'. It involved steel mandolin strings being used to slice through the testicles.[52]

★★★

When Rudolf Hess floated down by parachute from his Me 110, low on fuel, in the night sky over Scotland on 10 May 1941 he had no real idea what awaited him. He landed in a field of Floors Farm, Eaglesham, south of Glasgow. He was met by ploughman David McLean after landing only 200 yards from his cottage. David had heard the aircraft pass low overhead and crash into the ground. He rushed outside to see the flames and a man coming down by parachute. Taking a hayfork with him, he made his way to the field where the man was lying on the ground, his parachute nearby. 'I helped him unloose his harness and get to his feet.' Hess told him he was Hauptmann Alfred Horn, that he wanted to go to Dungavel House and that he had an important message for the Duke of Hamilton.[53]

McLean had to help Hess hobble to his cottage as he could not put weight on his damaged ankle, the result of getting out of the plane and/or landing. He was made comfortable and offered tea by McLean's mother; he declined but took a glass of water. Two Home Guard lookouts had seen the plane come down and were quickly at the McLean cottage. More Home Guard arrived, who took him to Busby village in a car. He was moved again to the Headquarters of the 3rd Battalion Renfrewshire Home Guard. He asked for Hamilton again and that he had a message for him. He was soon on the move again, to Maryhill Barracks, Paisley, where he arrived at 0230. There the duty doctor attended to his ankle.

At last Hess got his wish of meeting Hamilton, a serving RAF officer at Maryhill Barracks, at 1000 on 11 May. Hamilton wrote a report on the meeting but continued to deny he had ever met Hess before. Hess outlined the Führer's peace terms, but Hamilton pointed out this was far too late and there was little hope of a peace agreement now.[54]

Later that day Hess was driven to Drymen Military Hospital in Buchanan Castle on the shores of Loch Lomond, where a 100-strong guard was soon in place. Hamilton took a Hurricane fighter from RAF Turnhouse and flew south to report to the prime minister, who was at Ditchley Park near Oxford. When Hamilton made his report Churchill said: 'Well, Hess or no Hess, I am going to see the Marx Brothers.' Churchill went to see the film in the host's private cinema. After midnight he spoke with Hamilton again for three hours.[55]

The next day Churchill and Hamilton were driven to London, where top-level meetings with various people took place in Downing Street. Sir Stewart Menzies, 'C' of SIS, was one, another was Lord Beaverbrook, who having met Hess several times was able from photographs to confirm the man in question was the Deputy Führer. It was decided to send Ivone Kirkpatrick, who worked for the Political Warfare Executive, to Scotland with Hamilton to see Hess. Kirkpatrick had been at the Munich talks in 1938, knew the Nazi leaders and spoke German. That night, 12 May, the first announcement of Hess's arrival was made. The Germans had already announced that 'party member' Hess was missing.[56]

The overriding objective for Kirkpatrick was to find out if the British deception plans had worked, in that Germany would turn away from Britain and attack the Soviet Union. The Nazis believed peace could be obtained with Britain through a 'peace party' coming to power and overthrowing Churchill.

There is evidence that Hitler never saw the invasion of Britain as anything but a ruse to secure peace; then he would be free to settle with the Soviets. In fact the preliminary planning for Operation Barbarossa, the invasion of the Soviet Union, started two weeks after he had signed directive No. 16 for Operation Sealion, and even the movement of troops to the east began in the summer of 1940. The Führer had highlighted the need to avoid war on two fronts in *Mein Kampf*: 'We can oppose Russia only when we are free in the west.' He had been shaken by Soviet moves in the east while the Battle of France was in progress. The Baltic States were annexed with no recourse to

Berlin, and then pressure was put on Romania to cede territory to the Soviet Union.[57]

With his ankle healing, Hess was taken by train to London on 17 May and spent a few days in the Tower of London. Four days later he was moved again to Mytchell Place, a house near Aldershot adapted for him that had been a residence for senior Army officers. It had been fortified with high barbed-wire fences, machine-gun pits, and spotlights. A suite of rooms were prepared for him, all bugged, and in the house was a sound room where everything he did or said could be recorded.

Lord Simon, a former lawyer, MP, foreign secretary, home secretary and chancellor of the exchequer, was persuaded by Anthony Eden to pose as a peace negotiator. However, all talks were under the control of MI6. On 9 June, Simon, accompanied by Kirkpatrick, began with a German witness present as Hess had requested. The negotiations were a veiled continuation of the interrogation begun in Scotland. It was from the Simon interviews at Mytchell Place that the DNI received the Foreign Office memo that Ian Fleming wrote his comment on.

There is little firm evidence that Ian and for that matter Peter Fleming were ever involved in the Hess affair, other than in Ian's case being on the fringes of the deception fostered by Hoare and Hillgarth in Spain. John Pearson, Ian Fleming's biographer, felt that Ian's idea to engage Crowley in the talks with Hess 'had to be one of Fleming's bright ideas which never came off ...'[58] As far as Naval Intelligence and the 007 plots are concerned, the great benefit of the Hess affair was that Ian met Crowley and later used him as the model for Le Chiffre.

As far as the Hess affair is concerned, the threads of the deception plan run through it. Most of these threads run back to 'C', Stewart Menzies, and his intervention, it can be argued, changed the course of the war.

In December 1940, Menzies saw Dusko Popov, code-named Tricycle, who was in London having flown in from Lisbon. His cover for the trip was that he was representing some Yugoslav banks. Popov had started off as an Abwehr agent, but never had any intention of spying for the Germans. Rather he became a double agent when he was approached by the SIS in Belgrade. His control was passed to the XX Double Cross System run by MI5. His code name Tricycle was apparently because of his 'fondness for three-in-a-bed sex'.[59] He would become the centre of a large network of false agents. By establishing an espionage ring in England, it enhanced Popov's standing in the Abwehr and led to what Menzies wanted, which was information on Canaris.

Menzies invited Popov to spend the New Year weekend at Dassett, near Woking. Popov described the house as 'a Victorian mansion set in a large park, the lawns perfectly manicured'.[60]

Over the New Year weekend, even though the house was full of guests, Popov spent several hours speaking with Menzies in his study: 'Deep armchairs, a fireplace where the flames were miraculously steady, book-lined walls – it was the traditional and perfect setting. What followed was not commonplace,' says Popov. Menzies regretted that Popov was no longer an MI6 man. He thought he had the makings of a good spy but would need to curb his tendency to ignore orders or he would end up 'a very dead spy'. Menzies explained that Churchill had met Canaris in 1938 and had come to the conclusion that the admiral was a catalyst for the German resistance against Hitler. He went on to say he wanted to know all he could about Canaris and about his lieutenants, Hans Dohnanyi and Colonel Hans Oster, both of whom were 'not dyed-in-the-wool Nazis', but were 'patriotic Germans'. Menzies thought Popov could get the information through Jebsen (Johann Jebsen), another XX Committee double agent and the Abwehr representative in Lisbon, who Popov knew well. Menzies' idea was that Popov was to oust Hitler through Canaris. He told Popov that he was 'handling this matter myself' and that: 'All information you pick up is to come directly to me with no intermediary.'[61]

When Popov returned to London from Surrey after Menzies' party he met with Lieutenant Commander Ewen Montagu RNVR, another of Godfrey's recruits from civilian life. He was a barrister by profession, who was by then the DNI's representative on the XX Committee. Montagu gave Popov his cover story to feed to the Abwehr, which included him as a friend in the circle he had cultivated. Knowing Popov was a keen yachtsman, he gave him a personal letter he could show the Germans in which he commented on Popov's boat the *Nina*, saying he would like to see it 'as she sounds a grand boat' which he hoped to see in 'the Solent after the war'.[62] Later in the war Montagu would largely be responsible for the deception plan Operation Mincemeat.

Popov was soon back in contact with his Abwehr colleagues on his return to the Iberian Peninsula. Colonel Oster, who was later recruited by Tar Robertson as a double agent code-named Artist, told him Hess was talking of powerful people in Britain seeking contact with Germany.[63] After the war Popov would speculate in his memoirs whether Hess was influenced by reports from Britain of low morale, and whether he was enticed to fly to Scotland by British Intelligence via the Abwehr.[64]

It is apparent that Menzies, like many of his friends, believed the Soviet Union to be a greater danger to Britain than Nazi Germany. Stalin was extremely worried at the time that Britain and Germany would conclude a peace and turn on the Soviet Union. After the war, when the Allied powers agreed to the release of the ageing Hess from Spandau prison on humanitarian grounds, the Soviets refused. They believed Hess had flown to Britain to gain support for the attack on their country, which had cost them 20 million dead. They cited that German air raids on Britain largely finished after the night of 10–11 May 1941, not returning on a large scale until 1943. On 18 May the Soviet double agent Kim Philby informed his masters at the NKVD, the Soviet People's Commissariat for Internal Affairs, that: 'Hess will be the centre of intrigues for the conclusion of the compromise peace and will be useful for the peace party in England and for Hitler.'[65]

It would seem to be likely that Hess arrived at the invitation of Menzies with the co-operation of Canaris, with the aim of replacing Hitler, albeit Hess would not have known that was the ultimate aim or agreed to it. As Peter Padfield reflected in his book, 'that is probably as close as it is possible to approach to the truth'.[66]

Another reason we can conclude Ian Fleming was not at the heart of the Hess affair is that the Foreign Office note to DNI refers to an interview with Hess on 22 May. Yet two days before, Godfrey and Fleming had flown out to Portugal on the first leg of their mission to the United States to help develop links between the two countries on intelligence matters.

8

ARCHITECT OF US INTELLIGENCE

On 20 May 1941, a Tuesday, Godfrey and Fleming, in civilian clothes, took the Dutch KLM flight from Whitchurch near Bristol to Lisbon. Six Dutch Douglas DC-3 aircraft had escaped from the Netherlands in 1940 and by then were operating a scheduled flight for BOAC four times a week. Godfrey and Fleming were on the first leg of their trip to the USA, there to help develop collaboration on intelligence between the two countries. They would fly on from Lisbon on the Pan Am Clipper service to New York via the Azores and Bermuda. But first they would spend two days in Lisbon to check on the progress of Operation Golden Eye with the heads of station. Fleming was not impressed with the service rivalry that was hindering headway.[1]

Portugal, and in particular Lisbon and Estoril, 10 miles from the capital on what is known as the Portuguese Riviera, was a hotbed of spies and informers at that time. Early in the war the red light district of Lisbon, the dock area of Alcântara fronting on to the River Tagus where the prostitutes obliged the sailors, was controlled by the Germans, their agents run by the Abwehr keen to find out the movements of Allied convoys. Thus the olive-skinned ladies of the night got paid twice.

On their arrival they checked into the Hotel Palacio in Estoril, with Fleming registering as a 'government official'.[2] The hotel was built in

1930, with an entirely white facade and extensive exotic gardens. In 1969 it would be used in the Bond film *On Her Majesty's Secret Service*. By 1941 the ballroom and casino nearby were favoured meeting places, and were often full of glamorous refugees or royal families on the run. The Palacio and Inglaterra hotels were regarded as Allied, while the Atlantico was German. All three were rife with rumours, intrigue and bribery. Most of the staff were on the payroll of one side or the other or both.

Watching all this activity was the PVDE, Portugal's secret police, from their headquarters at Rua Victor Cordon in Lisbon. It was run by Captain Agostinho Lourenço, known as the Director, an ardent fascist utterly loyal to the 48-year-old Antonio de Oliveira Salazar, Portuguese prime minister but in effect dictator. Lourenço had fought with the British in the First World War and was considered a man not to be crossed. He was not overly concerned what the foreign intelligence services got up to as long as it did not affect Portugal.

The Lisbon *London Times* correspondent, Edward Lucas, found out what happened if you displeased Lourenço in December 1940. He had written articles for a US magazine insisting that the Portuguese people were pro-British while the government was pro-German, and that nothing much was done to curb Nazi espionage within Portugal. He was arrested by the PVDE on Christmas Eve and subjected to interrogation for six hours, before being deported in January. For good measure, and to appear even-handed, the Italian journalist Dr Cezare Rivelli was also expelled.[3]

On their second evening in Estoril, Fleming and Godfrey went to the casino. There Ian tried his hand at the table, playing a long, unsuccessful game until he was cleaned out of a modest amount by the Portuguese with whom he played. During the game he was supposed to have whispered to Godfrey: 'Just suppose these fellows were German agents. What a coup it would be if we cleaned them out entirely.'[4] Fleming's own experiences must have impacted on the opening lines of *Casino Royale* in 1953. First he described the atmosphere: 'The scent and smoke and sweat of a casino are nauseating at three in the morning. Then the soul-erosion produced by high gambling – a compost of greed and fear and nervous tension – becomes unbearable and the senses awake and revolt from it.'[5] The narrative moves on to the second paragraph to introduce James Bond and how tired he feels at three in the morning: 'when his body or his mind had had enough and he always acted on the knowledge'. This helped him to 'avoid staleness and the sensual bluntness that breeds mistakes'.[6]

Donald McLachlan, who worked with Fleming at NI and later wrote the book *Room 39 Naval Intelligence in Action 1939–45*, also becoming editor of the new *Sunday Telegraph* in 1961, wrote an article in that paper about the night in Lisbon. He wrote that it was Fleming's idea to go to the casino and play the Germans. There they found they were playing *chemin de fer* (a French card game also called Shimmy or Chernay): 'The Admiral did not know the game so Fleming decided to sit it out himself and gamble against these men in the hope, as he put it, of reducing German secret service funds. With only £50 in travelling money, he was quickly defeated and cleaned out. The DNI was not impressed, but this was how the whole Bond business started.'[7] Others have claimed that their experiences in casinos were used by Fleming in *Casino Royale*, when 007 takes on the evil Soviet spy Le Chiffre at the baccarat table. Perhaps the most compelling was that of Dusko Popov.

The British double agent run by MI5 and the XX Committee, Popov was often in Lisbon during the early years of the war. He came up with the audacious idea to milk the Abwehr of funds. The operation was called Plan Midas. He convinced his Abwehr handler in Lisbon, the Austrian Major Ludovico von Karsthoff, that he had a sure method to finance the growing network of German spies in Britain. Almost by accident he had come up with something that had great appeal to the Abwehr, who were finding it difficult to get funds to their agents. MI5 supplied a bogus front with offices in Piccadilly and a bank account in the name of Eric Glass, a wealthy theatrical agent, who often moved funds abroad and lived in Hampstead. The cover story Popov gave Karsthoff was that Glass felt Britain would lose the war and he was worried about protecting his fortune; helping the Abwehr was his insurance. The funds would first move to the USA and then to Britain. Another Abwehr agent who had been turned by MI5 would confirm the funds had arrived in the UK, where they would be deposited into an MI5 account.

Von Karsthoff was taken by Popov's plan, which appeared a fool-proof system, and he could make some money himself as he had an eye on Popov's 10 per cent handling fee. First he had to get approval from Berlin, which took several weeks. Approval and the money, £20,000, came through in July, and Karsthoff demanded half of Popov's commission.

On 31 July, Popov sent a coded telegram message to the Piccadilly address, although he made a mistake in the name by referring to Eric Sand instead of Glass. The message also contained details of the exchange rate obtained: 'Tilly had yesterday a Daughter weighing 3 Kilos please inform Harry when you meet him. Maria Concalves.'[8]

Dick White, Director of B Division MI5, was not impressed with Popov and wrote in a memo to MI6 on 2 August:

> You will see that in addition to giving the wrong name which might have been catastrophic, he has made another mistake which might have resulted in disaster, he has given the weight of the child as 3 kilos and according to the plan this would indicate that he had negotiated the deal at a rate of exchange of $2 to the £, which is 25 cents below the minimum we authorised.[9]

Even given White's misgivings, it all went smoothly. Von Karsthoff gave Popov the $40,000 less commission, which he would deposit in New York in the account of Eric Glass.

A few weeks later Hans Hansen, a Danish Abwehr agent working in Britain who had been turned by MI5, reported to Karsthoff that he had received from Mr Glass £18,000 in cash.

Dick White might have burst a blood vessel had he known what Popov got up to with the money the evening he was given it. As usual he headed for the casino in Estoril carrying the $38,000 on him. He thought it better to keep it on him rather than draw attention to himself by depositing such a large amount in the hotel safe; rather odd reasoning given his later actions.

Popov says as he came down from his room at the Palacio Hotel carrying the money in the breast pocket of his evening jacket: 'I noticed Fleming in the lobby but thought nothing more about it.'[10]

And he goes on to claim that Fleming followed him to a café, where he had a drink, and then went to a restaurant, where Fleming was 'skulking about outside'.[11] He saw him again in the casino, which he found 'amusing' as he felt he was being watched because of the money. All of which is highly unlikely, although Fleming was in Lisbon at the time, returning to the city from the USA on 29 July to check on Operation Golden Eye, this time more extensively through Spain, Gibraltar and Tangier. However, on this occasion he stayed with David Eccles, who worked for the Ministry of Economic Warfare, and not at the Palacio Hotel.[12]

In the Estoril casino, Popov found a 'wealthy Lithuanian named Bloch'. He had come across him before and knew he took great pleasure in humiliating other players by raising the stakes to high levels to show off. He did this when he had the bank calling '*Banque auvente*', which means the bank has no limit. Popov took the entire contents of his breast pocket out 'and started counting the sum out on the green felt covering of the table. Even for the Estoril Casino in the fever of war, it was a lot of money.' Silence descended on even the other tables: 'I glanced at Fleming. His face turned bile green.'[13]

Bloch is stunned speechless at the sight of so much money. Popov asks the croupier if the casino is backing the Lithuanian, who is still staring into space, knowing full well that they would not. He picks up the money and asks in a loud voice that such players should be banned from playing, then leaves Bloch to enjoy his humiliation. Popov said of Fleming, who he says had been watching the whole episode: 'I'm sure he had seen through and was appreciating my comedy.'[14]

Was Fleming there that night or did he just hear about it? Perhaps there is an echo of Popov's action in *Casino Royale* with Felix Leiter's rescue of Bond at the baccarat table – where he stares defeat in the face while playing against the villain Le Chiffre – with the supply of an envelope of money 'as thick as a dictionary' along with a note that explains it is 'Marshall Aid. Thirty-two million francs. With the compliments of the USA.'[15]

Plan Midas was a significant success for MI5 and the XX Committee. The Abwehr laundered about £85,000 through Mr Glass to maintain their networks in Britain, which in fact largely funded the XX Committee's operating costs throughout the war.[16]

As for Tricycle being the model for James Bond, other people might have thought so but not Popov. 'As for me, I rather doubt that a Bond in the flesh would have survived more than forty-eight hours as an espionage agent.'[17]

The Pan Am Clipper service terminal was located on the River Tagus, a purpose-built port for the huge Boeing 314 Clipper flying boats. They had the range to cross the Atlantic or Pacific at a cruising speed of 188mph. The aircraft could reach New York from Lisbon by refuelling at the Azores and Bermuda. The plane provided the passengers with the height of luxury unsurpassed in air travel, with bar, dining room and even a turn-down bed service. Did this opulence provide a hint of the opening line of *Live and Let Die*, but substitute naval officer for secret agent? 'There are moments of great luxury in the life of' a naval officer.[18]

Popov was also impressed with the great luxury of the Clipper service, feasting on 'beautifully prepared fish fresh from the Atlantic' and in the afternoon 'American dry martinis' in frosted glasses.[19] Whereas Peter Smithers, who was sent by Godfrey to Washington in 1940 to take up a post within the embassy to liaise with the US Navy, found the arrival in New York moving. 'At 2,000 feet I watched the sky scrapers of New York arising out of the sea. In view of what I had left behind and of what lay ahead it was a moment of overpowering emotion never to be forgotten.'[20]

Even given the luxury of the Clipper service and the amount of air travel Fleming, and for that matter his hero Bond, indulge in, there is an impression neither are overly fond of it. They much prefer cars and trains, even the sea. Air travel is uncomfortable, the Clipper excluded. Fleming wrote in *Thrilling Cities* of the prospect of twenty-four hours to Hong Kong: 'the hot face and rather chilly feet', the sickly smell of 'cosmetics that B.O.A.C. provide for their passengers' and 'endless chain smoking'.[21] Bond says in *Quantum of Solace* that if he were to marry he would like to marry an air hostess because of their devotion.[22] Yet Bond combats his fear of flying in *From Russia with Love* on his journey from London to Istanbul via Rome and Athens. He chooses to fly on

Friday the thirteenth if possible as there are fewer passengers, or is he tempting fate? BEA Flight 130 flies into an electric storm over the Adriatic: 'Bond smelt the smell of danger.' He withdraws into himself, closes his mind to the noise, flashing lights and bucking of the aircraft, and then they are through it flying straight and level. Bond 'heaved a deep sigh', reaching for his cigarette case, and he was 'pleased to see his hands were dead steady as he took out his lighter and lit one of the Moorland cigarettes with the three gold bands.'[23]

Fleming and Godfrey took the service to New York aboard the Dixie Clipper NC18605. They stayed two nights in Bermuda to catch up on correspondence and Godfrey hoped to explore the renowned reefs of the island after bringing 'underwater goggles with him'.[24] On the afternoon of 25 May the Dixie Clipper arrived at the La Guardia flying boat dock in New York, where they were met by a sea of photographers. However, they were not interested in the two shifty-looking naval officers in civvies but rather Elsa Schiaparelli, the Italian fashion designer. Their cover story for going to America was to inspect the ports, but more important was to help William Stephenson, who had only taken over as director of the British Passport Control Office, which co-ordinated intelligence operations on that side of the Atlantic, a few months earlier. Another objective was to establish better relations with US Intelligence organisations.

The man chosen to lead the British Security Co-ordination (BSC), the name for all British intelligence operations in the USA, was the Canadian William S. Stephenson, known as 'little Bill'. He was brought up on the prairies of western Canada, was a fighter pilot hero after winning the Military Cross and Distinguished Flying Cross in the First World War, and a skilled boxer. He was a millionaire by age 30, largely due to his invention of the first radio photograph transmitter. He was single-minded and a man of few words, and he was code-named Intrepid. Fleming was fascinated by him, even more so because he mixed the 'largest dry martinis in America and served them in quart glasses'.[25]

It had been at Stephenson's suggestion that Colonel William Donovan (Wild Bill) had gone to Europe to assess the chances of British survival in the war on the behest of President Roosevelt. Stephenson made himself available to the DNI and his assistant and put an office next to his own in the Rockefeller Center at their disposal, complete with a secretary.

Much to Fleming's delight, Stephenson took him on a raid on offices in the same building:

> One floor down was the Japanese Consul-General. We knew he was sending coded messages by short-wave radio to Tokyo with two assistants; I broke into the Japanese consular offices at three in the morning. Fleming came as an onlooker. We cracked the safe and borrowed the code books long enough to microfilm them.[26]

Fleming was delighted to be involved in a field operation and being able to view 'the spectacle of the greatest of secret agents at work'.[27] He was able to use this later in *Casino Royale* as a means for Bond to gain his double-0 classification. This is explained in detail in Chapter 20, The Nature of Evil, where the Rockefeller Center is mentioned, and Bond kills the Japanese cipher expert by shooting him from the 'next-door sky scraper'. You had to kill two people to gain the licence; for the second – a Norwegian double agent – he used a knife but 'he just didn't die very quickly'.[28]

Shortly after Godfrey and Fleming arrived in New York, they were struck by the harrowing news of the loss of HMS *Hood*, sunk by the German battleship *Bismarck* in the Denmark Strait. Even worse, out of a crew of more than 1,400 only three survived the icy waters of the North Atlantic. To Godfrey, Ian, although shocked like him, soon regained his optimistic air. 'You wait and see,' he told Godfrey, 'and sure enough within forty-eight hours *Bismarck* went to the bottom.'[29]

Fleming may well have been aware of the direct help Stephenson had obtained from Roosevelt to aid the British in the Battle of the Atlantic. The US Navy made a direct contribution to the sinking of *Bismarck*. Under Lend-Lease, PBY Catalina flying boats had been supplied to the British but not only that; kept highly secret, in some cases US personnel were manning the aircraft. Flying from their base at Castle Archdale on Lough Erne, Northern Ireland, one with Ensign Leonard B. Smith from Missouri at the controls spotted the German battleship on 26 May.

Not only that, US radio direction-finding stations had picked up radio transmissions from *Bismarck* and relayed this to London.

The American playwright Robert Sherwood, who helped Stephenson obtain fifty old US Navy destroyers for Britain, saw Roosevelt on 24 May. The President was then pondering any further help he could give Britain. He contemplated American submarines attacking the German ship, observing that, if it ever came out: 'Do you think the people would demand to have me impeached?'[30]

As for the city of New York, Godfrey and Fleming stayed at the St Regis Hotel overlooking Central Park. Ian made sure he used his $40 allowance on off-duty moments in the bars and clubs. However, over the years he felt the city lose its sparkle. He wrote in *Thrilling Cities* that 'each time I come back I feel it has lost more of its heart'.[31] On Bond's first visit since the war, while being driven into the city he observes 'the beautiful prospect of New York hastening towards them until they were down amongst the hooting teeming petrol-smelling roots of the stressed-concrete jungle'.[32]

Godfrey and Fleming soon moved on to Washington. Often when in the capital Ian would stay with his friend Peter Smithers: 'My tiny frame house on 28th Street in Georgetown had been newly renovated, rescued in fact from collapse.' He found Fleming: 'Relentless in his determination to win the war, he was a dynamo of creativity in intelligence operations.' He was even too busy according to Smithers to give several young ladies 'more than passing though certainly exciting attention'.[33]

The wooing of the Federal Bureau of Investigation (FBI) and its crusty director J. Edgar Hoover did not go so well. Hoover was watchful of the FBI position, and did not like the BSC sidestepping US laws by using Canadians in operations to get around using US citizens working for a belligerent in a foreign war. The Soviet double agent Kim Philby observed: 'Stephenson's activity in the United States was regarded sourly enough by J. Edgar Hoover. The implication that the FBI was not capable of dealing with sabotage on American soil was wounding to a man of his raging vanity.'

Even worse, he felt: 'Stephenson was playing politics in his own yard, and playing them pretty well. He foresaw that the creation of OSS (Office of Strategic Services) would involve him in endless jurisdictional disputes. The new office would compete with the FBI for Federal funds. It would destroy his monopoly of the investigation field.'[34] He would never forgive Stephenson for his part in creating the OSS, in which Fleming would play a leading role.

On 6 June, Fleming found that he and the DNI were received politely by Hoover, 'a chunky enigmatic man with slow eyes and a trap of a mouth'. He listened patiently to what they had to say and then told them he was 'uninterested in our mission'. The entire interview with Hoover lasted sixteen minutes. They were shown over the building's various departments, ending up in the basement shooting range where weapons were being tested. 'Even now I can hear the shattering roar of the Thompsons in the big dark cellar as the instructor demonstrated on the trick targets. Then with a firm, dry handclasp we were shown the door.'[35]

This had been half expected by Godfrey and Fleming; trying to impart their hard-won experience of the folly of inter-service rivalry fell largely on deaf ears. The branches of US Intelligence, Military Intelligence G2 under Brigadier-General Sherman Miles, the Office of Naval Information under Captain Alan Kirk, and the FBI under Hoover had no joint intelligence committee in Washington. Donald McLachlan wrote: 'nothing gave these three officers more pleasure than to scoop one another – which meant doing another department's job for it in order to show off.' And as for closer co-operation with the British, it was looked on as aiding a lame duck.[36]

Godfrey discussed his problem with Bill Stephenson and Sir William Wiseman, the former head of British Intelligence in the USA, and was advised to resolve the dilemma; he must go to the top and see Mr Roosevelt. With the help of the editor of the *New York Times*, Arthur Sulzberger, it was arranged that Mrs Roosevelt would ask him to dinner and make sure he had some time with the President. The prickly admiral was also warned that Roosevelt liked ribbing people and it was better to take it in good humour. 'All went according to plan,' wrote Godfrey. He was suitably dressed in a dinner jacket, and suffered being subjected to being told how much better the Americans would run the 'West Indian Islands; we're going to show you how to look after them …', to which Godfrey forced a laugh. Later he went with the President into the Oval Office, hoping there in a private setting to make his points. However, first he had to listen to the President reminisce about his admiration for Blinker Hall. Roosevelt had been under-secretary of the Navy in 1917 and remarked: 'Of course, Hall had a wonderful Intelligence Service but I don't suppose it's much good now.' Godfrey, frustrated, listened politely and: 'At last I got a word in edgeways and said my piece.' In between more reminiscences: 'I said it a second time and a third time – one intelligence security boss, not three or four.' Then Mrs Roosevelt came in and it was time for bed.[37]

Driving away that night from the White House, Godfrey 'felt doubtful if I'd really made the point …'[38] Godfrey says he did not support Donovan for the role, but Wild Bill had other people in his corner.[39] John G. Winant was one. He had replaced Joseph Kennedy as US Ambassador to Britain and soon became a confidant of Godfrey; often dining with the admiral at his flat at 36 Curzon Street in Mayfair.[40] Stephenson was also working through his own contacts behind the scenes. He signalled Churchill on 19 June when he learned Donovan had been appointed to be Co-ordinator of Information (COI), which would become in 1942 the Office of Strategic Studies (OSS): 'You can imagine how relieved I am after three months of battle and jockeying for position at Washington that "our man" is in a position of such importance to our efforts.'[41]

Another Donovan supporter was David Eccles, who worked for the MEW and was a friend of Ian. He was often in the White House in the early months of 1941 to brief the President's principal advisor, Harry Hopkins. He paints an interesting picture of a visit in April:

It's a thrill going in through the gate and up to that famous porch. When inside the most terrific n**** waiters seize hold of you and whisk you upstairs. Hopkins was in his bedroom. He said that FDR wanted to know all about North Africa. The Secretary of the Navy was with him. I said my piece – three quarters of an hour – and they were most helpful and saw the real point at once.[42]

With his main objective in the bag, Godfrey left Washington, leaving Ian behind to help Donovan get his new project off the ground. On

24 June, Eccles wrote to Roger Makins at the Foreign Office about the new CSI that Bill Donovan was setting up, and he was sending him a memorandum on the new agency. 'Bill offered me a copy of his paper to the President but I thought it better the DNI should have it. In order not to break the continuity of collaboration between us and Bill on this subject, I have installed Ian Fleming in my bed at Bill's house. He knows much more about the details of intelligence work than I do.'[43]

Ivar Bryce, a lifelong friend since he had met Ian and his brothers on a Cornish beach holiday when they were boys, a member of the SIS and having worked for Donovan and Stephenson, recalled Ian telling him: 'He had been whisked off to a room in the new annexe of the Embassy, locked in it with a pen and paper and the necessities of life, and had written, under armed guard around the clock, a document of some seventy pages covering every aspect of a giant secret intelligence and secret operational organisation.'[44] A blueprint for US Intelligence, in later life Fleming claimed tongue-in-cheek that much of it was used to create the Central Intelligence Agency (CIA). The deputy head of BSC, Charles Howard Ellis, known as 'Dick', felt Fleming's role was greatly exaggerated.[45] However, whatever his contribution was, Donovan valued his input and gave him a .38 Police Positive revolver, inscribing it 'For Special Services'. It remained one of Ian's prized possessions.

Yet Ian's time in Washington was not all work, there was the round of Embassy parties to be endured, and picnic trips into Virginia and Maryland. On 18 July he reported his progress to Godfrey that Donovan should be starting operations in a month with a small staff and a grant of $10 million. He felt the new COI would be heavily reliant on Stephenson, and there were rumours that Donovan was a lackey 'and hireling of British SIS is spreading and should be carefully watched'.[46]

★★★

By 29 July Ian was back in Lisbon to check on the progress of Golden Eye. As we know, he stayed with David Eccles, who had returned from Washington at the end of June. In their talks Eccles despaired of the petty squabbles between the various British agencies operating on the Iberian Peninsula. 'The FO are all right.' But, 'The others, the amateurs and minor departments there has been and will be trouble without end.'[47]

When Ian moved on to Tangier he came across what Eccles had described. The NID Golden Eye agent, Henry Greenleaves, was doing good work, but found the SIS man, Toby Ellis, to be 'an undesirable individual'.[48] Greenleaves had written to Commander Geoffrey Birley of NID Gibraltar to say he would have no further contact with SIS in Tangier. He had not found Ellis 'to be very reliable and, in addition, have found the open criticism of this Department by members of the supposedly uninstructed public to be most disconcerting'.[49] However, he found the SO2 man Robert Schelee, with whom he shared an office: 'useful to me in many ways, particularly through his existing business contacts in the French Zone …' He was happy to continue on alone, providing Gibraltar did not fall.[50]

In a letter to Godfrey, 'C' Stewart Menzies argued that Greenleaves lacked training in intelligence operations and, in view of what happened next, he may have had a point.[51]

Greenleaves would be arrested after a drunken night spent with Ian in which they broke into a bullring and drew a large 'V' sign in the sand. Fleming apologised to Commander Birley because he might 'have received something of a shock on hearing of my escapade with Greenleaves, of which I admit I was thoroughly ashamed, but it appears to have created nothing but the most ribald mirth in London and so perhaps it was not such a shameful affair as I thought it was'.[52] To get back to England as soon as possible to report to Godfrey, he chartered a special plane from Tangier to Lisbon at a cost of £110 to the Admiralty.[53]

When back at Room 39, Fleming wrote to Greenleaves that: 'Operation "Catastrophe" has been greeted with the most unseemly mirth in the Foreign Office and Admiralty, and there will certainly be no reaction whatsoever from London. I hope there have been no backlash with you locally.'[54]

Ian Fleming at the 1932 Alpine Trial he navigated for Donald Healey, who is behind the wheel of the 4.5-litre Invicta. (*Motor Magazine*, September 1932)

Ian Fleming in RNVR uniform from the photograph album of Maud Russell, *c.* 1940. (Courtesy of Ian Fleming images ©Maud Russell Estate Collection)

Ian Fleming publicity photo for *From Russia with Love*. The film was released in October 1963, less than twelve months before he died. (Moviestore Collection Ltd, Alamy)

Admiral John Godfrey, Director Naval Intelligence 1939–42, photo taken by Cecil Beaton in the Red Fort Delhi when Godfrey commanded the Indian Navy. (IWM IB-1-IB200)

Admiral Reginald 'Blinker' Hall Director Naval Intelligence 1914–19 was a great help to Godfrey when he took the reins of NI. (Photo Colin Simpson)

Admiral François Darlan, commander of the French Fleet in 1940, who Ian Fleming was ordered to track down and stick to as France collapsed. Darlan was assassinated in North Africa in 1943.

William Donovan (Wild Bill). Fleming first met him in Spain; he would later become head of OSS, the forerunner of the CIA. (US National Archives NAID 6851006)

Dudley Wrangel Clarke, known as the pioneer of military deception. Maybe this was a deception that went too far when he was arrested in Spain for cross-dressing. (The National Archives Kew)

Fleming intended to use a Heinkel III bomber like this in Operation Ruthless; his plan would later emerge in the plot of *Thunderball*. (World Image Archive, Alamy)

Rudolf Hess and Joachim Von Ribbentrop at the Nuremberg War Crimes Trials. (Alexander Charles Harry S. Truman Library)

Aleister Crowley, who Fleming suggested might be consulted on the Hess affair. He became Fleming's model for Le Chiffre in *Casino Royale*. (Granger Historical Picture Archive, Alamy)

Benito Mussolini and Adolf Hitler, Munich, June 1940. Mussolini's appearance is often compared by Fleming in the Bond books to some of his villains', particularly around the eyes. (US National Archives)

Estoril Casino, a hotbed of spies in the 1940s.

Fleming and Godfrey took the Clipper service to fly to the USA from Lisbon, the height of air travel luxury at the time. Peter Smithers and Dusko Popov also used the service. Pictured is a Clipper 314 Yankee. (Library of Congress)

William Stephenson (Little Bill), head of BSC, who Fleming considered a true spy compared to his creation James Bond. (CIA Library)

5)   In connection with the unfortunate incident, of which I am giving you a separate report, if there are unpleasant consequences for Greenleaves I would like to suggest that he be transferred to Captain Benson's staff, where he would be most valuable.   Captain Benson concurs and would provide a relief for Greenleaves at Tangiers, but it is to be hoped that nothing more will be heard of the matter.

6)   The problem of Admiral G. has now been satisfactorily cleared up.   Lady G. is shortly returning to England.   I will give you a verbal account of the whole affair.

7)   In order to get back to England as quickly as possible it was necessary for me to charter a special plane from Tangiers to Lisbon.   My quick departure is also necessary in view of the incident referred to in para. 5 above.   The cost of this plane was £110, and the bill is being paid by P.C.O. Lisbon.   It will be necessary to obtain repayment of this sum through Mr. Morgan for C.S.S.   The total amount required for the purposes I mentioned in this report will, therefore, be £310.   If you agree I will prepare the usual request to the Secretary.

Yours sincerely

Ian Fleming

Fleming's report on Operation Golden Eye chartering a plane to get back, and his signature. (The National Archives Kew)

Badge of Italian Naval Commandos X Flottiglia MAS.

HMS *Repulse*, Admiral Godfrey's last sea-going command, which was sunk by the Japanese off Malaya in 1941. The ship is mentioned in the Bond books. (USN Historical Center)

Badge of 30 Assault Unit.

Commander Lionel Crabb RNVR at Gibraltar. (IWM A23270)

Friend of Ian Fleming Peter Smithers, seen here at his wedding in the uniform of lieutenant RNVR, at the time naval attaché in Mexico. (Denny Lane Private Collection)

Dusko Popov, a double agent who worked for MI5. Could Crabb, Smithers and Popov have been models for 007? (US National Archives)

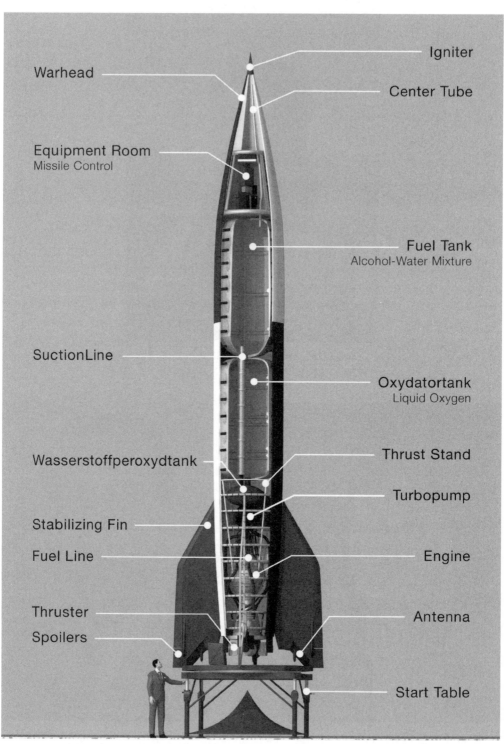

Igniter

Center Tube

Warhead

Equipment Room
Missile Control

Fuel Tank
Alcohol-Water Mixture

SuctionLine

Oxydatortank
Liquid Oxygen

Wasserstoffperoxydtank

Thrust Stand

Turbopump

Stabilizing Fin

Fuel Line

Engine

Thruster

Antenna

Spoilers

Start Table

Diagram of a V2 rocket, the inspiration for *Moonraker*. (US Army)

Camp X from the air, 1943. Did Ian Fleming ever visit here? (Lynn Hodgson)

Hoagy Carmichael, Fleming's idea of how Bond looked, was mentioned in *Casino Royale*.

This "golden" typewriter belonged to Lady Dojean Smithers, wife of the dashing Sir Peter Smithers, who worked closely with Ian Fleming for British Naval Intelligence. Smither's exploits, it is said, contributed to Fleming's vision of the Bond character. Fleming so admired his friends' golden typewriter that he purchased one for himself, and used it to write several novels.

Courtesy Colonel Denny Lane

Golden typewriter similar to that used by Ian Fleming. (Denny Lane Private Collection)

9

GIBRALTAR

It is barely 3 square miles in total area and since 1981 has been called the Overseas Territory of Gibraltar, but in the Second World War it was the Crown Colony of Gibraltar. According to ancient Greek myths, Gibraltar was the northern pillar of Hercules, while Jebel Musa, across the straits in Morocco, is said to have been the southern pillar. It appears the Berber Tarik ibn Zeyael called the Rock the 'Geb-el-Tarik', translated as the Hill of Tarik. He is credited as the author of the name Gibraltar.

Ian Fleming was often in Gibraltar during the war years, more often than not passing through in one direction or the other. NID had an office there that covered the straits and much of the Iberian Peninsula. Events within the Rock and in the waters surrounding it were to have a profound effect on the Bond books.

The British captured the Rock in 1704, although the defence of Gibraltar over the next few decades was no easy task, with one siege ending in March 1783 after three years and seven months. During this siege, Sergeant Major Henry Ince and his band of tunnelling builders constructed a whole new system of communication galleries 659ft long within the Rock. Food was always a problem during the sieges and the garrison often suffered from scurvy. Water was never an issue as rain water collected into a natural reservoir within the Rock and was piped down to the seafront. With the water filtered by the Rock, it was said to be of excellent quality.[1]

The highest point is on the eastern face, 1,398ft high, and near the cable car station. To the west lies the Atlantic, past the sprawl of Algeciras. To the north are the low hills of San Roque, to the south Morocco, and the Mediterranean Sea is east. Gibraltar is 1,100 miles from Malta and 2,000 miles from Alexandria.

In 1940, after the defeat of France, Adolf Hitler cast covetous eyes toward Gibraltar. The Germans did a lot of planning to capture the Rock, even some exercises for Operation Felix. Admiral Canaris, Hitler's 'Spanish expert', and a team from the Abwehr spent two days in 1940 looking at the Rock from Algeciras. They used three houses in the town: Villa Leon, San Luis and Villa Isabel. The first of these had a view of Gibraltar Bay. Ladislas Farago thought the number of visitors to Algeciras from the German Secret Services had reached comical levels, comparing the town to 'the popular tourist attraction of the Abwehr'.[2] In many ways it was a far easier proposition than Operation Sealion, the cross-Channel invasion of Britain, and would have sealed off the Mediterranean from the West. It would have made holding Malta even more difficult than it was and imperilled the Suez Canal. The trouble was that Hitler could not get Franco to co-operate. All the while the British were manipulating the Spanish through various schemes, some of which Ian played a leading role in.

Gibraltar was home from time to time to significant naval forces, and the notable Force H under direct Admiralty control that could operate in the Mediterranean or Atlantic. It was also a staging post for merchant ships and convoys. All of this made the anchorage a tempting target.

The Decima Flottiglia MAS, Tenth Light Flotilla of the Italian Navy, known as X MAS, was one of the best units of naval commandos to come out of the war. During the First World War, the Italian Navy had sunk an Austrian dreadnought battleship in the naval base at Pulo. Two frogmen had ridden a slow-speed torpedo with a detachable warhead into the harbour, before placing it under the keel and sinking the 20,000-ton ship. In 1935, the Italians began to update the device, resulting in the famous Maiale (pig) two-man human torpedo. During the course of the war, X MAS conducted its own clandestine war led by Commander J. Valerio Borghese against Allied shipping and would sink more than 200,000 tons with pigs and limpet mines for the loss of three men killed and three captured.

The first X MAS operation against Gibraltar, 'B.G.1', set off from La Spezia in northern Italy on 24 September 1940. The Adua-class submarine *Scirè* of 700 tons, launched in 1938, carried three Maiale in cylindrical containers on her casing. To accommodate them the tower was reduced in size and her deck gun removed. Her commander, Borghese, thought she was 'the strangest thing afloat'. She was painted pale green, and against this in darker green was painted the outline of a trawler, its bows pointing in the opposite direction to that of the submarine, so as to distort her profile. It would have been hard 'to conceive a clumsier or less seaman-like line'.[3] They reached the straits of Gibraltar five days later, to be told by radio that the British Fleet had sailed and they were to return to La Maddalena, Sardinia.

However, they returned again on mission B.G.2 on the next moonless night, 29/30 October, when the *Scirè* surfaced at two in the morning in Algeciras Bay. Borghese had eased the submarine between Algeciras to port and Gibraltar to starboard. He had to deal with a current of 1.5 knots on his approach, about half the speed of a submerged submarine, coming into the straits from the Atlantic. When the current was abeam it was a torrid business trying to keep a heading but once they turned into the bay and it was astern it was much easier. There were still whirlpools and eddies to deal with, and they banged into rocks as they hugged the rocky Spanish coast waiting for darkness. Once dark, they surfaced to check position and steered toward Gibraltar, brightly lit on the port bow. They were momentarily caught in the beam of a searchlight and submerged, steering by depth measurement and picking up the flashing light of a Spanish lighthouse in the periscope. By now there was a lot of traffic on the surface. A British destroyer passed directly overhead, its whirling propellers picked up by their hydrophones as they edged their way slowly to the north end of the Bay of Algeciras.

The *Scirè* reached the launch position at the mouth of the Guadarranque River off the Spanish coast and the operators began getting into their diving gear. Borghese was informed by Supreme Naval Command that two battleships were moored in Gibraltar harbour. At

0200 *Scirè* surfaced to release the three Maiales from their carrying pods. The six operators were wished good luck and the submarine submerged. Borghese retraced the route they had taken on the approach and by 0700 had reached open water on course back to Italy.

The six operators wore goggled face masks connected by a tube to a rubber breathing bag across the chest. This cleaned the carbon dioxide from their exhalations, while clean oxygen came from two bottles strapped across their stomachs.

Having mounted their 'Pigs' and set off, one was caught in the shockwaves of a random depth charge from a motor boat and sank, the crew abandoning their breathing gear and swimming to the Spanish coast. The second Pig got close to the North Mole of Gibraltar when one set of breathing gear failed. Forced to remain on the surface, they detached the warhead and headed for Spain. They reached the shore at 0710, where they destroyed their breathing gear and opened the flood tank on the Pig, sending it off to the south.

The third Pig of Gino Birindelli and Domas Paccagnini was slow in getting under way, trailing some way behind the others. Again they had trouble with their breathing gear and the Pig was slow, so they continued toward the target on the surface, taking their bearing on the lights of Gibraltar town and diving as they got near to the target, HMS *Barham*. Paccagnini's breathing gear then gave up and he was forced to surface, while Birindelli went on alone, although shortly after this the Pig broke down.

Surfacing, Birindelli found himself about 70m from *Barham*. He dived back down to the Pig and tried dragging the 300kg warhead toward the keel of the battleship. Birindelli wrote: 'After about 30 minutes of strenuous effort during which I had very little oxygen to breathe, I experienced the first symptoms of collapse due to excess of carbon-dioxide and consequently decided to give up. I set the time fuse going and returned to the surface.'[4]

Climbing on to a buoy, he got rid of his diving gear and set off to swim to Spain across the bay. However, he was gripped by excruciating cramp and he managed to climb out of the water on to the harbour's North Mole. From there he got on to the Spanish ship *Santa Anna*, where he tried to hide. However, he was discovered by a Royal Navy patrol. He was interrogated by several British officers but refused to give anything but name and rank. He did have the satisfaction of hearing the warhead he had set explode. It erupted with a huge spout of water cascading over *Barham* but caused little damage. The next morning, Paccagnini was also captured, still trying to swim to Spain, while the other crews reached there safely. Despite their technical difficulties the Italians had come close to their objective; X MAS would try again in May 1941.

On 'BG.3' X MAS addressed the problem of keeping the operators in peak condition. The long trip to Gibraltar in the bad atmosphere and cramped conditions of a submarine was far from ideal preparation. The interned Italian tanker *Fulgar* was in the harbour at Cadiz and the Maiale crews were sent in disguise overland as merchant seamen and crew replacements. Then *Scirè* would pick them up at night from *Fulgar*. The submarine left La Spezia on 15 May, picking up the operators eight days later and entering the Bay of Algeciras on 25 May. On this mission there were no large warships in the harbour but a number of merchant ships were a good target. However, once again all the Pigs broke down and the crews had to swim for the Spanish shore. 'BG.4' in September was a success, sinking three British merchant ships, one of which was the *Denbydale,* a tanker lying inside the naval base. All six operators got back to Spain safely.[5]

About the same time as X MAS were launching their second attack, Admiral Godfrey was becoming increasingly worried about Gibraltar. Not then about the Italian attacks, but rather a growing threat that the Germans would occupy the Crown Colony. The idea grew in his mind of a stay-behind team walled up in the Rock that could monitor shipping through the straits and relaying it through radio to the Allies. Operation Tracer, as it became known, was so secret and involved so few people that meetings took place in Godfrey's flat at 36 Curzon Street rather than in Whitehall.[6]

Commander Geoffrey Birley, the SOI of Gibraltar, with two engineer officers, Colonels H.M. Fordham and R.A. Hay, conducted a reconnaissance of the Rock to choose a site and start work on construction. The site chosen was in the existing tunnel system called Lord Airey's Shelter. This was high up on the southern ridge of the Rock, behind Lord Airey's Battery completed in 1891, and just north of O'Hara's Battery.

The accommodation would be for six men and their wireless systems and stores, as well as a water tank with 10,000 gallons that could last a year. It was estimated that it would take the Germans a year to eighteen months to find them. The chamber would be 45ft long, 16ft wide and 8ft high, with two narrow observation slits to overlook the Bay of Gibraltar to the west and the Mediterranean to the east.[7]

In December the head of NID responsible for the Mediterranean, Colonel John Cordeaux, Royal Marines (RM), went out to view the work, and to tell Birley what the Admiralty signals experts wanted. He also had several questions from Lord Thomas Jeeves Horder, who had been brought in by Godfrey along with Surgeon Commander George Murray Levick for advice on the men's welfare and their chances of survival.[8] Horder was a physician and advisor to the Ministry of Food during the war. Levick was a naval doctor and survival expert who had been part of Robert Falcon Scott's Terra Nova Expedition in 1911–12. Due to pack ice, Levick and five other members of the expedition were forced to spend the winter on Inexpressible Island in Antarctica inside an ice cave that he called 'a dismal hole'.[9]

In 1940, Levick came back to the Navy as a specialist in guerrilla warfare with the Commandos, who were training at Lochailort in Scotland. He taught fitness, diet and survival techniques, many of which found their way into Commando training manuals.

On 25 January, Godfrey met with Cordeaux, Fleming, Horder and Levick to consider the latter two's report, which had made recommendations for personnel, making sure they had exercise and recreation, clothing, ventilation, sanitation, food, alcohol, tobacco, and the disposal by embalmment and cementing up of anyone who died. The team, it was agreed, would consist of six: one officer leader, two doctors and three telegraphist ratings. Horder would find the doctors and DNI would find the rest. It is possible that Ian had a part to play in Tracer, especially given the details in some of the Bond books.[10]

Ian's short story *From a View to a Kill* may have echoes of Tracer in it. In the story, NATO dispatch riders from SHAPE headquarters in France are being ambushed and losing vital information to a Soviet GRU (Soviet Military Intelligence) 'left behind spy unit', which Bond uncovers. He finds the spy unit to be 'certainly the most professional that had ever been devised – far more brilliant than anything England prepared to operate in the wake of a successful German Invasion, far better than what the Germans themselves had left behind in the Ardennes in 1944'. When the story was published in 1962, Tracer was still classified as Top Secret, along with the Auxiliary Units, who would have been concealed in elaborate underground hideouts to strike at the Germans if an invasion of the UK had taken place.[11]

Peter Fleming was directly involved in raising the Auxiliary Units. General Andrew 'Bulgy' Thorne, also like Peter a Grenadier commander of the XII Corps, had the task of defending south-east England in the event of a German invasion. He wanted an officer to raise and train a body of troops to stay behind and harass the invaders. Peter, who Thorne had met before in Berlin in 1934, was given the job. He was well suited to the task, being a small-game hunter.[12] With typical modesty, Peter wrote in his 1957 book *Invasion 1940* that the War Office 'oddly enough' chose him for the task.[13] He soon had some twenty-odd Auxiliary Units under command. They were made up initially of one officer, usually a subaltern, and twelve soldiers. When 'wireless sets with the necessary range became available, two signallers were added'. Shortly after this: 'Loosely affiliated to the military nucleus, and dotted arbitrarily about its sphere of operations were small "cells" composed of members of the Home Guard, selected for their skill in fieldcraft. These men were trained, mostly at the week-ends, in sabotage and the use of high explosive; and as the dumps and hide-outs began to be established they assumed responsibility for them.'[14]

Most of their 'hides' were in dense woodland or scrub, some were purpose-built 'large dugouts, excavated, roofed and provided with bunks and ventilation by the Royal Engineers'. Other hides took advantage of existing underground sites, ruined buildings, enlarged badger setts; even an abandoned chalk pit was used. Peter doubted they would have been able to achieve very much as they would have been handicapped by the 'lack of communications'. They would have had to rely on 'messengers, moving cautiously across country at night, so that very little co-ordination would have been possible'.[15]

However, Tracer was strictly an intelligence-gathering operation but, again in *From a View to a Kill*, there is a hint of what would have taken place on the Rock when a 'pedal generator would get going deep down under the earth and off would go the high-speed cipher groups'.[16]

Work carried on at the site in the Rock in secret, with the labourers unaware of the exact location. All of the workers had been brought out from the UK and were returned as soon as the work was complete. However, the work did not go smoothly. The chamber became known as Braithwaite's Cave, named after the commanding officer of the construction gang, Major J.A. Braithwaite, who died in an accidental explosion while tunnelling.[17] The accommodation had a large main room with a water tank at one end and a wash pit. Toilets were placed beside the radio room, which housed the standard MK3 transmitter and HRO receiver, a HF (shortwave) communications receiver made by the National Radio Company of Massachusetts, USA. To provide power, three 12-volt batteries would be charged by one of two generators, one hand-propelled and one bicycle-propelled, which had the secondary role of aiding fitness. The bicycle was also used to drive the ventilation system. A rod aerial, 18ft long, would be thrust out through the observation apertures when required.[18]

Near the main chamber, a staircase led up to the east observation post, and it was decided that the aerial would be hidden in a pipe extending down the stairs when not in use. As originally conceived, the apertures would be slits of the same size. This was later changed so the eastern post aperture would be larger, overlooking a narrow ledge, so that a man could climb out for fresh air while being concealed from view. Part way up the main staircase, another set of stairs led up to the western post. The observation aperture could be sealed off with a wooden wedge. The chamber was plastered and the floor was covered with cork tiles to reduce noise.[19]

Another meeting took place at Godfrey's flat on 17 February 1942. Recruits for the team were discussed and, once chosen, it was decided that Levick would stay with them through their training. They hoped to have the 'expedition ready by the end of May, the period for rehearsal and training occupying two months'.[20]

Godfrey sent a memo, dated 13 April, to those involved. In it he said: 'Now Tracer is fairly launched, I should like Cdr Scott to adopt it and take it over as soon as possible but he will certainly need help from Fleming and Merrett for some time to come.'[21] Edward Merrett was Godfrey's private secretary, a solicitor by profession 'with a taste for drawing and a genius for friendliness and reducing tension'.[22]

By the end of the month, five members of the team had been assembled, including Surgeon Lieutenant Bruce Cooper, 28 years of age, and recruited by Levick while on shore leave from his Plymouth-based destroyer *Versatile*. In May 1940 his ship was bombed and damaged while helping evacuate the Dutch royal family. The destroyer lost all power and was dead in the water. Ten men were killed and a third of the crew wounded. Many were treated by Cooper, who earned a mention in dispatches.

Cooper was asked to recommend another doctor for Tracer and he suggested Arthur Milner, a civilian physician. The two had been friends since their medical student days. Milner was not keen to start with as he suffered from chronic seasickness. However, even though he was required to join the Navy, he was assured he would never have to serve at sea.[23]

Survival training took place in Scotland. Once this was completed, the team moved to Gibraltar, where they were established by August. There they were given 'cover' jobs. Cooper was a doctor aboard the docked HMS *Cormorant*, but the drafting officer there felt Cooper might be better employed on a fighting ship. That officer was quickly drafted back to the UK. Life on the Rock was pleasant as they waited. They conducted regular training stints in the chamber. Cooper recalled entering the Rock Hotel as an RNVR surgeon lieutenant and leaving as an Army sergeant to disappear into the Rock.[24]

By the end of August, Tracer was largely ready to go. Wireless telegraphy (W/T) had been fully tested and all stores were in place. A survival manual had been printed. There were even some games and a library in place, with a variety of books, one of which attributed *Anna Karenina* to Dostoevsky.[25]

Yet Tracer was made largely redundant by the German invasion of the Soviet Union in June 1941. With the failure of the Wehrmacht to take Moscow in October–November and the success of the Soviet counter-attack, as a result the required conditions to bring Spain into the war no longer applied. OKW issued instructions that political and military relations with Spain would continue to be cultivated, but Operation

Felix would have to wait until the Soviets had been dealt with. The operation was put on hold. Once resurrected, it would take longer to implement and the time was extended to six months. Hitler reluctantly agreed and OKW published orders to that effect in March 1942.[26] Although Felix would come up from time to time, it was doomed as Germany's position had weakened since 1940.

The story of Tracer ended on 20 August 1943 with a final W/T exercise, followed by the removal of stores and the sealing of the chamber. Godfrey and the First Sea Lord felt 'that the principle of Tracer should be permanently recognised and that, in future wars, Tracer teams should be organised and Tracer locations prepared throughout the world'.[27]

With Felix abandoned, Gibraltar's security was not seriously threatened again, although German and Italian aircraft bombed the city and harbour with little result. However, shipping in the port and naval base would come under renewed underwater attacks by the Italian Navy, and now the Germans got in on the act.

In the period December 1941–January 1942 a merchant ship and small patrol boat were blown up at anchor off Gibraltar. By July the team led by Commander Ewen Montagu at Room 17M NID, through Ultra decodes, began reading German Abwehr radio traffic. This led them to the activities of a sabotage group called Humberto Kosp and divers operating from Sesera, the code name for Seville, against Basta, the Gibraltar code name. Immediate action was taken that saved the SS *Imber* and, wrote Montagu, 'gave us the interesting limpet mine'. With continued vigilance and the Ultra decodes, they were able to thwart German frogmen by sending their own divers down into the harbour area to watch ships on the days of expected action. As a result: 'The Germans had no further success with limpet mining …'[28] However, the Italian threat was an altogether different proposition, not only because the British could not read their radio messages, but rather the skill of the men of X MAS was on a far higher level.

The Italian operators of the Maiale were closely associated, if not in many cases being one and the same, to the Gamma assault frogmen. X MAS had a large pool of excellent volunteer swimmers to call on. Gamma men wore the Belloni suit and used the same breathing equipment as the Maiale operators. Their main weapon was the limpet mine, which they attached to the target's hull. There were two main types, the first being the 2kg mignatta, which was secured by suction. A Gamma man could carry up to five of these in a bag. There was also a 4.5kg mine that was secured to the keel with a clamp. This was activated by a small propeller when the ship was in motion, arming the mine and exploding at sea. This would likely cause the complete loss of the target and create confusion as to how the attack was conducted.

With the success of 'BG.4' and the ability of the Maiale crews to operate from Spanish soil with impunity, the idea of operating from Spanish bases was perused. Aided by the Italian Consul at Algeciras, Giulio Pistono, the X MAS officer Antonio Ramognino rented the Villa Carmela at Puente Mayorga near La Linea under the ruse that his new Spanish wife Conchita was ill and needed to live by the sea. The villa had a clear uninterrupted view of Gibraltar and the shipping anchorages, and it was only a few metres from the beach.[29]

The newly married Ramogninos moved in, putting in a large window facing the sea from which a telescope could be used to study the anchorage across the bay and the North Mole at Gibraltar. Their first guests soon arrived: twelve Gamma frogmen, who came to Spain overland via the Pyrenees or by Italian merchant ships. All headed for Cadiz in the guise of Italian merchant seamen as replacements for the *Olterra*. From there, in ones and twos they reached the stricken ship lying at Algeciras and now interned. She had been scuttled in the early days of the war in an attempt to block the mouth of Gibraltar harbour, being beached in Spanish waters. From the beach near Villa Carmela on the night of 13/14 June 1942, the twelve frogmen entered the water and swam toward the anchored merchant ships 2,000m away. Each man carried three suction limpet mines. Four ships were badly damaged as a result of the attack and had to be beached to save them. All twelve men returned safely, although one had suffered a foot injury from the propellers of a British patrol boat and another concussion from depth charges. Seven were arrested by Spanish police on the beach. However, Pistono was soon in action and within hours they were released.[30]

Olterra had been refloated from her scuttled position at the suggestion of Borghese to her Genoese owners and moved to Algeciras harbour, where the ship would be refitted. Lieutenant Licio Visintini was a favourite of

Borghese for his 'determined will to succeed' and his 'courageous cool in danger'.[31] He had a burning desire to emulate his dead brother, Mario, a fighter pilot. He had shot down seventeen enemy aircraft before being shot down and killed in East Africa, and Licio felt he:'Aids and directs me from heaven.'[32] Visintini suggested they use *Olterra* as a forward base for Maiale operations. First a civilian crew was put back on the ship for care and maintenance. These were soon joined by X MAS technicians and Visintini, who was given command of the operation, and they set up a workshop deep within the bowels of the ship.

A large hole was cut in the ship 5ft × 8ft below the waterline and covered by a hinged trap door, through 'which the "pigs" could either enter or leave the vessel wholly unobserved'.[33] The Maiale were brought in sections by road from Italy and smuggled past the bored Spanish guards. While this was going on the Gamma attacks from Villa Carmela continued. They sank the 1,787-ton *Ravenspoint* with limpet mines.

In *Live and Let Die*, Fleming has Bond destroy Mr Big's motor yacht *Secatur* with a limpet mine that he attaches to the hull when the boat is anchored off Jamaica. Bond, after testing the 'thin black rubber frogman's suit' and the twin air cylinders, sets off for a night swim to *Secatur* armed with a 'Champion harpoon gun' and a Wilkinsons Commando dagger, with the limpet mine strapped to his chest.[34]

Bond sets off at 2200, enters the water off rocks and goes straight to the bottom. After having to deal with an octopus that grabs him around 'both ankles', it takes him an hour to reach the keel of the *Secatur*. He arms the mine with a seven-hour fuse, but the magnets drag him toward the hull and he has 'to pull hard against it to prevent the clang on contact'. Then he has to swim down hard because with the weight of the mine released he could easily break the surface.[35]

There is some suggestion that Ian attended an agent's sabotage course at Camp X Oshawa in Canada, on the north shore of Lake Ontario close to the US border. Fleming says Stevenson purchased the land in small lots 'and the title was transferred to the crown later'.[36] He also claimed that Fleming's course included the use of limpet mines. John Pearson, in his biography of Fleming, says that the school at Oshawa 'provided him [Fleming] with lots of the tricks he would pass on to James Bond' and in the long run helped him decide 'just what kind of an agent Bond must be'.[37] However, Fleming did not need this experience given the wealth of information and first-hand accounts he would have obtained about the underwater fight in the waters around Gibraltar. We will return to the question of Camp X later.

The first Maiale attack from *Olterra* took place at 2330 on 7 December. There were some prize targets in Gibraltar at that time in the shape of the battleship *Nelson* and aircraft carriers *Formidable* and *Furious*. Licio Visintini led the three Maiale on the raid and only one man came back from it. Two men were captured, and one fell off his Maiale and was never seen again. Subjected to various depth charges, Visintini and his crew man, Sergeant Giovanni Magro, got into the inner harbour. Barely on the surface, they were caught in the beam of a searchlight and their Maiale was sunk by a hail of gunfire, with the area then subjected to scuttling charges. A few days later Visintini's and Magro's bodies were recovered by the British. They were buried at sea with full military honours. The Gibraltar Underwater Working Party unit formed to combat X MAS sent a wreath. The unit was by then commanded by Lieutenant Crabb.

The month before, Lionel Philip Kenneth Crabb had arrived in Gibraltar to help with mine disposal. With the harbour and anchorage vital to Operation Torch, it had to be made safe. Crabb hated his nickname 'Buster' and the comparison to the super-fit American actor, athlete, Olympic gold medal winner and star of *Tarzan*. His friends called him 'Crabby'. Little in Crabb's background had prepared him for his wartime role. He had served in the Merchant Navy, worked for Shell Oil, pumped gas at a filling station in America and got entangled in various enterprises, none of which worked out. When in business with a friend, financing inventors, he came across 'rubber swimfins or flippers', invented by the Frenchman Louis de Corlieu, and agreed to demonstrate them at Marshall Street baths in London, even though he felt they would never catch on.[38]

In 1938 he tried to volunteer for the RNVR but at 28 was considered too old. When war came he went back to the Merchant Navy as a seaman, from which he transferred to the Royal Navy Patrol Service in 1940. The next year he was commissioned for the Navy but discovered he had a weak left eye, which ruled him out of sea service. He volunteered for special service duties, which got him into mine and bomb disposal, and for this he was sent to Gibraltar.

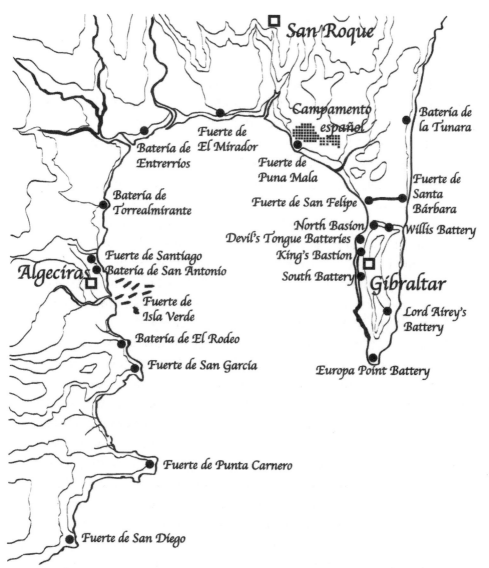

Map of Gibraltar and Bay of Gibraltar.

On arrival he learned he was expected to dispose of mines or whatever the divers brought up, and that there were only two of them,
Lieutenant William Bailey and Leading Seaman Bell, to whom he
volunteered his services. The team had no suits or fins and only rudi-
mentary breathing gear. They dived in swimming trunks and overalls
with weights in their tennis shoes. It seemed crazy to Crabb that these
two men would have to go up and down telling him what they had
found. He did not tell Bailey he could barely swim three lengths of a
swimming pool but suggested he should dive with them. He did one
short trial dive, putting on goggles that did not fit well.

Bailey showed him how the Davis Submerged Escape Apparatus
(DSEA) set worked, which was really for submariners to escape from
a submarine, and how to hold the mouthpiece, then he was led to a
ladder and was told to climb down it into 12ft of water to practise
breathing underwater. He had a string around one wrist to communicate with the surface. He went up and down the ladder several times.
He admitted not going to the bottom for he had heard octopuses were
in the harbour and he hated the thought of them. He soon felt a tug on
his wrist and returned to the surface, where Bailey told him there was
'a flap on in the harbour. Mines have been reported.'[39]

Crabb set off with Bailey to examine the hull of a ship suspected
of being mined. The dive exhausted him but he was duly accepted as
a member of the diving team. A week after his arrival Crabb found a
clamp mine on the keel of *Willowdale*; was it booby trapped was the
question? It took him and Bell forty-five minutes to loosen the mine
and get it off, exhausting both men. Finally they moored it between
two buoys at the same depth, fearing a change in pressure might set it
off. The two buoys were then towed by a launch to a mooring in Rosia
Bay. By then it was almost dark. The next day, after moving the mine to
the end of the airstrip where it could not be left close to parked aircraft,
Crabb nervously carried it ashore. There Crabb and Commander Ralph
Handcock defused it. Soon after this Bailey tripped and broke his ankle
and so Lieutenant Crabb, a poor swimmer, became the diving officer.[40]

On the night of the Visintini-led attack, 7 December, Crabb was out
examining the hulls of British ships for mines, but found nothing. He
had a torch attached to his wrist but it gave only a few inches of light in
the murky waters. He dived deeper looking for 'Pigs' but found none.

There was a launch above him keeping pace with him, and Leading Seaman Bell went with him, although he was diving at night for the first time. Crabb's greatest fear was that some trigger-happy matelot would start firing at wave ripples. They were at it all night, but of course found nothing.

Crabb was moved by the sight of the bodies of Visintini and Magro he saw in the morgue the next day, although he had no idea who they were, and the damage inflicted on them by various explosive charges. For that underwater war was 'a private war in which men respected their enemies'.[41] In 1945, while clearing German mines from Venice, Crabb gave Visintini's widow Maria, who spoke good English, a secretarial job.[42]

After Christmas 1942, Bailey and Crabb called for volunteers to join the diving team and were 'inundated with offers'. However, very few were suitable, many only being motivated by the extra pay.

The Italians had not been discouraged by the loss of five men, three killed and two captured; the concept was sound. Lieutenant Commander Ernesto Notari took over command of *Olterra* operation, and more Maiales were brought in. On the night of 8 May 1943, taking advantage of a storm, three 'Pigs' set off. The 'B.G.6' attack was a complete success as three merchant ships were badly damaged.

Even though the Gibraltar Underwater Working Party was scrambled under Operation Tadpole they encountered no one. This was hardly surprising, as Crabb, with just six divers, had some sixty ships to protect, a near-impossible job.

The finger of suspicion had been pointing at *Olterra* for some time. Colonel H.C. 'Tito' Medlam, the Defence Security Officer at Gibraltar, greased many palms around the bars and seedy clubs in the towns and villages that lined the bay of Algeciras, trying to find out where the attacks were coming from. The Villa Carmela was suspected. Alan Hillgarth came to Algeciras as well at the behest of Bailey. His protest to the local authorities resulted in *Olterra* being searched by the Spanish Navy but they found nothing, or turned a blind eye.[43]

Crabb and Bailey volunteered to swim around *Olterra* at night and perhaps mine her. Lieutenant Frank Goldsworthy observed that the proposal went right up the chain of command to the War Cabinet but was rejected as such action would infringe Spanish neutrality.[44]

On the night of 3/4 August, X MAS launched their last attack against Gibraltar, even though by then Mussolini had been dismissed as head of state on 25 July, Italy was still in the war. The three 'Pigs' sank three more merchant ships. On 8 September Italy signed the armistice with the Allies. In their campaign against shipping at Gibraltar, X MAS sank or damaged fourteen ships of more than 80,000 tons. By early August most of the men had returned to Italy. *Olterra* was then boarded by Spanish officials and all remaining Italians were ordered to leave. An attempt was made to dismantle the Maiale base and workshop, but on 11 October 1943 *Olterra* was towed out of Algeciras and moored in the commercial harbour in Gibraltar.

Goldsworthy recorded that there was an inquiry as to why 'we had not discovered the truth sooner'. Yet he went through all the intelligence reports and found 'nothing to link Olterra with the attacks. The secret had been well kept.'[45] Crabb went on board the ship soon after she arrived and salvaged a Maiale, which he called 'Emily', and learned to pilot it, even shaving off his beard to wear Italian breathing gear. However, he fumed about the security officers, even though he had several friends among them. If only he and Bailey had been allowed to examine the ship.[46]

At the end of November 1943, Ian Fleming attended the Sextant Conference in Cairo between Roosevelt, Churchill and Chiang Kai-shek to determine policy in the Far East. There he suffered a bout of bronchitis and returned to England on the cruiser HMS *London*, which he likened to a 'millionaire's Mediterranean cruise'.[47] They docked in Gibraltar on 13 December, where they had to wait five days for an escort they were to share with the battleship *King George V*. It is inconceivable that he did not learn about *Olterra* and the exploits of X MAS at this time. Maybe he even met Crabb, who was still there experiencing some 'dull months' before he was transferred to the Italian mainland as part of the 'clearance diving team' to help clear ports.[48]

Kingsley Amis put 'underwater swimming' at the top of Ian Fleming's list of interests and it appears in five of the thirteen Bond books. Amis thought it sent 'the emotional temperature soaring'.[49] Fleming even missed the launch of *Casino Royale* in April 1953 for the chance to go diving with Jacques Cousteau, such was his passion.[50]

10

IS YOUR JOURNEY REALLY NECESSARY?

In the wake of Operation Catastrophe, as Fleming called his drunken night out in Tangier with Henry Greenleaves, he was back in London in August 1941. Looking for a new challenge, he applied to join the British Military Mission to Moscow as naval representative. The leader of the mission was Major General Noel Mason-MacFarlane, known as 'Mac'. He had known Ian from Berlin in the late 1930s and their paths had crossed again when he had been second-in-command of the Gibraltar garrison up to March 1941. At the time, Mac was also head of the Joint Intelligence Centre on the Rock and the combined forces group ready to activate Operation Golden Eye. He was not impressed by Fleming, thinking he was 'gullible and of poor unbalanced judgement'. He told Major General Francis Davidson, the Director of Military Intelligence, that he did not want Fleming 'foisted' upon them. He felt that he was likely to harm the 'so far very co-operative and matey family' he had assembled.[1]

Mac need not have been concerned for the question never came up as Godfrey would not release his key assistant. Fleming was disappointed, telling Peter Smithers that he 'hoped to lose myself there for protracted winter sports, but I dare say skiing with a Panzer Division behind is less fun than the old-fashioned kind'.[2]

It was only a matter of days after his return that Ian got involved with the new Political Warfare Executive (PWE) and their remit to take over propaganda and deception, which he found fascinating and had ended up on his desk at 17F.[3] One of Ian's great skills was to delegate and for the day-to-day running of propaganda he set up a new section in Room 39, 17Z, to be run by Donald McLachlan in close co-operation with Sefton Delmer, who had set up PWE's 'black' propaganda machine, designed to confound and confuse the enemy, at Woburn Abbey. White propaganda was put out by the BBC. Ian's friend, Robert Harling, would also be roped into 'black radio' the 'subversive broadcasts to the German Navy'.[4]

Harling had first met Ian in the late summer of 1939 when he was an established typographic businessman publishing innovative magazines. Theirs was an unlikely friendship, given Ian came from Eton and the City, while Harling came from a working-class background and was a self-made man. However, Fiona MacCarthy wrote in the foreword to Harling's *Ian Fleming: A Personal Memoir* of their 'burgeoning friendship' and that they had much in common: 'The two men shared a certain inner loneliness, war suited both of them. They both had a taste for action, an almost boyish longing for adventure and escapade.'[5]

Harling was a keen sailor and at the outbreak of war he volunteered for the Navy. In the evacuation from Dunkirk he commanded a whaler shuttling men from the beaches to larger ships. After that he was a navigator on a corvette on convoy duties in the Atlantic. A bad bout of gastric flu left him ashore billeted on the old cruiser HMS *Caroline* of First World War vintage, the HQ of Atlantic escort craft moored in Belfast. In 1941, Fleming plucked him from there to work in the Inter-Service Topographical Department (ISTD), which worked closely with intelligence supplying details of ports and beaches and other likely targets. They met in a 'scruffy waiting room' at the Admiralty; Harling would later learn it was near the legendary Room 39. Fleming asked him if he had enjoyed life at sea, to which Harling replied that it was 'too boring and repetitive'. Ian then told him that the new job at the ISTD might be 'too land based' but nobody really knew. The next day he introduced Harling to Colonel Sam Bassett, RM, the head of the new ISTD. He told him: 'If Ian thinks you could be the man for the job, that's good enough for me.'[6]

Late that August Ian, with his good German, was speaking directly from the BBC to the enemy, on the special service for the Kriegsmarine. Leonard Miall, who ran the BBC German service, recalled Ian's boundless enthusiasm. One example was just after the Japanese attack on Pearl Harbor and Hitler had declared war on the United States. Ian was excited: 'The war is practically over, now this bloody fool Hitler's gone and brought the Americans in.'

Miall replied: 'I'm sure you are right in the long run, Ian, but we've got a lot of fighting still to do.'

'Oh! You defeatist lot in the BBC,' said Fleming.[7]

Before he started broadcasting for the PWE Ian had been trying to obtain information from German PoWs that might be useful for propaganda. He tried buttering them up with lavish boozy lunches in swanky London restaurants. On one outing he took Captain Werner Lott and his navigation officer from *U-35*, which they had scuttled when forced to the surface by British destroyers in the North Sea, to Scott's in Coventry Street, where he hoped to get them drunk and learn what he could. The party became noisy and so much of the talk was in loud German that the waiter raised the alarm and the restaurant was soon full of the Special Branch. He was on the carpet with Godfrey for this caper and recalled the DNI saying 'the only result of our secret mission was to mobilize half the narks of the Special Branch of Scotland Yard'.[8]

Scott's is also one of Bond's favourite restaurants. In *Moonraker* Chapter 19, Missing Person, he waits for Gala Brand at his favourite right-hand corner table, also Fleming's favourite, and watches 'the people and the traffic in Piccadilly and down the Haymarket'.[9] While in *Diamonds are Forever* in Chapter 3, Hot Ice, he offers to take Chief of Staff Bill Tanner to lunch: 'I'll take you to Scott's and we'll have some of their dressed Crab and a pint of black velvet.'[10]

About the same time in that summer of 1941 a report by Ewen Montagu crossed Admiral Godfrey's desk about 'German prepared Intelligence Commandos', the Abwehr Truppen who moved in with the lead troops of an offensive on the hunt for any intelligence material they could find: codes, ciphers, plans, anything that might give them the edge over the enemy. This was a fillip to the DNI to form a similar unit of Naval Intelligence Commandos when the Allies took up the offensive. More importantly for Montagu at the time, having broken the Abwehr Enigma codes, the Germans' use of this special unit 'gave us the first indication of a possible German operation'.[11]

The report was passed on to Fleming, who began to study the Abwehr Truppen. The unit had been formed in 1939 on the initiative of Admiral Canaris and was made up of men mainly from the Abwehr military intelligence Brandenburg Lehr Regiment. They were men who had been born, or spent much of their lives, abroad and had multiple linguistic skills, and their training was tough. The programme required they were marksmen, demolition and counter-demolition experts and specialist drivers with light vehicles and motorbikes. They were extremely successful in the Balkans and the invasion of Greece and Crete.

Lieutenant Commander Trevor James Glanville, known as 'Jim' or 'Sancho', was one of the first to bring back news of the Abwehr Truppen on his return from Zagreb, reporting on their activities against the Yugoslav 4th Army. He had been arrested with other members of the British Military Mission by pro-Nazi Croats but was later exchanged for some Italian prisoners. He told his story to Colonel G.F. Taylor, Assistant Director of SOE, suggesting a similar unit should be raised in Britain. Taylor was enthusiastic but felt it was not a role for SOE. Also, SIS had no operational troops on call; however, the DNI did. Glanville would later go on to serve in 30 Assault Unit (30 AU).[12]

With so much on his plate, Ian was glad to find a small flat to live in at Athenaeum Court not far from Godfrey's home at Curzon Street. He had been living in a string of hotels and clubs since he had left his flat at 22B Ebury Street, which he had moved into in 1937 from his mother's house. He had bought the lease from Oswald Mosley, who had used the former Baptist Chapel for meetings of his British Union of Fascists. Fleming had moved out at the start of the Blitz because the unusual skylights could not easily be blacked out. He was not overly fond of the Athenaeum Court flat, which he likened to a 'ratlike existence' where it was 'impossible to swing a cat', although it had a good location. Many other advantages he had taken for granted were now affected by wartime deprivations. He bemoaned the fact the Savoy Hotel was mixing Martinis out of 'bath-tub gin and sherry' and the restaurants were 'expensive and crowded'. Even his car he had to run on 'pool petrol, (which had a low octane rating, usually below 80 for private cars) water and moth-balls' to make it go further. But he still had his luxury cigarettes, Morland Specials from Morland of Grosvenor Street, made for him. Each bore three gold rings, as he wore on his uniform sleeve as a commander. He ordered 400 a week at 32s a hundred (about £85 today).[13] Of course, Bond smokes them as well, consuming sixty of this high-tar mixture of Turkish and Balkan tobacco a day. That is unless he is training, as in *Live and Let Die* under Quarrel's supervision, when he cuts it down to ten a day and cuts out the booze entirely.[14]

Life was not entirely grim for Ian; he even in a perverse way enjoyed the constant danger of the Blitz, not knowing what might happen next. He had plenty of female company; at the time he saw Ann O'Neill, as she was then, with or without her husband. Later she would become Ian's wife. Loelia, Duchess of Westminster, was another, a divorcee who thought him 'the most attractive man I've ever seen'. Joan Bright was introduced to him by his brother Peter, and he often went to the cinema with her. There was also Maud Russell, his stern mistress. At the Admiralty another girlfriend was Pamela Tiarks, who he called 'Silvertop'. Then there was Muriel Wright, 'Honeytop' because of her blonde hair, and it was she that he was probably closest to, having first met her in Kitzbühel in 1935. He had got her a job as a dispatch rider at the Admiralty and she would often pick up his cigarettes for him when on her duties around the city.[15]

The start of 1942 must have tested even Ian Fleming's optimistic nature with a string of Allied disasters, given no doubt he was shocked by the loss of the battleship *Prince of Wales* and the battlecruiser *Repulse* off Malaya on 10 December 1941. The loss of *Repulse* must have been particularly painful for Godfrey, being his last sea-going command.

In February the news got worse with the humiliation for Britain of what became known as the 'Channel Dash'. Three German ships, the battlecruisers *Scharnhorst* and *Gneisenau* and the heavy cruiser *Prinz Eugen,* were moved from Brest in France – where they were a constant target for the RAF – to Wilhelmshaven right under the noses of the British. The attempts by the Royal Navy and RAF to interfere were woeful. However, although it was not obvious at the time, despite this being a tactical success for the Germans it would prove a strategic failure as none of the ships were able to have much effect on the Battle of the Atlantic. That was just as well as a new four-rotor Enigma machine had been introduced for the U-boats which was harder to crack, which greatly increased Allied shipping losses. Both battlecruisers had hit mines during the 'dash' and *Gneisenau* would never put to sea again. Admiral Norman Denning, at the Admiralty's OIC, had warned that this was something the Germans were likely to try; he even outlined how it might be done.[16] Despite this, the Navy and its intelligence services received a slating in the press, *The Times* declaring: 'Nothing more mortifying to the pride of sea-power has happened in home waters since the Seventeenth Century.'[17] Gloom descended on Room 39, which was not eased when two days later Singapore fell with 80,000 men taken prisoner, which, Ian explained to Ann O'Neill over a dinner of lobster and beer at Wilton's Restaurant Jermyn Street, was because 'we no longer shoot deserters from the army'.[18]

In March, Ian put the idea to Godfrey to form a specialist Commando unit in a memo with the heading 'Most Secret', before outlining his proposal. He argued that the Commandos should be sent with the forward troops during a raid and if successful: 'Their duty is to capture documents, ciphers, etc before they can be destroyed by the enemy.'[19] Godfrey approved the concept.

In July, the Intelligence Assault Unit was formed. It became 30 Assault Unit in 1943, made up largely of Royal Marine Commandos, along with naval men and some specialist Army and RAF ranks from time to time. They were first bloodied at Dieppe. The unit became known as 'Red Indians' within NID, and later as 'Fleming's Red Indians'.

The first outing of the Intelligence Assault Unit (IAU) was the Dieppe raid of August 1942, where some 6,000 men were put ashore to destroy port facilities and radar installations, as well as boost morale back at home. However, the main requirement was to test the feasibility of an invasion in 1943. The landing was a disaster, with nearly 60 per cent of the landing force killed or captured. The RAF lost double the amount of aircraft compared with the Luftwaffe, and the Navy lost thirty-three landing craft and a destroyer.

Fleming was permitted by Godfrey to observe the action from a destroyer off the coast. In 1961 he wrote 'The Dieppe Raid', his account of the 19 August landings he witnessed from the deck of HMS *Fernie*.

It was based on the report he made at the time. He refers to *Fernie* as a *Hunt* because she was a Hunt-class destroyer. The weather was 'fine' crossing the Channel and the large fleet of small vessels passed through 'the enemy minefields as clean as a whistle'. He was woken from his doze in an armchair at around 0300 to the sound of gunfire. On deck, he and two other observers, an American general and a colonel of the United States Marines, witnessed a bright show of 'green and white tracer' in the distance to the north, which 'seemed un-dangerous and even friendly'.[20]

The IAU Royal Marine 33 Troop consisted of two officers, two sergeants, three corporals and twenty-one Marines. For this operation the unit was designated 10 Platoon X Company under the wing of 40 Commando RM. For the Dieppe raid they were transported there on the old flat-bottomed Yangtze River gunboat HMS *Locust*. It was captained by Commander Robert E.D. Ryder, known as 'Red', a former polar explorer who had won the VC during the raid on St Nazaire five months earlier that was intended to prevent the dry docks there being used by German battleships. At Dieppe 33 Troop were tasked with entering the Kriegsmarine HQ, which was housed in a dockside hotel, to seize whatever they could find there. They were under the command of Lieutenant Herbert O. Huntington-Whiteley.

Locust came in toward the shore at 15 knots heading for the mole to land the Marines but it was shrouded by thick black smoke and the gunboat was met by a blizzard of shell fire. Marine 'Ginger' Northern was killed before they got off *Locust*. Fellow Marine Paul McGrath, who was 19 at the time and facing his first time in action, recalled: 'The noise of the explosion was gigantic. The shock of it blew all the fuses in my nervous system. I was petrified with such terror it stunned my mind.'[21]

They went over the side via scrambling nets into landing craft 2,000 yards from the main beach. Covered by a smokescreen before hitting the shore, they entered into a brutal maelstrom of noise and confusion. The landing craft carrying 10 Platoon grounded on the beach and was immediately caught in crossfire. Lieutenant Huntington-Whiteley ordered his men to abandon their kit and swim for it back to the ships. Thus, Ian Fleming's first experiment with this specialist unit ended, with the men swimming away from the burning landing craft and carnage on Dieppe beach. Sergeant John Kruthoffer swam more than 2 miles before being picked up. McGrath thought he was going to drown when his life jacket deflated. He wrestled to get his trousers off, often going under. Luckily he was dragged into a small boat.

Out of the 5,000 Canadian troops that landed at Dieppe that day, only 2,200 came back. Along with Marine Northern killed on *Locust*, Marine John Alexander from 10 Platoon did not make it. Their parent unit, 40 Commando, suffered ninety-nine casualties, with twenty-three killed and the rest wounded and/or captured.[22]

Fleming observed this from the pitching deck of *Fernie*, getting glimpses through the billowing smoke. As they closed in on the beach he saw 'heaps of dead who, we rightly feared were our own men'. They remained 'about seven hundred yards away from the beach making smoke to protect the landing craft ...' Many stretcher cases and walking wounded were taken on board, Fleming talked to some of them; all showed 'outstanding cheerfulness and courage' after what they had been through on the beaches. They were still in danger on the destroyer, which was blazing away with her guns. The ship was hit near the funnel, killing one man and wounding several others. The anti-aircraft guns were very active, and during a particularly intense burst of fire while Fleming was standing by the port Oerlikon, he noticed 'one of the spare gun's crew sitting on a crate of ammunition engrossed in a book'. He looked over his shoulder and read the title of the book, '*A Fortnight's Folly*. The reader's eyes were popping out of his head with excitement as he greedily turned the pages.'[23]

It crossed Ian's mind that since his men had been unable to carry out their mission: 'The Government exhortation, "Is Your Journey really Necessary?" came to mind, heavily underlined by the shells from shore batteries which came zipping through our rigging.'[24]

The raid began at 0300, and by 1100 a withdrawal was ordered. *Fernie* was berthed at Newhaven sixteen hours later. Fleming left the ship 'with the American General and the Colonel of the Marines to find a welcome in the best hotel, which we stormed regardless of protest'.[25]

Later in his report, Fleming wrote: 'The machinery for producing further raids is there, tried and found good. Dieppe was an essential preliminary for operations ahead.'[26] But he also felt that 'the fortunes of war must be with us next time'.[27]

11

CHANGE OF COMMAND

The two American officers Ian Fleming rushed to beat to the enmities of the 'best hotel' in Newhaven were an example of a dramatic increase in US military personnel coming into Britain.[1] Roosevelt favoured an early cross-Channel invasion to pacify public opinion, and a prolonged debate took place over several months in 1941–42 over the merits of such action. Churchill favoured a Mediterranean strategy, his 'soft underbelly' of Europe theory. The Americans put forward Operation Sledgehammer, which would involve a landing to seize the French port of either Brest or Cherbourg during the autumn of 1942. Then it would be held as a springboard, building up troops before a breakout the following year. The original Allied concept, Operation Roundup, was a full-scale invasion of Europe in 1943. Sledgehammer was seen as too risky by the British, which the experience of the Dieppe raid confirmed.[2]

Troops were also needed in North Africa; in September, General Bernard Montgomery, the new 8th Army commander, had won the defensive battle of Alam el Halfa ridge on the Libyan–Egyptian border. This forced Erwin Rommel, the 'Desert Fox', to abandon his drive for the Suez Canal. Men and equipment would be needed to build up the desert forces to drive the Axis out of North Africa.

Ian was not impressed with the burgeoning American intelligence arm that had descended on London; he called the new OSS representative Bill Whitney 'completely useless except on the propaganda side'. In Washington as well, Donovan, given his apt sobriquet of Wild Bill, thrashed about widely 'with as much energy as ever, but very little comes from his activities except a moderate amount of smoke'.[3]

With the prospect of an Allied invasion taking place in Europe or North Africa in the not too distant future, Godfrey increased Ian's workload. He was put in charge, his bibliographical interest making him ideal for the job of forming a library of maps, information and personnel contacts in countries likely to be involved in Allied plans. All the while he kept Operation Golden Eye under review.

★★★

Another of Fleming's tasks was to liaise every week with SOE's Lieutenant Colonel Taylor on behalf of Godfrey, although increasingly he saw the Director of Operations, Brigadier Colin McVean Gubbins. Godfrey felt that SOE was 'fraught with countless petty troubles' largely of its own making. But given time it would 'emerge as a fully-fledged organization, quite capable of standing up for itself and doing a sound job of work'.[4] Fleming was much more sympathetic and fascinated by the derring-do of SOE.

Gubbins was code-named M and many have taken a leap of faith to equate him with Fleming's fictional 'M', which clearly he does not fit well. He was born in Japan, the son of an English diplomat of Irish extraction, and brought up in Scotland by his Scottish mother's parents on the Isle of Mull. In the First World War he served in the Royal Artillery, won the Military Cross on the Somme, and was wounded and gassed in 1917. In 1918 he was shipped home sick with trench fever. Given his strong constitution, he recovered and stayed on in the Army, serving in northern Russia in 1919 and Ireland during 1921–22. In Ireland he served as an intelligence officer, which began his interest in guerrilla warfare. The Anglo-Irish war he likened to 'being shot at from behind hedges by men in trilby's and mackintoshes and not being allowed to shoot back'.[5] In the inter-war period he served in India and at the Staff College at Camberley, and by the start of the Second World War he was with Military Intelligence at the War Office. He was sent to Poland at the start of the war, arriving far too late to aid the Poles and escaped via Hungary and the Balkans back to Britain, bringing with him intelligence of German Panzer tactics. He saw action in Norway, fighting delaying actions with the 'striking Companies', an all-arms early version of the Commandos, as German forces closed in on Narvik. When SOE was set up under Hugh Dalton, the Minister of Economic Warfare, Gubbins was appointed Director of Operations and Training.

Fleming was attracted to SOE and his creation James Bond has more characteristics shared with their agents than those from the SIS or NID. He was an assassin and uses a wide variety of weapons. Even the 00 number might be said to emanate from the numbering system at SOE; often having a 0 after a W meaning this agent was trained in silent killing and Commando skills. In *The Man with the Golden Gun* he even has 007 reply to Scaramanga's question if he is James Bond of the Secret Service: 'I thought the Secret Service packed up at the end of the war.'[6] And he says much the same thing to Blofeld in *On Her Majesty's Secret Service*.[7] The only secret service to be stood down in 1946 was SOE; even NID continued on into the 1960s. Even though by the end of 1942 relations between SIS, the three armed services and SOE had much improved, Sir Alexander Cadogan, permanent under-secretary at the Foreign Office, wrote: 'My secretary of state does not consider that there will be room for two Secret British organisations in Europe once hostilities have ceased.' All SOE personnel remaining in government service would be transferred to the War Office for 'overt duties with the military' or 'to the SIS if they are to perform underground work'.[8]

Gubbins remained a confidant of Fleming after the war, Ian encouraging him to write a history of SOE: 'Dear Colin,' he wrote to him in July 1949: 'I am wondering if you have thought over the idea of writing a popular history of SOE, both as a tribute to many gallant men and to preserve some of these great adventure stories for posterity ... The work of SOE really deserves such a monument.'[9]

★★★

As it became clear that North Africa would be the next target for Allied landings, NID's relations with OSS improved when Ian was appointed the division liaison officer working with Colonel Whitney H. Shepardson, acting head of the OSS office in London. The Americans were glad of his help and Commander Junius Morgan was given the job of dealing with NID. Morgan was a member of the banking family Ian knew well. Shortly before his second trip to Washington, in September, Ian offered his help through the DNI to Shepardson; 'if there are any private wars in which you are engaged I should be delighted to fire a salvo on your behalf in any direction you require'.[10]

Just prior to Godfrey's and Ian's departure for the United States, the news was received of the DNI's promotion to vice admiral. Yet on the same day, Admiral Sir Dudley Pound told him his appointment as DNI was over. Godfrey could be and was often bad-tempered and impatient, which had made him enemies within the Joint Intelligence Committee (JIC). He also had a difficult relationship with Churchill, who he felt interfered too much in things of which he had little knowledge. It remains ambiguous as to why Godfrey was sacked in September. Pound sent him a note the next day that said the JIC could no longer function 'as long as you were a member'.[11]

In June, Godfrey's old friend Admiral Andrew Browne Cunningham, known as 'ABC', was appointed to the Combined Chiefs of Staff Committee in Washington, from his command of the Mediterranean Fleet. He was not keen on leaving the fleet 'at a time when their fortunes was at its lowest ebb'.[12] Cunningham and his wife, Nona, flew from Bristol to Foynes to catch the flying boat for the transatlantic crossing. Their travel was supposed to be secret, and false passports described them as Mr and Mrs Bisselt-Christie travelling on government service. Irish officials questioned them before they were allowed to embark and, observing they had him listed as a 'naval officer', Cunningham answered: 'That must be a clerical error.' To which the official merely 'grinned and made no further ado, and we were soon on board'. The flight took twenty-five hours on a route often frequented by celebrities, politicians and military personnel. Much to his chagrin, the couple were subjected to an interview by US officials who 'after pulling my leg for some time knew quite well who we were'. The US Navy had a plane ready and waiting to take them on to Washington, although they still had to run the gauntlet of being 'bombarded by questions from a horde of pressmen with photographers' flashlights going off all round us …'They too seemed to know who he was – so much for security.[13]

It appears that Cunningham's appointment was the trigger that led to Godfrey's sacking, as he continued to send 'him intelligence summaries, which contained information on all three services. This had been approved when Cunningham was C–in–C in the Mediterranean but not when he went to Washington. The summaries continued, whereas Field Marshal Dill, on the same mission, was only getting assessments rather than full intelligence. It never occurred to Godfrey that this would upset the other services. It is possible that Dill complained, but the significant factor was that Vice Chief of the Naval Staff Admiral Henry Moore and Pound would not support Godfrey. Pound might well have had more pressing matters on his mind. He was extremely ill with a brain tumour, which seriously affected his concentration, and in a little over a year would be dead. He died on 21 October 1943, Trafalgar Day.[14]

The trip to the USA still went ahead but it had lost some of its sparkle. In New York Fleming and Godfrey visited the NID and BSC offices. Yet for Ian, meeting Ernest Cuneo, a leading member of the Roosevelt team, was to prove of far more significance. He would become a close friend, although they did not hit it off from the start. Cuneo was a lawyer by trade of Italian descent, who had told Churchill he was a direct descendant of the navigator namesake who had sailed with Columbus.[15] Born in 1905, in his youth he had been a college football star but by 1942 he had gone to fat and was almost as wide as he was tall.

Ian first met him at Bill Stephenson's apartment at the Hotel Dorset on West 54th Street, where they got into an argument about the Soviet convoys. Ian observed that the Americans, in the shape of Admiral Ernest King, Chief of US Naval Operations, needed to do more. Cuneo retorted that junior British officers were hardly in a position to advise the admiral. Ian sprang to his feet, pointed out he was a serving officer and asked if Cuneo doubted his 'bona fides'.

'No, only your patently limited judgement,' said Cuneo, to which both men burst into laughter, having enjoyed the verbal fencing.

Cuneo likened Fleming in build to a lightweight boxer. He soon realised he was one of Stephenson's special men and 'had privileges far and above his rank of the Commander in the Wavy Navy'.[16]

'Ernie Cureo', the wisecracking taxi driver, would appear in *Diamonds are Forever.* He is the undercover man who Felix Leiter gets to 'look after' Bond in Las Vegas.[17] Cureo gets rubbed out by the 'Detroit Purple Mob' and their hitmen, who drive a red Jaguar sports car. Cureo calls them a 'couple of lavender boys. You know pansies.'[18] Cuneo would help with the research and the plots of several of the Bond books. Fleming's dedication in *Thunderball* was 'To Ernest Cuneo Muse'.

Another important friend Ian made in this visit to the United States was Roald Dahl, who had arrived in Washington in the spring of 1942. He had been a fighter pilot whose flying career was ended by a crash in a Gladiator biplane fighter in the Western Desert, which put him in the naval hospital in Alexandria for six months recovering from concussion. His head had hit the plane's reflector sight at 75mph, fracturing his skull and breaking his nose. Pilots were in short supply and he was so keen to get back in the fight that, seemingly recovered, he joined 80 Squadron in Greece flying Hurricanes. He was soon in action against swarms of German aircraft. The British were soon forced out of Greece and Crete, whereupon Dahl's unit re-formed at Haifa in Palestine.

Again he was in the thick of the action, flying against the pro-German Vichy French operating from Syria and Lebanon. He was in the air every day: 'My Log Book records that on 15 June I went up five times and was in the air for a total of eight hours and ten minutes.' This began to bring on severe headaches, and steep turns soon resulted in agony and blackouts. Dahl duly reported to the squadron doctor, who grounded him as unfit to fly and said that in his opinion he was still suffering from the effects of the desert crash. He was sent back to Egypt and from there to Britain by sea.[19]

After a spell of leave, he was sent to the United States as part of a diplomatic delegation to become assistant air attaché at the British Embassy, his role to spread pro-British propaganda. At first he was not enamoured with the land of milk and honey he found himself in, given what he had left behind, Britain being blitzed and his friends shot out of the sky. He later admitted to Bill Stephenson that: 'Now almost instantly, I find myself in the middle of a pre-war cocktail mob in America. I had to dress up in ghastly gold braid and tassels. The result was I became rather outspoken and brash. The senior people decided I wasn't a very good fellow to have around. An RAF Air Chief Marshal there arranged that I get the sack and be sent home to England.'[20] The air marshal was William Welsh. At the end of October 1943, Dahl left the embassy after being recalled to London.[21]

However, his no-nonsense approach had impressed Stephenson, who had him brought back to Washington within a few weeks and promoted to wing commander. At a party he came across the same air marshal, who angrily asked him what he was doing there. Dahl replied: 'I'm afraid, sir, you'll have to ask Bill Stephenson.' This ended the argument with the senior officer, who knew he could do nothing against the power wielded by the head of BSC.

Another powerful friend Dahl was to cultivate was Eleanor Roosevelt, who had been captivated by his children's book *The Gremlins* after reading it to her grandchildren. Hearing he was in Washington, she invited him to dinner with the President. 'My job was to try and oil the wheels between the British and the Americans. After that first dinner with the President, I used to get out to Hyde Park at weekends. There were always Roosevelts there, and people like Henry Morgenthau. I was able to ask pointed questions and get equally pointed replies because, theoretically, I was a nobody.'[22]

Ian Fleming and Roald Dahl had an influence on each other's writing. In Dahl's introduction to the TV version of his short story *Lamb to the Slaughter* he reflected on how 'his friend Ian Fleming' had inspired the story while the two of them had spent the weekend at a house in Vermont. At dinner Ian had whispered to Roald about the lamb being so dry 'this ruddy thing must have been in the freezer for ten years she [the hostess] should be shot'.

'Not shot,' reflected Roald. 'There must be a more interesting story than that here.'[23]

After Ian's death, Roald was short of money and so was happy to write the screenplay for *You Only Live Twice*, although he was not impressed with the writing, thinking it 'Ian's worst book'. Dahl, though, had great respect for Fleming as a writer and friend, describing him as 'a sparky, witty, caustic companion, full of jokes and also full of odd obscure bits of knowledge'.[24] The screenplay earned Dahl $165,500, and he got another $125,000 for writing the script to Ian's children's book *Chitty Chitty Bang Bang*, transforming his finances at the time.

With the arrival of the Joint Staff Mission in Washington, Peter Smithers, who had been paddling a lone canoe, had his 'one horse show taken over by a staff of five naval officers'. Godfrey had been quick to employ his skills in another post; a fluent Spanish speaker, he was sent to Mexico City as the acting naval attaché at the British diplomatic mission. His job was to investigate U-boat activity in the area, in particular reports of refuelling on the Mexican coast. This meant Fleming had lost his bolt hole with Smithers in Georgetown.[25]

However, Ivar Bryce, Ian's childhood friend who he had first met in Cornwall on a family holiday, was in Washington at the time and Ian stayed with him. Bryce was even ordered to accompany the Assistant Director of Naval Intelligence to a conference in Jamaica and told to 'please arrange transport'.[26]

German U-boats had been enjoying one of their 'happy periods' off the eastern seaboard of the United States and in the Caribbean. In the early months of 1942, they sank twenty-five ships in ten days. In February, the Kriegsmarine had introduced a new four-rotor Enigma machine. This meant it took longer for Bletchley Park to break the messages, and so the Allies were unable to counter many of the attacks. Godfrey had sent many of his best people to America to improve intelligence and direction finding, which is the art of listening to high-frequency radio messages to obtain a fix on a submarine's position. Captain Rodger Winn, an expert on submarine tracking, managed to convince Admiral King USN to adopt the tactic. This was no easy task given that the US Fleet Commander could be notoriously difficult to please. Godfrey was thrilled when direction finding was adopted by the US Navy, and it was possibly his greatest contribution to the war.[27]

Later, Godfrey went to Canada while Ian went to Jamaica for the Anglo-American Conference to discuss further naval co-operation in the Caribbean, where more than 300 ships had been sunk. Bryce, who went with him, had been working for Stephenson in Washington and North America in the 'dirty tricks' department, encouraging anti-German feeling wherever he could.

Bond, with the undercover name Bryce, which he also uses in *Dr No*, takes the Silver Phantom train to Miami in *Live and Let Die* on a journey that will end in Jamaica. The train started running in 1939 as the Silver Meteor from New York and ran via Washington, Richmond, Savannah, Jacksonville and Tampa. Compartment H, in Car 245, is reserved for Bond under the name Bryce.[28] The early chapters take place in Harlem, where Bond meets Mr Big and as a warning gets the little finger of his left hand broken by Tee Hee. It was Ernest Cuneo who arranged for Fleming to spend a night in the Upper West Side on patrol with two local detectives. This demonstrates the lengths Ian went to in his research for the Bond books.[29]

Bryce gives us a picture of the work ethic of Fleming as he takes every opportunity to be well informed, even on the move: 'We climbed aboard the US Army transport aircraft and started hammering down the US East Coast on the 1,400-odd miles to Kingston's Palisadoes airport. Conversation did not flourish; between the violently noisy plane and the thick files that Ian was devouring one after another, it was impossible.'[30]

Arriving in Jamaica, it was hot and raining. Bryce persuaded Ian to stay with him at his Bellevue plantation in the Blue Mountains, which would be cooler and was only 10 miles from Kingston. The only trouble was getting there, something Bryce had never done in the rainy season or the dark. The road surface was reduced to like driving along 'a river bed and several of the endless hairpin bends were of the kind that can only be negotiated by reversing on the precipitous brink'. On arrival there was little to eat or drink, although Elizabeth, his resourceful housekeeper, rustled up a chicken, linen and towels, and beds were made. A solitary bottle of grenadine used to colour cocktails was found to complement the 'stringy, tasteless chicken' that made up the heart of the meal, with some yams and small tasty bananas. They went to bed early, needing to set off at dawn to be at the conference on time. It was the same routine for four long days spent at the hot stuffy conference in the Myrtle Bank Hotel, returning to Bellevue over the rough roads in the evening.[31]

Bond drives the same roads in *Dr No* in an Austin A 30, having got rid of the black Sunbeam Alpine that belonged to Commander John Strangeways, the local SIS man who Dr No has killed. The Sunbeam was too hot for Bond to use. Fleming's descriptive writing is evocative of the time and place: 'They were at the saddleback at Stoney Hill where the Junction Road dives down through fifty S-bends towards the North Coast. Bond put the little Austin A 30 into second gear and let it coast. The sun was coming up over the Blue Mountain peak and dusty shafts of gold lanced into the plunging valley.'[32]

There was little time, Bryce felt, for Ian to discover Jamaica or see much of Bellevue in the relentless rain of 1942. He had hoped that Ian would come and stay when the war was over but felt the weather might have scuppered that idea. Yet Ian had loved the island and told Bryce so on the plane back to the United States after working on his files for hours: 'he suddenly snapped his brief-box shut and turned to me sparklingly with enthusiasm. He paused: "You known, Ivar, I have made a great decision." I waited, nervous of the news to come. "When we have won this blasted war. I am going to live in Jamaica. Just live in Jamaica and lap it up, and swim in the sea and write books."'[33]

Ian was back in London in October to concentrate on Operation Torch. He had to make sure that Golden Eye was still in place and ready, and that his 'Red Indians' of the Intelligence Assault Unit would soon be storming ashore in Africa. Godfrey was still on hand, but had received a new job offer as flag officer commanding the Royal Indian Navy in Bombay, leaving his desk at NI in November. He thought about it for a day, seeking advice from his old friend ABC Cunningham, and came to the conclusion 'that in wartime you must do what you are told'. He had also wanted to see the East and the Pacific, and so 'India appealed to me strongly'.[34] He would be replaced as DNI in the New Year by Captain Edmund Rushbrooke, who was not keen on the job. Joan Saunders, who worked at NID, felt that Godfrey was 'too good' for the job while 'Old Rushbrooke was no good, and if it hadn't been for Ian Fleming the whole thing would have run down'.[35]

With Operation Torch scheduled for the early part of November, Golden Eye was activated ready to counter any German moves into the Iberian Peninsula. In Spain, Alan Hillgarth was ready and waiting to supervise and direct the agents of H section of the SOE. Hillgarth had a portable wireless transmitter and two cars in case his staff had to take to the road. One was a Humber Super Snipe 'with huge tyres'. He loathed that car after the steering broke on it one day at 40mph and nearly killed him.[36] It cost £196 18s 2d to repair.[37]

Hillgarth had recommended for a lorry to be ready at Madrid to carry the transmitter, along with a petty officer telegraphist. In a report from Commander Birley, the NID man in Gibraltar, to Hillgarth, he outlined the staff needed on the 'outbreak of hostilities': two officers, two telegraphists, and three Royal Marines, to join him by road. Birley noted that: 'Petty Officer Telegraphist Bowling is a wizard and all his W/T routines are accurately taped with Admiralty, Gibraltar and the Army set at Spanish Military GHQ (if required).'[38] Hillgarth wrote in his Golden Eye report in November 1941 that he wanted three officers in Gibraltar to be 'under my orders. I reckon that with this personnel and this means of communication and transport, I shall be in a position to maintain efficient liaison between the Spanish minister of Marine, wherever he may be, and Gibraltar.' It is clear that he thought they would be dealing with the Spanish against the Germans.[39]

On 23 October, Montgomery's artillery near the tiny Egyptian railway halt of El Alamein opened fire, beginning the second Battle of El Alamein. By 6 November the Afrika Korps was in full retreat. Rommel had lost half his army and nearly all his tanks, and he could not recover such losses.

12

30AU GET THEIR KNEES BROWN

When Admiral Godfrey ordered his assistant to press the Joint Intelligence Board over the formation of an intelligence assault unit in the early summer of 1942, Ian had little idea just how much time he would have to devote to it. He might have begun to realise when Godfrey sent a memorandum through the Admiralty to various departments for ideas of what they might like picked up from the Axis powers by the Commandos. He even added:

> The officer particularly concerned with this matter in the N.I.D is Commander I.L. Fleming, R.N.V.R, Ext 991, and he will be available to give any further information required on the machinery of Intelligence Assault Units as described in the attached paper …[1]

Within a few days, Ian was being bombarded with shopping lists, including weapons systems, mines, torpedoes, infrared equipment and sights, along with the more obvious ciphers, documents, codebooks, and of course coding machines.[2]

After the ill-fated Dieppe raid, 30AU settled down to a period of training, including house clearing and street fighting 'among the bombed houses of Battersea', recalled Marine Paul McGrath. Other lessons included working with explosives, bomb making and safe blowing. In this they were instructed by an elderly chief inspector at Scotland Yard, all arranged by Ian Fleming, as was the trip to the large house in Buckinghamshire where mines and small arms were covered. Dunstan Curtis recalled: 'Ian was immensely excited. You'd have thought he was the one who was going on the trip. It was an enormous adventure for him.'[3] They also began French lessons. The 'buzz' was soon going around that maybe they were going to France. All of which he thought 'good fun'.[4]

The unit by then had been given the cover name 'Special Engineering Unit', and Godfrey had decided that a small section would take part in Operation Torch, the Allied invasion of North Africa. In late July 1942, Roosevelt and Churchill had made the decision to land in North Africa. The President in particular was keen to have US troops in action that year. It would be largely an American affair because after the bitter conflicts between Britain and Vichy France, who controlled North Africa, it was felt the latter would be more willing to throw in the towel against US forces.

Lieutenants Dunstan Curtis RN and Quintin Riley would jointly command the first assignment for 30AU and the detachment of seven Royal Marines joined the cruiser HMS *Sheffield* on the Clyde. Also on board were 600 American troops. They sailed on 26 October. Training continued on the journey south with weapon handling and physical exercises, and the French lessons continued. They even gave unarmed combat demonstrations to the Americans, who thought them 'pretty rugged guys'.[5]

McGrath was armed with the .45 Thompson machine carbine, a US weapon that became famous during the Prohibition era and had a plethora of nicknames including the 'Chicago Piano'. The Commando Pocket Manual says it was a weapon 'especially useful when on patrol or for fighting in close country, such as woods and villages …'[6] He also carried a Colt .45 automatic pistol, a commando knife and No. 36 hand grenades. The Commandos on board *Sheffield* messed with their fellow sea-going Marines, who manned the ship's X gun-turret, with whom they: 'Shared the hammocks, food and grog' (the issue of Navy rum).[7]

When they reached Gibraltar, the destination was at last revealed as Algiers in French North Africa. There they were kept below decks, but the dozens of ships there were a bit of a giveaway that something was happening. Yet the Germans failed to grasp what the Allies were up to. The Abwehr and Admiral Canaris got much of the blame for the intelligence failure in not predicting the target of the Allied invasion. There had been warnings and the British had not woven together an elaborate deception plan for Torch, but had produced a lot of 'noise' about various possibilities including Norway, Dakar and Sicily, as well as a large relief effort for Malta.

Some fairly accurate Abwehr reports did reach German High Command, including one from the Vatican in October that indicated the Americans would land in Dakar, the British in Algiers. Canaris had also been supplied by the pro-German Muslim leader Hadji Amin Mohammed al-Husseini, the Grand Mufti of Jerusalem, who the admiral knew well, with a detailed report on the Allied landing in North Africa for early November between the 5th and 10th of the month. Nine American divisions would be shipped directly from the USA and a further five from Britain, which is pretty much what happened.

Canaris took the report to Field Marshal Wilhelm Keitel of OKW, who dismissed it, insisting that the Allies did not have enough ships or landing craft for such an undertaking. Canaris did not press the point. Colonel Friedrich Heinz, who served under Canaris, said after the war that the admiral had been intentionally vague with the facts, deliberately downplaying them in his plan to undermine Hitler about the North African landings.[8]

McGrath and his comrades were transferred to HMS *Broke* and HMS *Malcolm*, destroyers of First World War vintage, and along with American Rangers they set off toward the port city of Algiers. They were flying 'the Stars and Stripes upon which, it was hoped the French would not fire'.[9] It was a moonless night on 8 November. Commander Henry Fancourt commanded the two ships of Operation Terminal, and their mission was to seize the harbour and prevent damage to its facilities. The Commandos for this operation were known as the 'Special Engineering Unit' and came under Admiral Mountbatten's Combined Operations. Despite this, Fleming still kept a good eye on his protégés and their development. They were now commanded by Commander Robert (Red) Ryder VC, one of the heroes of the St Nazaire raid. He built up his unit around three sections from the Royal Marine Commandos, the Army and the Navy. The Navy troop initially only had five naval officers in it, who had a 'technical' role. Their job was to instruct the men from the other troops on what was the best 'loot' to grab. The two other troops also had a fighting role, with two officers and twenty men each.

The bow of *Malcolm* was reinforced with concrete to crash through the Algiers harbour boom. The American troops were to take and hold the port area, while other troops landing on beaches to either side of the town would soon relieve them. The Commandos' job was to get into the French Admiralty building on the mole and grab intelligence material.

Due to the dark night the two destroyers could not find the narrow entrance into the harbour. Both ships ran in close to the harbour wall on repeated sweeps. As *Malcolm* was about to finish a run she was lit up by searchlights and came under heavy accurate fire from French shore batteries. She was hit several times, three of her four boilers were put out of action, and on her crowded decks ten men were killed and scores wounded. The ship lost speed and listed to starboard, heading back out to sea. *Broke* came in, laying a smokescreen to cover *Malcolm*. On her fourth sweep, *Broke* found the boom that was covering the entrance. Ramming it, she sliced through and came alongside the mole. By then it was 0530 and getting light. The American troops landed and took the commercial port area. Two hours later the Vichy French started firing again. *Broke*, having been hit, was forced to leave at 1030.

Broke was hit again making her way out to sea, and was then taken in tow by the Hunt-class destroyer *Zetland* but sank two days later. The American troops, now on their own holding the harbour under Lieutenant Colonel Edwin T. Swenson, came under increasing pressure. Heavily outnumbered and facing tanks, they surrendered.

The Commandos managed to transfer from the crippled *Malcolm* to HMS *Bulolo*, the HQ ship, from which they got ashore 12 miles west of Algiers. From there they set off toward the city and the secondary target of the Italian Armistice Commission HQ. Lieutenant Curtis, in command, praised Fleming's detailed briefings and 'how much thought he had given to our whole show. He had organised air pictures, models, and given an expert account of what we were to look for when we got to the enemy HQ.'[10]

The next day the Commandos took the Italian HQ, capturing seven Italians. One was a cook who, the then Lieutenant Jim Glanville recalled, 'prepared a delicious Italian meal for us'. He also helped himself to a Beretta automatic pistol for a souvenir.[11] Admiral Darlan surrendered Algiers to the Americans, but the wily sailor said he lacked the authority to do the same with the rest of the country. In the German Armistice Commission, from where the Abwehr ran a cell, Curtis found an Enigma machine, which was no ordinary standard military job but 'a "KK" rewired multi-turnover Abwehr machine', along with six weeks' back traffic. The machine was flown back to England via Gibraltar and 2 tons of documents followed by sea. The 'back traffic was soon broken' and from it a detailed picture emerged of Spanish collaboration with the Germans.[12]

Many regard *From Russia with Love*, the fifth of the Bond books, as the best. In it, SMERSH (Death to Spies), the Soviet counter-intelligence department, attempt to take revenge on the British Secret Service by luring Bond to Istanbul to meet the beautiful Tatiana Romanova, who apparently wants to defect. She would bring with her a 'Spektor' machine that could decipher Soviet top-secret radio traffic. This would be a 'priceless victory' thinks Bond, and its loss to the Soviets 'a major disaster'.[13] Notwithstanding, this is clearly a trap and SMERSH have their assassin ready in the form of the psychopathic Irishman Donovan 'Red' Grant, who has 'violent compulsions around the time of the full moon'.[14] The Spektor described is very similar to an Enigma machine in that it is 'case size' and has 'three rows of squat keys rather like a typewriter'.[15]

Fleming went to Istanbul in 1956 to cover the Interpol conference. Darko Kerim, the extrovert Turkish Secret Service agent in the novel, was based on Nazim Kalkavan, the Oxford-educated ship owner who was his guide to the city. Fleming even copied down parts of their conversations, which were used in the novel.[16]

What happened next in Algiers unfolded like the plot of a spy novel. Two days after Darlan surrendered Algiers, he called a ceasefire in the rest of the country. The US Commander, General Dwight D. Eisenhower, gave him the authority by confirming him the political head of French North Africa, a move that infuriated the Free French under General de Gaulle, and Churchill who saw Darlan as a 'dangerous, bitter, ambitious man'. He warned Roosevelt that 'deep currents of feeling are stirred by the arrangements with Darlan' and that he had 'an odious record'.[17]

The SIS had smuggled General Henri Giraud out of France by submarine to take over in French North Africa. He had been taken prisoner at the fall of France, but had escaped from Königstein Castle, a German prison that was regarded as escape-proof, near Dresden on the left bank of the River Elbe, by means of a rope smuggled to him in cans of ham. It was quite an achievement for a man of 60. He got back to France in the spring of 1942.

An American officer watched Giraud approach the submarine *Seraph* in a fishing boat from the conning tower; he sat in the stern, a tall man: 'His gloved hands were folded over a walking stick and a raincoat was thrown over his shoulders like a cloak. It was the first time I had ever seen him and he looked rather like an old-time monarch visiting his fleet.'[18] He arrived in Algiers on 9 November to take over; the scheme was code-named Orange. Three days later, Sir Stewart Menzies, 'C', was asking about Giraud's relationship with Eisenhower.[19]

Menzies had told Sir Alexander Cadogan, permanent head of the Foreign Office, that Churchill's call for the French Resistance to 'set Europe ablaze' had little hope of success if they dealt with fascists such as Darlan. Cadogan began to wonder if they should liquidate Darlan. He wrote in his diary that the Americans had let 'us in for a pot of trouble' and that: 'We shall do no good until we've killed Darlan.'[20]

Fernand Bonnier de la Chapelle was born in Algiers; he was an ardent monarchist and detested the Vichy regime. He was a youthful 20 with a hint of humour in his face, and was under training at a joint OSS/SOE base at Ain Taya near Algiers waiting for a mission. On 8 November, with a group of resistance members, they had seized control of Vichy buildings. On Christmas Eve, after he and two friends drew lots, depending on which way you look at it he either won or lost, for he was chosen to shoot Darlan. He entered the Palace of State, hid and waited for his target. As the admiral returned from lunch, Fernand sprang from his hiding place into the entrance hall and shot Darlan twice, once in the head and once in the chest. It is said Darlan's last words were: 'The British have finally done for me.'[21]

Soon arrested, Fernand, when questioned, admitted he belonged to the Corps Francs d'Afrique, a resistance force formed by Giraud. Rumours swirled around Algiers that it had been a plot orchestrated by the SIS. Fernand was, with undue haste, convicted, condemned and executed. Right up until the end, Boxing Day at 0730, he did not believe the firing squad would shoot him, assuring the priest they would be using 'blank cartridges'.[22] The court martial was organised by Giraud and conducted in secret with no Allied officers present. Within hours, Giraud was appointed high commissioner of French North Africa, as Menzies had intended. What was strange was that Menzies, who seldom left London, was in Algiers at the time. On the day Darlan was shot he was having lunch with Squadron Leader Frederick Winterbotham, who was in North Africa on Ultra business, and two French officers. With coffee came the news Darlan had been killed only a few hundred yards away. Winterbotham felt the murder came as no surprise, and it was as if 'they could not have cared less'.[23]

The pistol said to have been used to kill Darlan was a .22 semi-automatic Colt Woodsman issued to Fernand from the SOE stores by SOE officers. They all denied having any role in the assassination. The gun weighs barely 2lb, and the barrel length varies between 4 and 6in. It has a ten-round magazine and was a favoured SOE assassin's weapon for ease of concealment. Raymond Chandler has one of his characters in the short story *Trouble is my Business* use one; it has 'a long barrel and the front sight filed off. That meant he was good.'[24]

James Bond uses a .25 Beretta in the first six books, the pistol making its first appearance in *Casino Royale* Chapter 8, Pink Lights and Champagne, where 007 uses the 'light chamois leather holster' to house the 'flat Beretta automatic with a skeleton grip'.[25] It is thought to have been the Beretta 418 model manufactured in 1919–22, although Fleming never made this clear. The Danish SOE agent Anders Lassen liked to carry a Beretta as a hidden weapon in the small of his back; he was also an expert with throwing knives. Lassen was a figure Fleming probably came across in his dealings with SOE.[26]

The pistol remained Bond's weapon of choice until Fleming was held to account by Geoffrey Boothroyd from Regent Park in Glasgow. He was a gun expert who had got 'rather fond of the Bond Books' but could not reason why 007 had a 'rather deplorable taste in firearms'. He reasoned that the .25 Beretta 'is really a lady's gun, and not a really nice lady at that'.[27] In reply to the letter, Fleming, rather tongue-in-cheek, says that Bond 'admitted to me that the .25 Beretta was not a stopping-gun, and he places much more reliance on his accuracy with it than any particular qualities of the gun itself'.[28] Their correspondence, which developed into a long friendship, started in 1956 and went on until Fleming's death. Boothroyd was hired on the film *Dr No* as a firearms consultant, and he also became a character in the book. In Chapter 2, Choice of Weapons, 'Major Boothroyd' is introduced as the 'greatest small-arms expert in the world'.[29]

Weeks after the Torch landings, Operation Golden Eye was stood down, along with the contingency plans Operation Backbone and Backbone II set up to counter any move by the Germans into Spain. The plan was to seize control of Spanish Morocco and the area around Gibraltar. However, the Germans had no troops to spare for Spain because on 19 November the Red Army launched its powerful counter-attack at Stalingrad. Hitler's response was to occupy the whole of France and to seize control of Tunisia to pour troops in to gain a final foothold in North Africa, at the expense of the Eastern Front.

★★★

In 1964, John Godfrey reminded Ewen Montagu by letter that it was from one of Ian Fleming's schemes that the basic idea that would kindle into Operation Mincemeat was gleaned 'of the dead airman washed up on a beach'. Godfrey gave the idea to Montagu when 17M was formed, after the latter was put in charge of naval deception. Montagu, however, could not recall Godfrey passing it to him.[30] He liked Fleming, even though he felt that he 'would sell his own grandmother'.[31]

In May 1943, after the Torch landings in Tunisia and the defeat of the Afrika Korps – which had been squeezed from the west by the 1st Army and from the east by 8th Army, resulting in more than 275,000 troops being taken prisoner, many only recently arrived in Africa – there was the question what the Allies might do next. The obvious move was to invade Sicily and try to knock Italy out of the war. However, this tactic was equally obvious to Hitler and his generals.

Thus, the deception plan Operation Mincemeat was born, where the body of a dead Royal Marine major would be washed ashore in Spain from a supposed crashed aircraft. The body was named Major William Martin, and he had documents on his person that indicated that the Allies would land not in Sicily but in the eastern Mediterranean. It was hoped the Spanish would photograph the papers and hand them to the Germans, while the originals would find their way back to Britain.

In 1953, Montagu's book *The Man Who Never Was* came out, in which he states: 'It all really started through a wild idea of George's. He and I were members of a small inter-service and interdepartmental committee which used to meet weekly to deal with questions of security of intended operations.' Later, George would be identified as Flight Lieutenant Charles Christopher Cholmondeley.[32]

However, Cholmondeley's idea came from the 'Trout Memo', which had fifty-one ideas in it mostly penned by Ian. 'Trout' referred to fishing, and in this case they were trying to lure the enemy to bite. Number twenty-eight on the list was one Fleming had come across in a novel by Basil Thomson, a former intelligence agent and police officer. The novel was called *The Milliner's Hat Mystery*, published in 1937. In this story a body is found in a barn and every document on its person is found to have been forged. Influenced by this, Fleming came up with the bare bones of Mincemeat: 'a corpse dressed as an airman with dispatches in his pockets could be dropped on the coast, supposedly from a parachute that had failed.'[33]

With Fleming's idea and the fate of the RAF Catalina flying boat FP119 fresh in his mind, Cholmondeley began to form a plan. The incident in September 1942 caused some alarm in Allied intelligence when it looked as if the invasion of French North Africa might have been revealed. The Catalina, en route from Plymouth to Gibraltar on

25 September, crashed into the sea during a violent electrical storm over the Bay of Cadiz. All ten people on board were killed. One of them was Lieutenant James Hadden Turner RN, a courier carrying letters for the Governor of Gibraltar containing details of the invasion set for 4 November.

The bodies were washed ashore south of Cadiz and were turned over to the Spanish authorities. A day later they were returned to the British. Turner's corpse still had the letters in his pockets. Experts were flown out to Gibraltar, and the body and the letters were minutely examined. The envelope flaps had been opened by the immersion in salt water, but the writing was 'quite legible'. The question was, could the Spanish or Germans have read them in such a short time? They came to the conclusion this was unlikely, as they had noted while 'unbuttoning the jacket that sand had fallen from the buttonhole'. Sand had gathered there while the body was rolled by the tide on the beach. It was thought the sand would not have been replaced after reading the letters and buttoning the jacket. This meant the Torch landings had probably not been compromised.[34]

Another passenger on the Catalina had been Louis Danielou, an intelligence officer with the Free French forces who was code-named Clamorgan, who had been on a mission for SOE. His notebook, written in French, was recovered from the aircraft, and it mentioned the British landing in North Africa. An Italian agent procured a copy from the Spanish authorities, which he handed to the Germans. They treated it with little value, even suspecting that it could have 'been planted as a deception'.[35] This affair revealed 'that the Spanish could be relied on to pass on what they found, and that this non-neutral habit might be turned to account'.[36]

Fleming had little direct involvement with Mincemeat, probably the greatest deception story of the war, whereby the body of William Martin RM was put into the sea off Huelva from the submarine *Seraph* and the prevailing tide carried it ashore. His documents were examined by the Spanish, photographed by the Abwehr and sent on to German High Command. Hitler at first doubted the documents, but came around to think them genuine. Subsequently, units were moved from Sicily to Crete, mainland Greece and Sardinia.

After Operation Golden Eye was stood down in 1943, Fleming's 'Red Indians', 30 Commando, came to dominate his remaining time with NID. With the change of DNI to the more staid and bureaucratic Captain Edmund Rushbrooke, there were no further exciting trips to Lisbon, Madrid and Tangier on which Ian had come near to his dream of being a secret agent. He became more desk bound and Room 39 was no longer the hive of ideas it had been. Edward Merrett said of Ian: 'He wasn't James Bond. He was a pen-pusher like all of us. All through the war I thought of him as a collector of rare books. Of course, he knew everything that was going on, but he never seemed to show any real inclination to take part in it.'[37] Yet Merrett must have noticed how often Fleming was not at his desk, often for long periods.

In May 1943, Fleming was in Washington for the Trident Conference, a strategy meeting at the highest level. During it the main theatres of the war were discussed, with particular focus on Operation Husky, the invasion of Sicily. Ian's brother, Peter, was also there with the Director of Military Intelligence Brigadier, Walter Cawthorn. They made a concerted albeit unsuccessful attempt to take over strategic deception in the Pacific area, which the Americans controlled.[38] The two brothers met there and were seen by Joan Bright, who was at the conference supplying the Commanders-in-Chief with the latest intelligence reports. She saw them as an 'attractive pair' and 'devoted to each other'. Ian also met his old friend Smithers, who told him about his impending marriage to an American woman. But Ian, although happy for Peter, felt marriage was not for him as he could not 'see anything in it for me'.[39]

The second conference, Quadrant, took place in Quebec in August and at it the invasion of France, Operation Overlord, was top of the agenda. It was during this visit that Ian is said to have attended an agents' course at Camp X, the Special Training School No. 103, opened in December 1941. The camp lay close to the US–Canadian border on the Toronto–Kingston highway between Whitby and Oshawa and on the shores of Lake Ontario, about 300 miles from New York and 700 from Quebec. It was chosen for its location, as potential agents could reach it without attracting attention 'but unauthorised visitors found it hard to reach'. To the south was a 40-mile waterfront and to the north dense woodland, while all approaches were well guarded by Commandos.[40]

It became a vital training centre for the fledgling SOE and OSS and was jointly administered by the Canadian Military and Royal Canadian Mounted Police (RCMP), although run by BSC. Vast areas of the Canadian wilderness were used for training and all the paraphernalia of dirty tricks was encompassed there. The camp also supplied life-and-death equipment, not romantic toys, to the spy trade, and had its own factories.[41]

William Stephenson claimed that Fleming did an agents' sabotage course at Camp X and was taught about limpet mines, which gave him the background used in *Live and Let Die* when Bond destroys Mr Big's motor yacht *Secatur* with such a weapon while it is anchored off Jamaica. The mine explodes at just the right time as Bond and Solitaire are being towed at speed toward a razor-sharp coral reef by the *Secatur*.[42] Stephenson wrote: 'The water there [in lake Ontario] is ice cold even in summer. Ian had a flair for the work. He had to deal with his own vivid imagination though.'[43] Yet there is some dispute among Fleming's biographers if he ever attended the course. Pearson supports Stephenson, citing being told: 'Ian Fleming was every bit as good as his hero and was one of the few trainees who succeeded in getting the mine firmly into place and escaping without detection.'[44] However, Andrew Lycett refers to: 'historian David Stafford, [author of *Camp X: Canada's School for Secret Agents*] who examined these claims, found no evidence that Ian had ever completed a course at the camp.' Yet Lycett goes on to say he may have 'taken a day trip there to view an important establishment'.[45] Nicholas Rankin is more scathing that Stephenson only claimed Fleming's attendance at Oshawa 'in his dotage', calling it 'pure fantasy'.[46]

How accurate is Stafford? In his 1986 book he devotes seven pages in Chapter 10, Camp X: Myth and Reality, to Fleming. He is rather dismissive of the help Fleming gave to Donovan in setting up OSS, questioning where it took place, as there are conflicting views on that, rather than if it did. However, the gift of an inscribed revolver 'For Special Services' rather confirms Fleming did have a hand in helping Donovan. He cites Fleming's Frisian Island scheme as 'Boy's Own Paper' stuff, and that he suggested it to SOE. As we know, Fleming saw this purely as an NI operation long before SOE even existed and it clearly came from Erskine Childers' *The Riddle of the Sands* (see Chapter 3).[47]

Later, Stafford examines the possibility of Fleming visiting Camp X, questioning when this might have taken place. Yet the only time Ian Fleming visited Canada during the war, August 1943, is well documented. He cites living camp commandants as having no recollection of Fleming having been there, but does admit he would just have been 'another short-term visitor from BSC' probably arriving with a group. A fairly junior officer may well have gone unnoticed.

The book is rather scathing of Stephenson again as he cites camp commandants who say he never even visited the camp, so how could he know what went on there? Marion de Chastelain, who was Stephenson's secretary during the war, has sprung to his defence. According to her, Stafford, following publication of *Camp X*, sent her a thank you letter 'for all I did for him. I didn't do a damn thing for him. I wouldn't have given him the time of day.'[48] She would not read *Camp X*, and was furious with Stafford's 1989 article in the *Saturday Night* magazine titled 'A Myth Called Intrepid', published after Stephenson's death, saying 'she could wring his neck'. In it he described Stephenson as a senile old man living in Bermuda whose memory was playing tricks on him.

She says he had a speech problem and there was nothing wrong with his memory. Stafford also wrote that the publishers of *A Man Called Intrepid* by William Stevenson had 'finally relented' and called the book a novel. However, this was untrue and led to legal action against the magazine. The matter was settled out of court, and the magazine printed several letters supporting Stevenson's account.[49] Other historians have criticised *A Man Called Intrepid*, most notably A.J.P. Taylor and Sir David Hunt, and the book was dogged by controversy from publication.

Pat Bayly, who was Deputy Director of Communications for the BSC and boss of Camp X, gets no more than a brief mention in *Camp X* and not that he was running the camp. Bayly insists Stephenson did go there.[50] He disliked Stevenson's book but thought Stafford's *Camp X* had 'made an attempt at accuracy', although it had made 'several mistakes or omissions'. One of the biggest was the date the camp was open, as it was fully operational 'before Pearl Harbor'.[51]

Where does that leave us? There is much circumstantial evidence to support Pearson. Again Stevenson, in *A Man Called Intrepid*, cites Stephenson as saying Fleming took part in exercise 'disposal of the tail' in which the trainee agent returns to a hotel room, which was housed in a 'mock-up hotel near Toronto'. He is to open the door fast and shoot the enemy agent he finds inside, for which is given a loaded .45 Smith and Wesson. According to Stephenson, Ian went up to the door and put his hand on the knob but could go no further.

'What's wrong?' asked Stephenson.

'Bill, you know I can't shoot a man in cold blood,' replied Ian.[52]

This implies the head of BSC would have been there while Fleming was taking the course, which seems unlikely. On the other hand, maybe he would have taken a group around the site from the Quebec meeting.

There are also examples in the Bond stories of trips around Canada. In *For Your Eyes Only*, 007 crosses the border into the USA having stayed at the 'Ko-Zee Motor Court outside Montreal'. He crosses the border on foot, his mission to kill the murderers of the Havelocks, husband and wife friends of M, who had been best man at their wedding in 'Malta. Nineteen-twenty-five'.[53] They had died because they refused to sell their beautiful Jamaican home to a crook named von Hammerstein, ex-Gestapo, who had escaped criminal charges at the end of the war and fled to Cuba. There he became head of Dictator Fulgencio Batista's Counter Intelligence and made a pile 'out of extortion and blackmail and protection'.[54]

Bond is instructed by Colonel Johns at the RCMP HQ in Ottawa, a character who seems right out of Camp X, how exactly to get to Echo Lake across the border, the luxury ranch of von Hammerstein. Johns recalls 'two sniping jobs' he had done in the 'Ardennes' during the war 'under Monty in Eighth Corps' and how similar that country was to that which Bond would have to cross.[55]

Also, in the much-maligned *The Spy Who Loved Me*, which Fleming defended in a letter to his editor Michael Howard at Jonathan Cape, his plan had been to dispel the heroic image of Bond: 'So it crossed my mind to write a cautionary tale about Bond to put the record straight in the minds particularly of younger readers.' But he admitted that the 'experiment has obviously gone very much awry'.[56] We find his heroine, Vivienne Michel, who is a French–Canadian born just outside Quebec, returning home to Canada after disappointing years in Europe and going on a road trip on a Vespa Gran Sport 150cc scooter. She reports: 'Route 2 from Quebec southwards to Montreal could be one of the most beautiful roads in the world if it weren't for the clutter of villas and bathing huts that have mushroomed along it since the war.' How did Fleming know this if he had not taken this route during the war?[57] Michel keeps heading south, crossing the border and joining US Route 9 into New York State, whereas Fleming in 1943 would have continued beside the St Lawrence to Lake Ontario and on to Camp X. Before we leave Vivienne Michel, Kingsley Amis, friend of Ian Fleming and keen admirer of Bond, felt her 'female viewpoint was treated with skill and imagination', but that *The Spy Who Loved Me* was 'not a secret-service story, except one short interlude'.[58]

Both these stories were also influenced by the time Ian spent on Ivar Bryce's farm Black Hole Hollow in Vermont; he spent a month there in 1952. It was no longer a working farm, and the two-storey clapboard house built around 1760 was surrounded by 500 acres of mostly tree-covered hills. Fleming says Bryce 'used to tramp alone for hours among the hills, and come back relaxed and brooding on some embryo new plot'. And: 'Several of the books owe their locations to the Farm and the wild Adirondack country across the state border.' He adds that *For Your Eyes Only* is set on the farm, albeit called Echo Lake, and 'described in minute but accurate detail'.[59]

The question still remains over whether or not Fleming went to Camp X in the summer of 1943? Probably on the evidence, but on a day trip, as Lycett indicates.

Did he take a swimming test? The answer to that is almost certainly not as Major Bill Brooker and Major Cuthbert Skilbeck, the two camp commandants, deny that underwater training ever took place at Camp X.[60] It is a mystery how this story came about in Pearson's book, about Fleming taking a swimming test at Camp X and attaching a limpet mine to an old wreck and coming top of the course.[61] Fleming would have learned all he needed to know about limpet mines on his frequent visits to Gibraltar from experts in underwater warfare.

★★★

Even when on his various trips Fleming kept a keen eye on 30AU, then operating in the Mediterranean, receiving a string of reports. After the Torch landings, a small section remained in North Africa to drive east with the Anglo-American forces. In Bone (now called Annaba), Sousse and Sfax, Royal Marine Allen 'Bon' Royle wrote: 'We got into Sfax well ahead of everyone and found the usual group of disconsolate I-ties. Again a busy time in various HQ's …' They commandeered an Italian 5-ton truck to hold it all but: 'Curtis seemed rather pleased with what we had picked up.'[62] They had captured a set of maps which detailed the enemy's minefields and defences in Sicily that would prove invaluable to the Allied invasion.

The men returned from North Africa to find that they had now been designated 30 Commando and had a new base at Amersham, Buckinghamshire, and the HQ in Cold Morham, a derelict farm near the town. Here they were reorganised into three troops, Naval, Military, and Technical, the latter composed of RNVR officers, specialists in mines and torpedoes, submarines, radar and secret documents.

The 30 Commando were one of the advance units to land in Operation Husky, the invasion of Sicily. Dunstan Curtis suffered from eczema, which was aggravated by the heat of the African sun, so he was sent home. He was replaced as CO by the now promoted Lieutenant Commander Quintin Riley. The Commando landed in Sicily near Cape Passero with the 8th Army XXX Corps. The unit's first targets were coastal radar. In a German-manned station they found many valuable documents, including the handbook of the Telefunken T 39 series of radar sets, which were used to direct fighter aircraft and anti-aircraft guns on to targets. This was sent to the RAF in Malta, who used it straight away to aid their bombing missions.

In another radar station a complete set of Italian Air Force ciphers were obtained virtually intact. Other notable finds took place at Syracuse, Augusta and Messina. In the naval base at Trapani, Glanville and the Marines captured the stores and maintenance department intact. Marine K.A. 'Jock' Finlayson helped Lieutenant Commander Lincoln defuse dozens of sea mines: 'All afternoon I was assisting him getting bits off, and quite petrified, my vivid imagination expecting booby-traps or time pencils blowing us and Trapani sky high.'[63]

For Ian Fleming, success on this scale meant that he might lose control of the unit. This happened to an extent with the Italian detachment, which became virtually independent when they continued with the invasion forces on to the mainland of Italy. Back in the UK, however, Ian was kept heavily involved with 30AU's activities.

At the end of November, Ian attended the Sextant Conference in Cairo, another high-level affair where Churchill, Roosevelt, and in this case Generalissimo Chiang Kai-shek of the Republic of China, met. The Mana Hotel close to the Pyramids was taken over for the conference. Chester Harrison, a reporter for the *Chicago Sun*, in a broadcast observed: 'Everything about this whole business was very secret except that nearly everybody knew about it …'[64]

A bout of bronchitis laid Ian low and he did not go on to the Tehran Conference two days later. Instead he recovered on a diet of fried eggs and orange juice. He spent much time with Joan Bright, who was there in her usual capacity. They both returned to England on HMS *London*, reaching home two days before Christmas.[65]

13

BACK TO FRANCE

Marine Jim Burns recalls seeing Ian Fleming at a parade in front of the Beach Hotel in the little Sussex seaside town of Littlehampton. The 30AU arrived there early in 1944, although there had been Commandos billeted in the town from September 1943: 'There we were drawn up in troops with "A" in the centre and me standing directly behind Red. In the midst of all this "bull", I couldn't help but smile when I noticed Red's blouse had parted company with his webbing belt and his trousers, and one of his gaiters was riding high on the top of his boot. Yet the Commander (Fleming) disdaining protocol, walked straight from his car to Red, took his hand and shouted something like: "Whiteley, my boy, how are you, how's father and the family?" much to the discomfiture of his aides and of course, our more senior ranks.' Herbert Oliver (known as Peter) Huntington-Whiteley RM, was a fellow Etonian. He had led a platoon of 40 Commando during the Dieppe raid, and was known affectionately as 'Red' by his men because of his red hair.[1]

There were certainly mixed views about Fleming from the members of 30AU. Lieutenant Commander Patrick Dalzel-Job found: 'He was quite kind to me, but somewhat cold and austere, very "Pusser" (went by the book) and on his dignity so far as the Unit was concerned. Although he had many friends, he gave me the impression of being essentially an egotistic person, with an eye to the main chance.'[2] Glanville found Fleming 'egregious' and 'always claimed he knew everything'.[3]

Yet his attention to detail in overseeing the forming of the 'Black Book', a compilation of hundreds of targets and key enemy personnel, was acknowledged to have been invaluable. Compiled mainly from PoW interrogation, SIS reports and signal intelligence and other sources available to the DNI, in the field it often led to targets or to a secondary source leading to other targets.[4] A team including Lieutenant Commander James Fawcett and Jim 'Sancho' Glanville worked with a team of Women's Royal Naval Service (WRNS, or 'Wrens') on the Black Book, while Captain Charles 'Quaker' Drake, the senior officer in Room 39, and Admiral Godfrey also contributed. It grew to more than 300 pages, which was broken down into handy area handbooks and relating maps for the troops.[5]

In the late months of 1943 there was a power struggle over who should control 30AU and what it should become. Colonel Robert Neville, of Combined Operations, had gone to Italy to inspect the unit and expressed the opinion that it should become part of the Royal Marines. Fleming argued it never was or never had been intended to become a Commando unit. It was too small, rarely exceeding 120 men, whereas a Commando unit was by then around 600 men. Its task was intelligence-gathering, in which it had excelled, and it should be part of NID. Fleming won this argument. It was reorganised into three troops designated A, B and X. All ranks when in battledress wore a shoulder patch with '30' in light blue on a naval dark blue square.[6]

All the fighting men were now Royal Marines, with the new CO Lieutenant Colonel Arthur Woolley, RM; the intelligence-gatherers were mainly RNVR officers. The 30AU now became part of Naval Intelligence as NID30 with its own office at the Admiralty. After his return from Italy, Glanville recalls being told by Fleming that the unit needed to shape up: 'You can't behave like Red Indians anymore. You have to learn to be a respected and disciplined unit.' Yet the largely desk-bound Fleming liked to hear stories of their adventures, which were all filed away for later use.[7]

Glanville had several run-ins with Fleming. He argued at the time of reorganisation that they should operate as small sections of up to ten men, who would be 'self-sufficient in transport and the men concerned qualified drivers. For special operations a number of such sections could be brought together with such larger formations as might be required.'[8] Curtis agreed with Glanville but Fleming did not and was willing to ignore the lessons learned in the Mediterranean. It seems Ian was preoccupied with losing control if the unit operated with other larger ones. Also, he had not been impressed by the disastrous Leros campaign, where 30 Commando came in for some criticism, after which there had been 'a good deal of witch hunting.' Sometimes referred to as 'Churchill's Folly', Operation Accolade in September 1943 was planned to capture the Dodecanese Islands in the Aegean, which was largely garrisoned by Italian troops at the time. This, it was hoped, would induce Turkey to join the Allies.[9] With the Italian armistice coming in the same month, Churchill wanted to seize the opportunity of a new front, and ordered troops in Egypt to launch an immediate invasion. The Americans opposed the operation.

General Eisenhower was far from happy and thought the scheme was a distraction, writing: 'If the decision to undertake Accolade depends on a firm commitment for the diversion from our own operations of a material portion of our air force, then, Accolade will have to be postponed.'[10] The Germans pre-empted the British planning by taking Rhodes and they were able to operate aircraft from Crete to hold the upper hand. The British landings on Kos and Leros were a fiasco, with a lot of the forces involved being captured and several Royal Navy ships being sunk. The 30AU element taking part achieved none of their aims during the landing. Glanville wrote: 'Thus ended a singularly ill-conceived and largely unplanned operation and, although the men had conducted themselves extremely well, had achieved no results respecting the basic objectives of the Commando. Moreover, it had incurred the loss of five valuable men, including an outstanding officer in Tom Belcher, and one severely wounded NCO who was unfit for further active service.'[11]

The author Alistair MacLean based his 1957 novel *The Guns of Navarone* on the ill-fated Operation Accolade. He was a leading torpedo operator on the cruiser HMS *Royalist*. The ship cruised the area in the summer of 1944, although he admits to not risking 'anything worse than a severe case of sunburn ...' However, he did 'come across and hear about, both in the Aegean and in Egypt, men to whom danger and the ever-present possibility of capture and death were the very stuff of existence; these were highly trained specialists of Earl Jellicoe's Special Boat Service and men of the Long Range Desert Group, who had turned their attention to the Aegean islands after the fall of North Africa.' To this we can add the men of 30AU.

MacLean went on to add: 'here obviously was excellent material for a story ... But the determining factor was neither material nor the islands themselves: that lay in the highly complicated political situation that existed in the islands at the time, and in the nature of Navarone itself.' In the relationship between the Germans, Italians, Greeks and the Allies, of course there was no such island as Navarone; that was a figment of MacLean's imagination. However, there were a few that bore more than a passing resemblance to it 'inasmuch as they were (A) German held, (B) had large guns that dominated important channels and (C) had these guns so located as to be almost immune to destruction by the enemy unless a small team should attack them'.[12] Later, MacLean would go on to write Cold War thrillers in the vein of Fleming, including *Ice Station Zebra* in 1963.

★★★

In March 1944 personal tragedy struck Ian when his long-term girl-friend Muriel Wright, who he had known since 1935, was killed in an air raid. Her flat at Eaton Terrace Mews was undamaged, but some debris from the bomb blast flew through the window and struck her head, killing her instantly. She had been doing her bit as a dispatch rider, a job Ian had got her, and the evening before she had gone to get cigarettes for Ian, 200 Morland Specials from Grosvenor Street, while he played cards at the Dorchester. He was called by the police to identify the body, rather than her elderly parents, and was shocked to find her still in her nightdress. Ian kept Muriel's bracelet on his key ring, and later wrote: 'Nostalgia is dangerous unless you are certain of never seeing the subject of your nostalgia again.'[13] He refused to visit the places they had frequented. Dunstan Curtis questioned his grief: 'The trouble with Ian is that you have to get yourself killed before he feels anything.'[14]

Robert Harling was rather more sympathetic as he saw Ian was 'utterly shattered' and that: 'Everyone in Room 39 was deeply depressed by Muriel's death. She had seemed so gentle and joyous a creature, all too rare in this world.' The popular dispatch rider had been regarded by all the officers 'as an enchanting and beloved mascot'.[15]

Bond never succeeds at any long-term relationship. The American heroine Tiffany Case, who appears in *Diamonds are Forever*, lasts the longest. Bond does warn her on board the *Queen Elizabeth* on their way back to the UK when she asks him if he is the marrying sort: 'Matter of fact I'm almost married already. To a man. Name begins with M. I'd have to divorce him before I tried marrying a woman.'[16] Tiffany lives with Bond 'for so many happy months'. But we are told in *From Russia with Love* that she has left him: 'He missed her badly and his mind sheered away from the thought of her.'[17] One suspects Fleming locked the memory of Muriel away in the recesses of his mind.

Yet James Bond does say 'I do' at the end of *On Her Majesty's Secret Service*, but Teresa di Vicenzo, Tracy, only lasts a few hours after the wedding. They are on their way to honeymoon in Austria when Ernst Stavro Blofeld shoots up the Lancia the couple are travelling in from a red Maserati. All Bond sees is a 'snarling mouth under a syphilitic nose'. The Lancia leaves the road and hits a tree. Bond survives as always, but Tracy dies, 'her face buried in the ruins of the steering-wheel'.[18]

Does Bond's loss reflect on Fleming's loss of Muriel in this case? There are comparisons, as Tracy's death at the wheel of the Lancia is unlucky, being hit by a stray shot, similar to Muriel being struck in the head from fragments of a bomb while the house she was in remained almost undamaged.

Fleming does allow Bond some domestic bliss with Kissy Suzuki in *You Only Live Twice*, albeit he has lost his memory. She belongs to the Ama people, on the island of Kuro, from which Bond gains access to the neighbouring island of Kyushu, where the mysterious Dr Shatterhand has a castle. There he runs a weird cult of death, luring people there to commit suicide. Bond has already realised Shatterhand is Blofeld and is there with his wife, Irma Bunt. Having at last dealt with Blofeld, who he strangles with his bare hands, he blows up the castle with Bunt in it, making his escape by clinging to the mooring line of a helium balloon. As the building explodes, he is hit on the side of the head and the balloon is punctured, Bond falls into the sea. Kissy sees a figure enter the sea: 'she sensed that it was her man, and she covered the two hundred yards from the base of the wall as fast as she had ever swum in her life'. Bond doesn't recognise her, he stays more than a year with her and she becomes pregnant but does not tell him. On a piece of lavatory paper he sees the word 'Vladivostok' and this kindles something in his memory. Kissy then reluctantly helps him return to his world.[19]

After the death of Muriel, Fleming was able to absorb himself in the work to build up 30AU for D-Day and was often seen at the training grounds. It seemed to Glanville when preparing for D-Day as if 'we had to start afresh'. The unit engaged in the usual Commando training of speed marches, field craft, weapon training and section drills. Men were selected to be drivers and went to the transport section: 'In addition to basics, selected men and sometimes whole troops were trained in specialized subjects, usually in conjunction with officers of the Naval Wing, who were either specialist or general duties officers, generally fluent linguists with experience in naval intelligence and the particular requirements of the Unit, in several cases acquired during operations with 30 Commando in the Med.'[20]

Marine Bon Royle, by now promoted to corporal, joined the intelligence section of 30AU at the new HQ in Littlehampton. He was issued with a Zeiss Contax II camera and sent on a four-week course to the Army Film and Photographic Unit at Pinewood Studios. Returning to Littlehampton in May 1944, he found there were many new recruits and the 'old hands were split up between troops' while: 'Somewhere above us, still on cloud nine sat Fleming, now a full Commander RNVR.' Littlehampton also hosted two battalions of US infantry at the time. Royle found: 'There was no fighting or nonsense of that kind between us and them; we were too interested in each other and in what we had done, and the pubs were peaceful places.'[21]

The strength of 30AU grew to more than 300 men. A week before D-Day, Curtis held a dinner at the Gargoyle Club for the unit's naval officers, and Fleming was invited. Harling says that the party 'went with a swing' straight away. There Harling learned from Pamela Tiarks, who worked in Room 39 and came with Fleming, about the elusive nature of Ian. She said that he was like water running 'right through one's fingers and past as smoothly'.[22]

The 30AU were only a tiny part of the Normandy landings. Code-named Operation Neptune, it was split into three sections. The first to land on Juno Beach with the Canadians was X Troop Pikeforce, led by Captain Geoff Pike, RM. Their target was straight inland to the radar station at Douvres-la-Délivrande. Second to land was Curtforce, led by Dunstan Curtis, with twenty-one men. They landed on Gold Beach on D+1. The main body under the unit CO Colonel Woolley landed on Utah with the Americans on D+4; their target was Cherbourg.

At 0835, X Troop was ashore on the Nan Red sector of Juno Beach. Captain Pike, on the run-in to the beach, wondered about his 'capacity to take it knowing half my troops had been under fire and I had not'. Jim Glanville was beside him and Pike was heartened by his cool demeanour: 'he never seemed to be frightened just interested in what was going on.' With water only coming up to their knees, their landing went well as they raced ashore to the nearest cover under the promenade along the front. Next to them on the left 48 Commando was having a hard time, attracting the fire.[23]

In just over an hour X Troop moved off the beach, not having lost a man. They spent that first night in some abandoned German trenches before they arrived at the radar station. Its 130ft tower had been damaged by the naval bombardment, but much of the station was underground, protected by barbed wire and minefields. It was too hard a nut for X Troop to crack alone. Finally it fell to a textbook attack by 41 RM Commando. By then there was only a handful of men from 30AU there under Glanville, most of X Troop having re-joined the main body. When he eventually got into the station, Glanville was exasperated to find the amount of looting that had taken place. As a result, 30AU's haul was small: some wheels from an Enigma machine and a used cryptographer's pad. Meanwhile, Fleming sat in London, fretting and reading the disappointing reports coming in, with the Germans having destroyed most of the valuable materials.

Part of Curtforce with Lieutenants Guy Postlethwait and Tony Hugill, both RNVR, and nineteen Marines had landed on D+2 at Arromanches, moving west toward Port-en-Bessin. On the way they captured a radar station and hit the jackpot. The station was taken intact together with a top-secret listing of all German radar installations in north-west Europe, along with the technical data on wavelengths, polarisations, pulse repetition frequency and aerial display. Once back with the Admiralty it was regarded as the most important radar intelligence to have been seized during the war and within thirty-six hours all German radar in that group had been successfully jammed.[24]

Patrick Dalzel-Job landed at Utah Beach with the main body on 10 June, D+4. He was an adventurer and ideal officer for 30AU. In 1940, using his special knowledge of the north Norwegian coast gained before the war and with the aid of local small boats, he had moved 10,000 men of the Allied Expeditionary Force without the loss of a single man. Then, disobeying orders, he had used the boats to evacuate all the women, children and old people from Narvik just before the town was attacked by German bombers and reduced to rubble. He escaped a court martial because the King of Norway thanked him personally and presented him with the Knight's Cross of St Olav. He is often cited as a model for James Bond, as he was a marksman, parachutist and diver, but he ruled himself out as 'unlikely'. He did meet Fleming's mother in a train during the war, and she confided in him 'that Ian hoped to be an author after the war, but she did not think he could ever make a living that way …'[25]

On Utah Beach, Dalzel-Job found it difficult to move his unit inland with their vehicles past masses of American troops. An hour after dark, they halted near Sainte-Mère-Église for the night and although there were no orders to 'dig in' some of the older hands did. Almost all the aircraft they had seen that day were Allied, so they paid little attention when they heard aircraft low overhead. Dalzel-Job recalled:

Suddenly, there was an explosion like a bomb blast immediately above us, followed by a peculiar fluttering noise in the air. For a while nothing else happened then the whole field was lit by sharp flashes, the explosions, like heavy machine cannons firing sporadically around us. The explosions did not last more than half a minute. In that time the unit lost thirty per cent of its strength in killed and wounded.

They had been hit by an early type of cluster bomb called a 'butterfly bomb' because they fluttered down to land before exploding. The 30AU suffered three men killed and twenty-one wounded, some seriously.[26]

Robert Harling observed a dozen of the wounded being shipped back to hospitals in England. He knew few would 'be passed fit for active service again in under three months'.[27] Within a week of Harling landing in Normandy he crossed back across the Channel in a 15cwt van 'loaded to the gunwales with papers, equipment, and two naval specialists'.[28]

Fleming was relieved to see his friend still in one piece and questioned him for an hour. He soon sought out Harling again, who by then was in the Citadel deep within the Admiralty. The 30AU casualties had shaken Ian and he wanted more information about what had happened. 'Quite clearly, he was holding himself ultimately responsible for the unit losses. Quite an unreasonable and unjustified reaction, but understandable. He was, after all, basically officer-in-charge of all elements in the unit although comfortably seated in Room 39,' says Harling.[29]

The stress and frustration levels on Fleming at the time were high. Harling settled down to life in the Citadel, he much admired Margaret Priestley, the young Cambridge history don, the 'blue-stocking', who seemed calmly and coolly to be able to cope with all that was thrown at her. However, the Cherbourg campaign was dragging on; the port was supposed to have fallen within a week. Two days after Harling's return, Fleming appeared in the Citadel again. That morning they had 'plotted the unit's likely whereabouts on a huge wall-map of northern France'. When Fleming asked where they were, Harling, with a ruler, pointed at the map: 'These seem to be their likely positions.'

Fleming erupted: '"Seem" and "likely" are not words I'm prepared to accept.' He then proceeded to verbally lay into Harling, who tried to explain it was impossible to say exactly where the unit was. Fleming had what Harling described as 'the most explosive brainstorm I have witnessed', verging on 'manic fury'. Margaret said nothing but 'had lowered her head down on her desk as if determined to burrow her way through the stalwart timber'. Fleming then left but they could hear his ranting 'fury still echoing in the corridor'.[30]

The next day Fleming took Harling to lunch and there was no mention of the bawling out. He told him that he would be going back to 30AU as they agreed Margaret was extremely capable of holding the Citadel. The two became friends during the war and would remain so in peacetime. Fleming's wife, Ann, told Harling that Ian had told her about his outburst. She sympathised with him and that: 'she had suffered a few on her own account, but thought mine had probably been closer to an H-bomb than hers'.[31]

Like several of Ian Fleming's friends, Harling's name appears in the Bond books. In *Thunderball* the Commissioner of Police in Nassau, capital of the Bahamas, is called Harling.[32] In *The Spy Who Loved Me* he is Harling the printer who worked at the *Chelsea Clarion*.[33]

By July, 30AU had assembled at Carteret, south of Cherbourg on the Normandy coast, to await its next task. Fleming flew over with the DNI to visit them. He took them to task over a lack of discipline – Admiral Cunningham had labelled them 30 Indecent Assault Unit after some incidents during the invasion of Sicily. Harling came to know some of the Marines well and found: 'They were merry, courageous, amoral, loyal, lying toughs, hugely disinclined to take no for an answer from foe or fraulein. Fleming always enjoyed anecdotes concerning their wayward ways.'[34]

Generally Fleming was not popular with the rank and file, though often he had their best interests at heart. Bon Royle had seen Fleming several times before he saw him at Carteret. He could hardly miss him as he was 'dressed in blues, which made him stand out as everyone else was in khaki. The rumour was, as reported by the batmen who doubled as flunkies in the officers' mess, that Fleming had had a stand up row with Woolley over the casualties, which he regarded as avoidable.'[35]

After Fleming and the DNI Admiral Rushbrooke visited 30AU, the two went on a tour of the V-2 rocket sites and installations. It was a visit from which Ian drew inspiration for one of his most accomplished

Bond books, *Moonraker*: 'The shimmering projectile rested on a blunt cone of latticed steel which rose from the floor between the tips of three severely back-swept delta fins that looked as sharp as a surgeon's scalpel. But afterwise nothing marred the silken sheen of the fifty feet of polished chrome …'[36]

Hugill also recalled Fleming's visit and his wanting to see the 'Crossbow Sites' where the V-1s were launched. It is clear he was another one who at the time was not overly fond of Ian: 'We had captured in a German HQ some Polish vodka, which we plied him, but – with justice – he suspected it. We also had some vin ordinaire which – we agreed with him – was extremely ordinaire. But when he belly-ached about the brandy (I admit it was only Three Star) I became very angry and abusive and had to be shushed down.'[37] In later life Hugill mellowed his view of Ian.

His was another name used in the Bond books. In *The Man with the Golden Gun*, Mary Goodnight tells Bond in Jamaica: 'The top man at Frome is a man called Tony Hugill. Ex-navy. Nice man. Nice wife. Nice children. Does a good job … Has a lot of trouble with cane burning and other small sabotage – mostly with thermite bombs brought in from Cuba.' In later life Hugill had become the managing director of Tate & Lyle in the Caribbean.

In *The Man with the Golden Gun* Bond even uses Commander John Strangeway's black Sunbeam Alpine, which we first came across in *Dr No* (Chapter 1 Hear you Loud and Clear). The station has brought the car and Goodnight uses it; 'The tank's full and it goes like a bird.'[38]

Paul McGrath, now a sergeant, led a section that pushed 15 miles beyond the American bridgehead at Omaha Beach looking for possible V-1 flying-bomb launch sites. They found one near Neuilly-la-Forêt. Dalzel-Job described it as having a: '"J" concrete runway and all around were scattered hurriedly abandoned German equipment and belongings.'[39] The following day, 13 June, the first of more than 8,000 V-1 flying bombs, known as doodlebugs, landed in Britain at Swanscombe in Kent. On the same day the first one to hit London came down at Grove Road, Mile End, with the resulting blast killing eight people. The Air Ministry response was to try and identify their launching sites and attack them with fighter-bomber aircraft.[40]

Rushbrooke and Fleming were later taken to see US General George Patton, who greeted the admiral personally and conducted him into his canvas HQ. The general was on form with his flamboyant style, and Harling saw him standing 'tall, the impressive warrior, duly dressed for his heroic part in heroic garb' right down to the pearl-handled revolvers on his hip.[41] The admiral and his aide were invited to take lunch, but Fleming feigned that important naval matters needed his attention. Harling had a jeep waiting and the two set off with his Marine driver Gordon Hudson, who had a secluded spot picked out where the two officers would not be disturbed only a few minutes away. Like all good Marines, Hudson had scrounged some American K-rations and a bottle of the local Calvados apple brandy. On arrival Hudson laid out a ground sheet, saluted, and left them with a promise to return in an hour. It was a sunny cloudless day, ideal for a picnic, the spot shielded by woodland from the road with an expansive view of fields.

The two men, easy in each other's company, ranged widely over many subjects including 30AU, of which Fleming was protective: 'If they're also fighting men they're welcome if not keep them out. My men are the fastest-moving action troops in the world and want no hold-ups.' On Patton, Fleming enjoyed his bravado and his 'unabashed pride in his men'.

The one subject not touched was the death of Muriel. Toward the end they discussed what they might do after the war. Harling thought he would return to 'designing books, magazines, and advertisements'. He asked Fleming what he had in mind, to which he replied that he was going to 'write the spy story to end all spy stories'. After all, he had the 'background' and he hoped that he had 'the talent to tell a tale and a publisher to make it public'. Harling almost choked on his food at the audacity of it, much to Fleming's amusement, but he never forgot it.[42]

Fleming's fast-moving troops of 30AU were often right up with the forward troops in the advance, and for such a small unit they often achieved startling results simply by bluff and guile. Such was the case of the radar station near Saint-Pabu. Tony Hugill was told by French civilians that 1,500 Germans were there, so they went to take a look. He decided to try and bluff them into surrender by pretending they were a big force. He felt that as the Germans were surrounded by a hostile population bent on revenge they might be inclined to surrender to regular Allied troops. Hugill, Sergeant McGrath and Marine Sandy Powell went forward to the gates under a white flag; it was a lonely 300-yard nervous walk out in the open. The guards called for the Commandant, a Luftwaffe officer, and after five minutes he arrived accompanied by ten armed guards and four other officers. Hugill asked him in good German to surrender but he refused, not wanting to surrender to such a small force. However, Hugill shrugged his shoulders and said that it did not really matter as they were part of a much larger force and they would be calling for an air bombardment in less than half an hour. By the time the Americans arrived the Germans had surrendered, having stacked their arms, and were sharing cigarettes with the handful of Marines.[43]

General Philippe Leclerc's Free French 2nd Armoured Division was granted the honour of liberating Paris on 24 August. The 30AU, amounting to about seventy-five men, went into the city with them and were greeted by enthusiastic happy crowds. However, Colonel Woolley was determined not to get involved with the celebrations and was fixed on their main objective, the French HQ of the Kriegsmarine, which had taken over the Rothschild estate bordering the Bois de Boulogne. Marine Bon Royle recalled: 'As we got nearer to it into Paris proper the crowds thinned noticeably.' Then they were alone and all was deathly silent apart from the noise from their own vehicles. Royle stopped his scout car off the Boulevard Lannes, as did others, to 'recce' the area. It was screened by trees. They advanced toward the trees to get a better view, but were greeted by a burst of cannon fire. It hit the scout car, sending tracer flying into the air. Royle dived over a wall, followed by his 'oppo', Bert Morgan, chased by 'a burst of Spandau fire'. A French civilian told Royle about the German positions, and he then sent his driver back to Woolley with the news. The Staghound armoured cars of 30AU started racing along the boulevard, directing the fire of their 37mm cannons into the grounds of the estate, which was 'swarming with Jerries and had some very imposing concrete bunkers'. Woolley brought all his men up, which had the desired effect: the German Commandant threw in the towel. A total of 560 Germans surrendered and the 'loot' taken was impressive; several truckloads of documents and technical equipment were shipped back to the UK.[44]

They had also hoped to capture Admiral Karl Dönitz, who was said often to be at the Château de la Muette, but the intelligence in this case was wrong; the C–in–C of the German Navy was not there.

The bluff approach used successfully by Hugill and Woolley was risky. On 12 September, Captain Huntington-Whiteley, Ian Fleming's friend, was killed at Le Havre while trying to talk the Germans to give up under a white flag. Along with the German officers he was negotiating with he was gunned down by some hard-line Nazis; he was 24. Dalzel-Job wrote of him: 'In my memory, Peter sits on the edge of a camp bed, plunking a banjo gently and singing one of Edward Lear's nonsense rhymes quietly to himself.'[45]

By the end of September, 30AU was back in Littlehampton. Royle recalls the unit being assembled on their parade ground the local bowling green. There Woolley stood on a chair and showed them the DSO he had been awarded 'and told us that we had won this. There were dark mutterings of "yes and you're the bugger who's wearing it", but on the whole we were pleased for him.'[46]

The 30AU now began to hone their skills for the final push into Germany. With the bulk of the naval war switching to the Far East, Ian Fleming set off on a new mission to assess the intelligence arm of the Pacific Fleet for the DNI.

14

THE FINAL PUSH

In December 1944 Ian Fleming set off for the Far East on his mission to review the British Pacific Fleet intelligence arm. He flew via Cairo and on to Ceylon, where his old friend from Spain and Operation Golden Eye, Alan Hillgarth, was now Chief of British Naval Intelligence Eastern Theatre (CBNIET). He had gone out the year before and had first worked in Delhi from the headquarters of Lord Louis Mountbatten. Early in 1944, that HQ was moved to Colombo, the capital of Ceylon. Alan spent most of his time at HMS *Anderson*, a land-based signals intelligence centre named after the Anderson golf course about 10 miles from Colombo. There Japanese radio traffic was monitored and analysed and shared with Bletchley Park. It was so secret Mountbatten knew little about it.

HMS *Anderson* was laid out on an open site, with lots of single-storey, bungalow-like structures with verandas surrounded by jungle. The radio direction-finding hut stood alone, in a 200-yard clear space, marked out by a mass of aerials. By the use of high-frequency, direction-finding 'Huff-Duff', they monitored Japanese radio traffic. Using it, skilled operators were able to identify individual Japanese ships from that vessel's 'finger prints'. They could identify the ship's individual radio men often by the way they used their keypads. Not only that: even the W/T equipment had distinct traces.[1]

Two days before Christmas, Fleming got to Ceylon. Alan Hillgarth was pleased to see him. He wrote to his wife: 'My friend Ian Fleming here on a brief visit …' and went on to say Ian would 'solve' a lot of problems at home: 'It's nice seeing him, because he brings a breath of the big world.' His assistant, Wren Clare Blanchard, took to Ian and he was instantly attracted to her. Here was a 'thirty-six and beautiful' naval officer in his tropical uniform, she confided in a letter to her brother. Everything about him was 'right'.[2]

Ian took Clare to a Christmas dance at the Galle Face Hotel, where he was billeted. She was thrilled, although he was not a good dancer. He in turn was stunned by her appearance in a long white silk dress. Seventeen years later he sent her a postcard of the ballroom, marked it with an X and wrote: 'I'm behind the palm tree on the right, watching you in the white dress …' The two explored the island together; Ian enjoyed the tropical heat, and confided to her that he would never 'spend the winter in England again'.[3]

However, it was not all festivities. Ian sent two reports to the DNI about the intelligence structure Alan was setting up.[4] Clare typed them up and was surprised when she found Ian editing them. He explained to her it was wise to 'make one or two corrections in a report otherwise no one will know you've read it'.[5]

In Delhi, Ian caught up with his brother, Peter, who was on Mountbatten's staff and ran a small deception team, D Division, which had managed to convince the Japanese that Allied strength in India was greater than it was. He was not above comical abuse either: one of his agents continually told his 'Japanese contact that his commanding officer was living with a prostitute, and that the ruling family of Japan had short, furry tails, of which they were inordinately proud'.[6]

In January, Ian returned to Colombo, and then set off for Australia on 23 January 1945, accompanied by Alan and Clare. Ian, never overly fond of flying, was annoyed when the Catalina flying boat had to turn back with engine trouble after only two hours. He threatened to go back to England if they did not set off in the morning. Two days later they were in the air again. The journey took twenty-six hours in an unheated plane at 10,000ft. They wore flying suits, overcoats and were covered in rugs, yet still felt cold.

In Sydney, Ian and Clare enjoyed the good life, staying at Petty's Hotel, frequenting the nightclubs and taking trips to Whale Beach for swimming. It was as if there was no war. Yet all too soon Ian left and headed for Pearl Harbor. From there he sent a personal letter to Alan thanking him: 'You could not have been more kind from the moment I stepped ashore in Colombo to the day I left Sydney.' He praised the job he was doing, and that he should be 'very proud'. He added: 'Please give my best love to the angel Clare.' He said he would write to her and she was a 'jewel and I miss her protective wing very much'. He finished by promising to fight Alan's 'battles in London'.[7]

It is revealing that Bond calls another Wren an 'angel' in *The Man with the Golden Gun*. Mary Goodnight is a capable crutch for 007 to lean on after tangling with Scaramanga.[8] He first comes across her in *On Her Majesty's Secret Service*, and she has 'blue-black hair, blue eyes, and 37-22-35, was a honey …' Office gossip has it she is more fond of 006, the former Royal Marine Commando. She is Loelia Ponsonby's replacement.[9]

★★★

By early February 1945, after his round-the-world trip Ian was back at his desk in Room 39. Colonel Humphrey Quill RM, who had commanded 30AU in the Mediterranean, was now to lead the unit as they went with the Allied Armies across the border into Germany. The main targets on Ian's blacklists were the advanced U-boats built and designed at Kiel. The 30AU was the first Allied force to enter the town. Ian kept them busy with constant requests from his shopping list, of which some items were openly questioned to even exist. Much evidence was found about the fast Type XVII U-boats, or 'Walterboats' as they were known, named after the Walter drive system powered by hydrogen peroxide and designed by Doctor Hellmuth Walter.

I.G. Aylen, known as 'Jan', then a commander serving with 30AU, came across two of the Walterboats in Hamburg on 3 May. *U-1408* and *U-1410* had both been 'heavily damaged by bombs' as they lay on the jetty. They resembled 'a gigantic fish rather than a conventional submarine … It was clear that certain parts, mainly the "boiler" unit of the turbine drive, had been cut away with a blow torch and removed.'[10]

In Kiel, 30AU caught up with Doctor Walter: 'a rather heavy, flabby-cheeked man'.[11] He talked freely but only about generalities. He would reveal nothing about using the liquid hydrogen peroxide in the combustion chambers, and confessed to being a loyal Nazi.

Colonel Quill rushed off to Admiral Karl Dönitz's HQ on the Danish border. Germany had officially surrendered on 4 May and all U-boats were ordered to return to base the day after. Quill obtained written orders from the admiral, the last leader of the Third Reich, that nothing was to be withheld from 30AU. Dönitz also sent one of his aides to see Walter with the same message. Walter then co-operated fully, ensuring that submarine test units, various torpedoes, aircraft jet engines and V-1 launch ramps were ready to demonstrate for Allied VIPs.[12]

Aylen got to know Walter and his immediate staff well and says:

> though our relationship was of necessity coolly formal, mutual respect was established, and he worked loyally for UK interest. This was perhaps in keeping with his background as an entrepreneur par excellence who would have employed his undoubted technical ability in the service of whatever political system happened in the ascendant. His close friendship with Dönitz helped, and he had, I believe the ear of the Führer in so far as Hitler had any interest in anything naval.[13]

A Dr Walter is a character in *Moonraker*; he is German and a rocket expert. Would Ian have met Hellmuth Walter? Unlikely. Would he have known about him? Almost certainly, not that Hugo Drax's chief scientist looked like the one 30AU captured. Fleming's character is 'thin elderly' with a head of black hair and pronounces his name 'Valter', whereas the one captured in Kiel was heavy and flabby-cheeked. Yet Ian's fondness for using real people's names in thinly veiled characters makes him a good candidate.[14]

Kingsley Amis felt Hugo Drax was Fleming's best villain 'because the most imagination and energy has gone into his portrayal'.[15] His full name was Graf Hugo van der Drache and Fleming gave him a comprehensive background. He serves with the Brandenburg Regiment initially raised by the Abwehr. Then later he is with SS Obersturmbannführer Otto Skorzeny, who commanded the 150th SS Panzer Brigade in the Ardennes in 1944, from which Drax gets cut off 50 miles behind enemy lines. He falls in with a small section of the Hitlerjugend Werewolves; a guerrilla forced raised by Heinrich Himmler of fanatical Nazi volunteers. Their leader is Krebs, who had 'certain gifts which qualified him for the post of executioner and persuader …'[16]

Drax has fifty German guided-missile technicians, who under the guidance of Dr Walter develop a ballistic missile system located on the cliffs between Dover and Deal. Drax, a mysterious multimillionaire, has convinced the government it is to protect Britain, but his aim is to use it against London. His mother was English and he was educated in England until 12. But he despises Britain, a country of 'useless, idle, decadent fools, hiding behind your White Cliffs while other people fight your battles', he tells Bond.[17]

M draws Bond's attention to Drax in the beginning because he cheats at cards, and he doesn't trust him. He is not prepared to 'chance anything going wrong with this rocket of his'.[18] At Blades Club, where M plays cards, Bond soon works out how Drax cheats at bridge using a highly polished cigarette case to read the cards before the dealer puts them down on the table. Bond himself cheats to trap Drax, who loses £16,500.

Bond and Gala Brand, an undercover policewoman working for Drax, discover his plan. The two become trapped beside the rocket when it is about to launch but manage to reset the co-ordinates, targeting the Soviet submarine Drax and his cronies are escaping on. Drax is a SMERSH agent.

Jan Aylen, later a rear admiral, visited a V-1 and V-2 factory at Nordhausen that was built into a hillside with 4 miles of tunnels: 'Components entering at one end and the completed missiles emerging on railway wagons at the other. The huge V-2's, 6 foot diameter cylinders, reared up thirty feet as if in some Wagnerian devil's kitchen, as indeed it was since it was largely staffed by slave labour.'

Many of those Aylen saw were walking skeletons. The factory even had cremation ovens and a gold filling abstraction slab. He was filled 'with a blind and sickening rage against the Nazi regime'.[19]

The 30AU, like many Allied units, had to deal with the arrogance of mostly the junior German officers, who were mainly ardent Nazis. In Kiel, the Royal Marines dealt with some 25,000 German soldiers and sailors. The senior officers were more contrite while the men generally did as they were told. Two SS guards were executed when the prison ship *Athen* was found to have 6,000 people locked in the hold. They had been there for twelve days without food or water.[20]

With the items on Ian's blacklist near fulfilled by 30AU, he got in on the hunt himself. Commander Jim 'Shanco' Glanville, in Bad Sulza in the Weimarer region, came across evidence of the German Naval Intelligence archives. Some of these had been destroyed but other parts had been sent to '25KL/KA'. It took Glanville some time to discover that meant they had been sent to somewhere called Tambach. The only problem was that there were several places of that name in southern Germany. They thought it might be near Ingolstadt in Bavaria as there was a naval base there used to service mines and torpedoes. The route there took them past the concentration camp at Buchenwald. They were shocked by the living skeletons and piles of corpses. Arriving at Ingolstadt, they found no records and realised the base was just a staging point for U-boat crews on their way to the Atlantic ports.

Glanville then thought it could be Tambach Castle 'west of Coburg on the fringes of the Thuringian forest'. They backtracked almost to their starting point, and avoided shattered Nuremberg. The journey was difficult because of downed bridges and wrecked roads. 'The whole area was in a state of chaos, with SS units fighting it out, the Wehrmacht fighting or surrendering and with bands of escaped POWs, mainly Russians and Poles, roaming the countryside, or deserters from the German Army.' They reached the castle at sunset and found their way in, only to be confronted by a single German naval rating who immediately surrendered when challenged by Marine Booth's Tommy gun. When asked who was in command, he replied 'Kontradmiral Gladisch'. Admiral Walter Gladisch was a veteran of the First World War.[21]

They were in the right place. The old admiral had by that time served in the German Navy for forty-seven years and now had charge of the entire German Naval archives since 1870. He confessed he was delighted by the arrival of Glanville and his men. Admiral Dönitz had ordered him to hand over the records to the Allies, but he had doubted his ability to comply as some of his staff, notably the 'Kriegsmarine Helferinnen', similar to the Wrens, some of whom were hard-line Nazis, wanted him to burn them. They were led by the 'formidable' Fraulein Androde, who had been trying to contact the SS.

Lieutenant Jim Besant had to confront the Helferinnen. After meeting Androde, he thought she should 'have been drafted to Ravensbruck as the wardress in charge'. He had to keep them all confined and only had a few Marines with which to do so. He decided to arm some of the German sailors loyal to Admiral Dönitz and unite them on watch with a Marine Commando. 'They had strict instructions to make sure the women did not leave their quarters and that nobody from outside got in.'[22]

Concerned about the fate of the records, Ian set off for Tambach Castle via Hamburg. He told Harling two weeks after his return that: 'For so chair-bound an officer such an excursion promised to be an unusual tail-end bonus to his personal war.'[23]

After the war, Ian, while researching his book *Thrilling Cities*, came to the conclusion Hamburg was 'one of my favourite cities in the world'. Yet this was tinged with guilt as he recalled how it was devastated during the war. In 1942, over nine days of raids by the RAF 48,000 people were killed in the resulting fire storms. Fleming remembered how 'in those days, studying the blow up photographs from the Photographic Reconnaissance Unit and reading the estimates of damage, we in the Admiralty used to rub our hands with delight. Ah me!!'[24]

On the journey to Tambach, Fleming was chauffeured in a staff car, while two Marine Commandos rode shotgun in a naval patrol car. Royal Marine Commandos are mentioned several times in the Bond books, and we know 006 was a former Commando. However, in *Octopussy* we do come across the more rounded character of Major Dexter Smythe RM, retired and living like Ian Fleming in Jamaica. During the war, Smythe had been given 'the unenviable job of being advanced interrogator on Commando operations'. His German was excellent as his mother had come from Heidelberg. At the end of the war he joins the 'Miscellaneous Objectives Bureau', their job being to clean up the 'Gestapo and Abwehr hideouts when the collapse of Germany came about'.[25] He is given the Tyrol area of Austria to ferret out Nazis on the run. In one location with a lot of documents he comes across an envelope containing a single sheet of paper that tells the whereabouts of two bars of gold hidden under a cairn near Kitzbühel.

It has been estimated that the Nazis might have hidden as much as £35 billion in gold in the Austrian Alps. The US Counter Intelligence Corps investigated the matter in 1947. Lake Toplitz, not far from Salzburg, was one of the suspected sites. Here counterfeit notes were dumped into the lake from Operation Bernhard, whereby slave labour forged British and American notes worth billions.[26]

Smythe memorises the location and burns the note. Having found the place, he forces a local man, Hannes Oberhauser, to guide him to the spot. After a long trek up into the Alps, they find the cairn. Smythe then shoots Oberhauser with two bullets in the back of the head. The impact knocks the guide off his feet and he falls over the edge of a cliff, landing on a glacier. Smythe then sets about dismantling the cairn rock by rock, at a frenzied speed and ignoring his cut and bleeding hands. He finally finds an 'old grey Wehrmacht ammunition box' and sits on a rock looking at it for a quarter of an hour. Smythe drags it to a nearby hut, where he consumes Oberhauser's sausage; 'a real mountaineer's meal – tough, well fatted and strongly garlicked'. He throws the ammunition box over the cliff, watching where it lands, and he does not mind if the impact opens it. Then he climbs down the face, testing all the hand and footholds with his weight on the way down. Reaching Oberhauser's body, he throws it into a deep crevasse. The ammunition box lid has been sprung open by the impact. The two bars of gold 'glittered' in the sun. Both had the marks of 'the Swastika in a circle below an eagle' as well as 'the mint marks of the Reichsbank'.[27]

He marries a Wren, Mary Parnell, and they set up home in Jamaica. After removing the Nazi markings from the gold, he cuts off a piece and approaches the Foo brothers, local Chinese traders, to sell it. However, they still know it is Nazi gold because it is 10 per cent lead, a sure giveaway. The Nazis always tried to cheat and swindle: 'Very bad business, Major very stupid,' says one of the Foos. Of course, even with 90 per cent gold, the bars are still worth a fortune.[28]

When Bond arrives at Smythe's house asking what happened to Oberhauser twenty years ago, Mary had been dead two years and now he was 'fifty-four, slightly bald and his belly sagged'. He had known one day someone would come. He tells Bond what happened and wonders how a Secret Service man is involved. Bond tells him that Oberhauser had taught him to ski and had been a father figure for him, 'when I happened to need one'.

Smythe asks him if he wants a written confession. Bond says no, he will send his report to the Royal Marines and Scotland Yard. They should be in touch shortly and will send someone out to arrest him. Swimming is one of Smythe's favourite pastimes, and after Bond leaves he goes out to feed his octopus. He is distracted by what has happened and, suffering chest pains, he is stung by a scorpion fish he has speared to feed his octopus. He knows he will be dead within fifteen minutes and it will be painful, but it is the penance he must suffer. He continues out to the reef to feed the octopus but he too becomes its meal.[29] *Octopussy*, a collection of short stories including *The Property of a Lady* and *The Living Daylights*, was published after Ian's death.

Gold crops up many times in Fleming's Bond books, often in the form of buried or lost treasure; a subject that had fascinated him since childhood. The hunt for Rommel's treasure is mentioned in *On Her Majesty's Secret Service*, where it is 'supposed to be hidden under the sea somewhere off Bastia (on the east coast of Corsica).[30]

Goldfinger is the seventh book and the longest, in which Auric Goldfinger, a SMERSH agent, plans to steal all the gold held in Fort Knox and thus throw the United States and the Western world into chaos. He plans to steal it away on board a Soviet Sverdlovsk (Sverdlov)-class cruiser while the US lies poisoned with 'GB', a Trilone nerve poison developed by the Wehrmacht in 1943. His Soviet masters had captured the German stocks. It would work well if introduced into the water supply.[31]

Where did this idea come from? Maybe the cruiser to carry away the gold is a giveaway. Captain Charles Brousse, a French naval officer after the fall of France, revealed to the American Elizabeth Thorpe, with whom he had an affair, the whereabouts of a huge amount of gold. She was code-named Cynthia and worked for the SIS and BSC. She was an attractive woman of 30 with 'bright auburn hair, large green eyes, and a slender voluptuous figure'. Marion de Chastelain worked closely with Cynthia, being fluent in French, when the agent was working to infiltrate the Vichy Embassy. Charles Brousse raided the safe regularly and handed over the contents to Cynthia. De Chastelain thought: 'She was the type who revelled in espionage. She really loved it. And came from a good Washington family so she had entry to all the embassies and places.' Cynthia told her that on one occasion when she and Brousse were almost caught by a guard she took off all her clothes to make it appear that they were engaged in 'other undercover activity'.[32] She learned from Brousse that 286 tons of gold had arrived on the island of Martinique aboard the light cruiser *Emile Bertin*. As the situation in France got worse, the cruiser was ordered to take the gold to Halifax, Nova Scotia.

However, by the time the ship got there the armistice had been signed. It escaped internment and went to Martinique, which was then controlled by the Vichy regime. The gold was transferred to an old fort and stored in the old magazines. The *Emile Bertin* joined the substantial forces there, ready to defend the island against a British attack.

BSC devised a scheme using disaffected sailors and soldiers aided by British agents on the island to launch a rebellion against the Vichy regime. Gaining control of some French ships, they would take the gold and head for Canada. However, the British action at Oran scuppered that idea as it fostered resentment among the French crews. Churchill was still keen on the idea, but by mid-1941 Martinique was firmly in the grip of Vichy powers. However, with the United States' entry into the war, a watching blockade was maintained and no evidence could be found that the gold was aiding the enemy. The powerful French Fleet at Martinique did not move until in June 1943 they joined the Allied navies. No doubt it was another scheme Fleming would have come across.[33]

Cynthia's exploits for BSC are said to have greatly assisted Allied operations. However, the story of her obtaining Italian naval ciphers could not have aided Admiral Cunningham at the Battle of Cape Matapan. She is supposed to have obtained Italian codebooks from Admiral Alberto Lais, her lover. But when Lais told her where to find the codebooks, the lovers were bidding each other farewell on the ship that was to take Lais back to Italy. That departure was recorded in the *New York Times* and took place on 26 April 1941, almost a month after Cunningham was supposed to have used Lais's codebooks at Matapan. Also, the admiral's son was serving in the Mediterranean and it is extremely doubtful he had access to the Italian Fleet's codebooks in the US anyway. After the war, Admiral Lais strongly denied this ever happened.[34]

Robert Harling asked Fleming if when he got to Tambach Castle he was welcomed with open arms. Not really, he felt, although the location was picturesque 'mountain background, forest clearing, lake and so on'. As to the castle, he found it: 'Cold. Dismal. Comfortless. Ghastly Count Dracula stuff.' He found the old admiral to be 'quite helpful' and that the possible destruction of 'those priceless naval records had been causing him quite a few sleepless nights'. The entire archives were brought to Hamburg in a convoy of 3-ton trucks, where they were loaded on to a fishery protection trawler for the voyage to London.

Harling observed that Fleming only spent four days at Tambach, leaving the convoy responsibility to Glanville, which rather proved his own theory 'that the somewhat basic and care free life of 30AU in the field was not for Ian'.[35]

Later, Ian admitted to having enjoyed the trip to Germany and seeing a part of the country he had not seen before. Regarding 30AU, he felt that, compared with others serving at the front, his 'Red Indians' had 'enjoyed a far more light-hearted war'. It was more of an adventure than his war had been. Harling observed that there were grim moments and they had suffered casualties.

'I agree,' said Fleming, 'that 30AU had its sharper moments and had lost a disproportionate number of its men, but the rest of you got away with far more than a fair share of unadulterated entertainment.'[36]

For Fleming the war was winding down. He had little to do with the German Naval archives once they arrived in London. The end was close in the Far East. After some mopping-up operations in Norway, the end came for Ian. On 10 November 1945, Commander Ian Lancaster Fleming, RNVR, was released from the Royal Navy, granted fifty-six days' resettlement leave.[37] After six years in Naval Intelligence, a job that he had loved, Ian had emerged as a far more mature man with a wealth of experience, though it had been exhausting. An established pattern to his life was gone. What to do next was the question?

15

CASINO ROYALE

Before Ian Fleming walked away into Civvy Street he briefly considered whether to stay in the Navy or alternatively transfer to MI5 or MI6. He discussed his options with Stephenson, but decided that the world of the peacetime secret service were not for him after 'the wartime variety-show of Room 39'.[1] Bond often bemoans the fact that: 'He was a man of war and when, for a long period, there was no war, his spirit went into decline.'[2]

However, Ian did not rush off and start writing the Bond books. He needed a period of gestation. He needed a bolt hole, a place to write with the right atmosphere. Yet he had to earn a living. He thought about returning to the City stockbrokers where his job had been kept open for him, but Lord James Kemsley had offered him a job far more to his liking in his newspaper group as foreign manager. This came with an attractive salary of £4,500 a year, plus £500 in expenses and an agreed two months' leave a year that he could take all at the same time.[3]

He had also contacted Ivar Bryce as the war was running down and asked him to find a place in Jamaica of about 15 acres, with cliffs and a secluded bay, and no road between house and sea. Bryce got the local land agent Reggie Aquart on the hunt and he soon contacted him: 'I have found the right place for your friend the Commander. Would he go up to £2,000 do you think?' Bryce had no idea as they had not even discussed money. They went off to view the site, which was on the north coast close by the village and harbour of Oracabessa. There was a small bay protected by a reef some 20 yards out. The land rose high above the water. Bryce and Aquart crawled out to the cliff edge to take a look. There was a strip of white sand below and about 10ft out to sea was a small rock covered with a single white Portlandia. Bryce knew this was the place for Ian. He cabled London and received a prompt reply from Ian, who transferred £2,000 to the land-owner, an Irish Jamaican named Christie Cousins, and the land was his.[4]

It was not until January 1946 that Ian managed to get away to Jamaica, where the weather was much better than his first visit. He was thrilled with the site Ivar had chosen for him and he eagerly set in motion the building of his home. Aquart was to manage the project and the local architects Scovell and Barber were engaged to work on the sketches Ian had brought with him. They had started life on an Admiralty blotter, so confident he had been that he would live in Jamaica.

The building was to be basic, with shutters instead of glass in the windows. He wanted to feel those warm tropical breezes and had visions of birds flying in and out. The building work would cost £2,000 and would include a garage and staff quarters. A local carpenter was brought in to construct stout chairs and tables, again to Ian's own design. Noel Coward called it 'Goldeneye, nose and throat'. He thought it a ghastly home that 'had all the discomforts of a bad hospital'.[5]

The naming of the dwelling, according to various accounts, went through several choices before settling on 'Goldeneye'. It had been called 'Rock Edge' or 'Rotten Egg Bay' and 'Rum Cove'. Bryce urged Ian to call it 'Shame Lady', but Fleming settled on Goldeneye and probably intended to do so before he even set eyes on it, after what he had done in Spain and Portugal. Bryce agreed that it was named 'after the code name of a wartime operation …'[6] Aquart was of the opinion that it did not matter much what Fleming called the place as the locals would always know it as 'Rock Edge'. Little did he know that Goldeneye, one day, would become the most famous residence in Jamaica.

By 1948, Ian's single-storey bungalow Goldeneye was finished. Reggie Aquart did Ian another big favour by obtaining for him the services of Violet Cummings, who would become the housekeeper and was the 'mainspring' of Goldeneye, thought Bryce. Violet became devoted to Fleming and remained with him until his death.[7]

In the last few years of the 1940s, Ian tended to bury himself in his work for ten months of the year at the *Sunday Times*. As at NID, he became the 'ideas man'. Harry Hodson, the editor, rather like Admiral Denning had observed, felt that of his ideas for articles and features, out of six 'maybe one would come to fruition'. He did little writing himself during this time as the mundane reporting of news did not appeal to him; he got others to do that. Rather he busied himself with the appointments of overseas correspondents and keeping in touch with them, rather like the agents and naval attachés he ran during the war.[8]

In December he would head off for Jamaica, crossing the Atlantic on the *Queen Mary* or *Queen Elizabeth* to New York and spending a few days there catching up with friends before heading south. The two liners had been used as troop ships during the war and Bond in *Diamonds are Forever* recalls *Queen Elizabeth*: 'when she had zig-zagged deep into the South Atlantic, as she played a game of hide-and-seek with the U-Boat wolf packs …' Crossing in peacetime, the 'boredom and indigestion would be the only hazards of the voyage'.[9]

Ian had known Lady Ann O'Neill for several years. She had been Ann Charteris, her maiden name, when they first met. When she was 21 she married Shane, the third Baron O'Neill, in 1934. She was described as: 'Slim, dark-haired, fine features, with a mildly imperious presence.' She was also a woman of 'vivacity, wit, charm and brains'.[10] Ann found Ian to be 'immensely attractive', yet 'there was something defensive and untamed about him, like a wild animal'.[11] Ann had two children with Shane. In 1941 he set off for North Africa with his regiment the North Irish Horse Guards. Ann and Ian began going out together, soon becoming lovers. While staying with Esmond Rothermere, another of Ann's lovers, in his house at Ascot in October 1944, news came that Shane had been killed in Italy. Ann, racked by guilt, was distraught at her husband's death; she turned to Ian for support. Harling met Ian and Ann for lunch at the Etoile only a week after the news of Shane's death. He observed them closely for half an hour and found: 'Her gift for prompting gaiety in others was unquenched.' As time passed, he could not help surmising what 'this loss would really mean to herself and her two admirers. Would Rothermere's wealth prove too enticing, or Fleming's more puzzling personality prove too tempting.'[12]

Ann had expected Ian to propose marriage, but this did not happen, so she accepted Esmond's proposal. Rothermere was the owner of the *Daily Mail* at the time. She told Ian while they walked together in Hyde Park at the end of June 1945 that she had decided to marry Esmond. She wrote later that if Fleming had proposed marriage, 'I would have accepted.'[13] She moved into Warwick House, Viscount Rothermere's London mansion, where she would become one of the city's leading society hostesses. Yet the affair with Ian was soon rekindled, first through secret assignations and later more openly.

In January 1948 she arrived at Goldeneye accompanied by Loelia Duchess of Westminster for appearance sake, another member of the close-knit group. At first she was not impressed with Goldeneye: there was no hot water, and during the night there were lots of animal noises from frogs and crickets. However, she recorded her first day there was a 'wonderful day of birds, flowers and fish'. In the evenings before dinner they would watch moths and beetles, which were attracted by the lamps. Then after dinner he would take his guests out to the cliff overlooking the sea, where they would gaze at the waves. Ann wrote that they 'watched the spray of the reef and the high bright large stars of the region'. The two women would leave Ian 'smoking and wallowing in the melancholy'.[14]

On her return to England, Ann discovered that she was pregnant, and she knew the baby was Ian's. The baby girl was born prematurely in Scotland, named Mary, but she lived only a few hours. Their affair continued into 1949, though Esmond warned Ann on her return from Jamaica that she must stop seeing Fleming or face divorce. Yet their tempestuous relationship continued. She wrote to Ian the following year after a short visit to Goldeneye that he was 'a selfish thoughtless bastard, but we love each other'.[15]

However, the affair began to affect Ian's prospects with Lord Kemsley and his various newspapers. He was fond of Ian, they had played bridge together at the Dorchester often during the war, and he had been a regular guest at dinner parties at Chandos Place. Others at Kemsley House were jealous of this close relationship. For the first two years things went well. However, by 1948 the foreign news desk was coming under economic strain, the competition was fierce: 'And Fleming, for all his debonair charm and his zest for living and his friendship with the old Tsar himself, began to suffer the disillusion and sadness inherent in a declining regime.' He had hoped for a directorship but it was not offered. Then there was his affair with a married woman, which did not fit with the 'high moral tone of Kemsley House'.[16] He began to feel a failure as he approached 40, yet his prospects were about to take a turn for the better.

Soon Esmond had had enough and the couple agreed to divorce. Ann was soon pregnant again by Ian. This time he married her and the wedding took place in Jamaica. On 24 March 1952, they married at the magistrate's office in the town hall at Port Maria. Noel Coward and his secretary, Cole Lesley, were the witnesses. Ian's closely guarded bachelor life was over. He had warned Ann about marriage with him, it would be no bed of roses. He could be selfish and he had no money or title, hardly an enthusiastic proposal. As to money, they would not be destitute, since Rothermere, as part of the divorce settlement, had given Ann £100,000, a fortune in 1952.

They had been living together at Goldeneye since January. It was a quiet time, although with an undercurrent of tension. To amuse herself, she took up painting. According to her, she suggested that Ian should write something rather than get bored. He agreed and said to her that he could not be idle 'while I screw up my face trying to draw fish'.[17]

Ian no doubt had his thriller firmly in his mind before this. He had brought his trusty 20-year-old Imperial typewriter with him, and had purchased a ream of good folio typing paper in a shop just off Madison Avenue on the journey over. He already had the name of his hero, he told Ivar Bryce, although he had no title for the book, and showed him *Birds of the West Indies* by James Bond; he had wanted a plain name.[18]

His biographers disagree as to when Ian started writing *Casino Royale*; Pearson is precise, claiming it was after breakfast 'of the third Tuesday of January 1952', which would have been the 15th. It was just a month before King George VI died, heralding the start of a new Elizabethan age. Fleming had swum that morning before settling down at his roll-top desk with a good supply of cigarettes.[19]

However, Lycett points out Ann's statement about Ian starting work after Noel Coward came to dinner. Coward arrived on the island on 16 February. Given the fact that Ian produced 62,000 words of *Casino Royale*, it took him either eight weeks or four, the latter equating to 2,000 words a day, as the book was finished on 18 March.[20] He started with no notes and no written plan, he just started typing. It must have all been in his mind already, though perhaps within his subconscious. He worked from nine to twelve. After lunch he slept for an hour and then at five returned to his desk to read what he had written, before putting the manuscript away in the bottom left-hand drawer of the desk. Around ninety minutes later, he began thinking about cocktails.

When Ian Fleming started writing what would become *Casino Royale*, whether it was January or February, most of the strands of the plot were there ready from his NID experiences. It has more than most of the other James Bond books, with the exception of *Moonraker*. Right from the start the main ingredients of gambling and casinos emerge, fuelled by his experiences at Estoril on his trips to Portugal to oversee Operation Golden Eye.

Lieutenant Commander John Hugill was sent to Lisbon by DNI. The son of Rear Admiral R.C. Hugill, at the beginning of the war he had joined the RNVR. A chemist, he was drafted into the Admiralty Miscellaneous Weapons Division, where he helped develop anti-submarine weapon systems. In early 1942 he was ordered to report to the NID and 'entered the old smoke grimed Admiralty building through the spring garden entrance'. First he was interviewed by a 'charming elderly' Royal Marine colonel, after which he was sent to Room 39. There a man in his early thirties, with a 'melancholy, compelling sort of face and a brisk, dégagé but kindly air took command and led me into a side room for an interview'. This was Ian Fleming, who told Hugill they were going to send him to Lisbon as naval attaché, and oddly asked him: 'Do you gamble by the way?'

Hugill thought it rather an odd question, perhaps some sort of test, but replied, 'occasionally'. To which Fleming murmured what sounded like the need to be careful, as 'chaps' could get into trouble with 'that sort of thing'. Then he was taken in to see the DNI, Admiral Godfrey, who asked him straight away, 'Do you gamble?'

Feeling once again that it was some sort of test, Hugill replied, 'Oh no sir.' 'I do, I enjoy it,' Godfrey said.

Rather bemused by the whole thing, Hugill said, 'Oh I see, sir.' But he did not.

He saw Fleming several times in Lisbon, a place that was 'humming' with 'espionage and sabotage'. He was usually in civilian clothes, sometimes with Admiral Godfrey and he knew they went to the casino in Estoril. He spent more than a year in Lisbon before being recalled. Back at NID, Fleming asked him what he would like to do next. Hugill had a vague idea of something on an aircraft carrier. Ian suggested he join 30AU, given his background, as a technical officer, which for Hugill would prove a worthwhile role.[21]

Of course, Dusko Popov also bore witness to seeing Fleming at the Estoril Casino. Commander Ralph Izzard, who served in 30AU, told Ian a story that while he was working for NID in South America he had played against Nazi agents in the casino at Pernambuco on Brazil's Atlantic coast. Izzard's report had crossed Ian's desk. This prompted him to take Izzard out to dinner, during which he quizzed him about the incident right down to the smallest details.[22]

Ian moved the action from Portugal to his fictional town of Royale-les-Eaux in northern France, based loosely on Deauville in the Normandy region, which had a grand casino. It was influenced by Le Touquet in the Pas-de-Calais area, renowned for its wide beach and lively nightlife, and in the 1920s Noel Coward and the smart set spent weekends there. Ian went to the casino in Le Touquet in the 1930s with Bryce, who did most of the gambling.

We are told Royale-les-Eaux started as a 'small fishing village'. The discovery of a natural spring made it fashionable. Casino Royale had 'a strong whiff of Victorian elegance and luxury …' It had been refurbished in 1950, repainted 'in its original white and gilt and the rooms decorated in the palest grey with wine-red carpets and curtains'.[23]

As Bryce gambled, Ian, like a sponge, absorbed the atmosphere of the casino and the people. It was all about 'the long game' winner takes all: 'Then the enigmatic cards would be burnt or defaced, a shroud would be dropped over the table and the grass-green baize battlefield soak up the blood of its victims and refresh itself.'[24] Bond might risk all on the turn of a card, that's if he was not cheating, to teach someone a lesson, but not Ian; he was too cautious, more bent on finding a perfect system, a sure thing rather like his cheating villains.

His first villain is Le Chiffre, the Benzedrine-sniffing, 18-stone mound that moves like a 'big fish' and has a 'cliff of reddish-brown hair' above the 'unsmiling wet red mouth …'[25] He is grotesque, as was his model: the drug addict, arch-Satanist of England Alistair Crowley, who Ian came across in 1940. Le Chiffre was thought to have a lineage of 'Mediterranean with Prussian or Polish strains'.[26] He is a Soviet agent controlled by Leningrad Section III. His cover is that of a French union boss, but he is working for SMERSH and has misused Soviet funds. If Bond can bankrupt Le Chiffre his stock as a Soviet agent will plummet.

SMERSH, 'Smert Shpionam' meaning 'Death to Spies', was a real Soviet counter-intelligence organisation in the Second World War. Its roots lay in the Cheka Special Division 'Chastny Otdyel', formed during the Russian Civil War to assassinate White Russians and other enemies of the Revolution at home and abroad. It was originally proposed that the new intelligence arm should be called SMERNESH, 'Death to German Spies'. However, Stalin not noted for his trusting nature, felt it needed a wider remit. 'Do not other intelligence organisations work against our armies? Let us call it "Death to Spies".' It started operating on 19 April 1943 as a department of the NKVD, with the Army and Navy having branches.[27]

The army directorate of SMERSH became the most feared. It has been held responsible for the arrest, torture and execution of thousands of Soviet soldiers, few of which were guilty. It was even said to have murdered Leon Trotsky in Mexico in 1940, although this would make SMERSH older than officially admitted. In 1946 it was disbanded and its duties were taken over by the People's Commissariat for State Security, the NKGB.

Fleming was able to obtain much first-hand material from Lieutenant Colonel Grigori Aleksandrovich Tokaev, code-named Excise, about SMERSH. He was a renowned aeronautical engineer who defected to the West in Berlin in October 1947. MI6 would try and use him to encourage other Soviets to defect, with mixed results.[28] Ian was able to talk with Tokaev through his links with NID and he told him about the

SMERSH headquarters at 13 Sretenka Street, Moscow. Ian would use this in *From Russia with Love*, even placing a note at the beginning of the book that 'the background to this story is accurate'. In Chapter 4, The Moguls of Death, there is a two-page description of 13 Sretenka Street, 'a very large and ugly modern building'.[29]

Ross Napier of Fife, a reader and fan of Bond, went to Moscow and picked Fleming up about Sretenka Street, sending him a picture of No. 13 and pointing out that on the ground floor were two small shops, a grocer's and a butcher's, while the other two storeys were flats. This was clearly not and had never been the HQ of SMERSH. Ian wrote back, admitting that No. 13 could not have had any connection with SMERSH, and said that he was under the impression that the organisation had not been closed down. He felt he had been misinformed by his source, 'a colonel of the M.W.D.', and that he, Fleming, 'was not being intentionally misleading'. All the same, *From Russia with Love* remains one of the most popular of the Bond books.[30]

Another event he would embellish from his days in NID is depicted in *Casino Royale* as the killing of the Japanese cipher expert in New York, mentioned in Chapter 9, The Game is Baccarat. It explains how Bond got his double 0 number, his licence to kill, which was another invention of Fleming's, taken possibly from the double 0 numbers used in secret documents, or maybe the zero used to prefix the numbers of SOE agents, some of whom were assassins. During his 1941 visit to the USA with Godfrey, he observed Stephenson breaking into the Japanese Consul-General's office to open the safe, microfilm the ciphers books and replace them without the Japanese being aware.

Later in *Casino Royale*, Bond explains in more detail the killing in New York. First he booked a room in an adjacent skyscraper from which he could observe the 'cipher expert'. Then, with a colleague from the New York branch, 'and a couple of Remington thirty-thirty's with telescopic sights and silencers', they waited for days watching the room. Then their chance came: 'He shot at the man a second before me. His job was to blast a hole through the window so that I could shoot the Jap through it. They have tough windows at the Rockefeller centre to keep the noise out. It worked well.' Bond's shot comes a split second after the first: 'I got the Jap in the mouth as he turned to gape at the broken window.'[31]

The blowing up of the Bulgarians in the book was inspired by the bungled attempt by the Soviets to kill Franz von Papen, the German Ambassador to Turkey and once chancellor of Germany before Adolf Hitler. At about ten in the morning, in Ankara on 24 February 1942, von Papen and his wife had been walking from their house to the embassy along the tree-lined Ataturk Boulevard, which was deserted when: 'Suddenly we were both hurled to the ground by a violent explosion.' His wife was unhurt, but he had cuts and bruises and a temporary loss of hearing. 'Don't go a step further,' he warned her, thinking they might have set off a mine. Both were covered in blood. The explosion had shattered windows along the street and a crowd began to gather. The Turkish Security Police were quickly on the scene and soon got to the bottom of the mysterious explosion. Human remains were found over a wide area, including a shoe and a foot hanging in a tree. Two Macedonian students recruited by the Soviets had failed in the attempt, with the bomb going off before it was thrown. One got away but was later found hiding in the Soviet Embassy. First suspicions fell on the British SIS as they were known to have an observation post opposite von Papen's residence. However, even 'the Gestapo seemed a distinct possibility, and this suggestion was reinforced by accounts of mysterious telephone calls that various people claimed to have heard'. Finally the attempt was laid at the Russians' door.[32] Bond endures a similar attack against him in *Casino Royale*, Chapter 6, Two Men in Straw Hats. In this case, both Bulgarians manage to blow themselves up by mistake, and Bond is thrown to the ground by the blast; 'a ghastly rain of pieces of flesh and blood-soaked clothing fell on him and around him'.[33]

Many of the staple Bond ingredients were introduced in *Casino Royale*. His love of swimming, shared with his author, comes out in his rehabilitation in Chapter 23, Tide of Passion. His only hobby is his car, not an Aston Martin DB 5 – that first appeared in the *Goldfinger* film – rather Bond's love is one of the last 4.5-litre Bentleys with the supercharger by Amherst Villiers in battleship grey. Ettore Bugatti famously described Bentleys as 'fast trucks'. Bond had bought it almost new in 1933 and had kept it in careful storage through the war. He has it serviced by a former Bentley mechanic. Given in the James Bond obituary that appears in *You Only Live Twice* and using the timeline whereby he joins the RNVR in 1941 claiming to be 19 although more likely 17, then he would have bought the car aged around 10. But no matter; today, taking his lineage from Ian's creation, he must be well into his nineties.

Bond wrecks the car in *Casino Royale* but it is repaired by 'coach builders at Rouen'.[34] However, in *Moonraker* the Blower Bentley is written off for good. He then progresses to a Bentley Mark VI at the end of *Moonraker*, bought with his winnings from the card game against Drax, although the car is not mentioned again.[35] However, by *Thunderball* he has a MKII Continental Bentley, which he has painted battleship grey and calls it the 'Locomotive'.[36] In the book *Goldfinger*, he drives an Aston Martin DB III from the secret service car pool. He could have had a Jaguar 3.4 but the Aston Martin had a few of Q-branch's optional extras like reinforced bumpers and a tracking device, and Bond loves his gadgets, and it too was grey.

Then there are the Bond girls, in many ways the least interesting ingredient in the mix. They have unusual names, and all are, of course, beautiful given they might have the odd defect such as Honeychile Rider's broken nose in *Dr No*, or Domino Vitali in *Thunderball* limps because one of her legs is an inch shorter than the other. Vesper Lynd's name came out of a visit Fleming made with Bryce to a neighbour called 'The Colonel' in Jamaica, where they were served what the Colonel called Vespers, a drink of frozen rum with fruit and herbs: 'So the heroine – or possibly the villainess, to be more precise – was christened Vesper, and we invented a new drink to bear the name. Gin with a splash of Lillet, instead of dry vermouth, shaken, not stirred, with lots of ice and lots of vigour.' The copy of *Casino Royale* Ian gave Bryce was inscribed: 'For Ivar, who mixed the first Vesper, and said a good word.'[37]

Vesper had all the usual attributes of Bond girls: hair long, 'very black'; her eyes 'deep blue'; her skin 'lightly sun-tanned'; a 'wide and sensual mouth'; and, of course, 'fine breasts'.[38] She is a former Wren working for the Secret Service. Yet she is unusual for she betrays Bond, she is a SMERSH double agent and has been blackmailed into working for them for more than five years because of the hold her former lover, a Polish fighter pilot, still has on her. At the end of the book she commits suicide rather than face certain liquidation by SMERSH after she refuses to supply more information on Bond, knowing this too will mean the death of the Pole. She takes an overdose of sleeping pills.

Fleming claimed that he started writing *Casino Royale* to take his mind off his looming marriage, as if he was doomed, which naturally annoyed Ann; even more so as he would often peddle out the anecdote in company. However, another motive lay in the fact that the situation of the country in the early 1950s depressed him. Winston Churchill had returned to power in 1951, but his government was weak with a majority of only sixteen. His policy of strengthening the Empire was outdated. There was trouble in Egypt and Cyprus.

Even worse for Fleming, British Intelligence had been rocked to the core by the defection of Guy Burgess and Donald MacLean to Moscow, tipped off by the third man Kim Philby, who had been a Soviet spy since the Spanish Civil War. This could explain why he used Vesper Lynd as a double agent to reflect the times. Bond is suitably betrayed and telephones MI6 in London to tell them: '3030 was a double, working for Redland.'[39] British Intelligence was a laughing stock at the time and not to be trusted by Britain's American allies. Fleming's brother, Peter, had written *The Sixth Column: A Singular Tale of Our Times*, published in the summer of 1952. The novel was dedicated to Ian. It was the story of an attempt by the Soviets to undermine what was left of the British national character with a subtle propaganda campaign organised by their agents to infiltrate the highest places of the establishment. It was a call-to-arms for Ian to unleash James Bond 007 into the world and restore national pride.[40]

One question that comes up with monotonous regularity is who Bond was based upon. This is a fruitless quest. The list of people who might have influenced Fleming is large. Peter, his brother, would probably top the list, followed in no particular order by Merlin Minshall, Patrick Dalzel-Job, Lionel Crabb, Sir Fitzroy Maclean, Biffy Dunderdale and Dusko Popov. Some of his close friends could be included: Ralph Izzard, Peter Smithers, Robert Harling, and even Ivar Bryce, all had some input. My own particular favourite was one Ian never met, but might be nearer to his creation. He was suggested by Leonard Mosley, foreign correspondent and espionage writer, who recalled chatting to Ian in April 1953 at the *Sunday Times*. Fleming had told him he had been inspired to create James Bond after reading about the exploits of Sidney Reilly, which he had found in the archives of British Intelligence during the war. Reilly was not as well known then as he is now.[41] Mosley had written *The Cat and the Mice*, which was the story of the German spy John Eppler and Operation Kondor, the plan to infiltrate the 8th Army HQ during the desert war.

★★★

Mr and Mrs Fleming headed for home from Jamaica in March 1952. In his briefcase Ian carried the manuscript of *Casino Royale*; he had no intention at that point of publishing it, rather he would play with it with his editing pen. On route in New York he asked his old girlfriend, Clare Blanchard, to take a look at it. Her opinion was: 'You can't publish this. It will be a millstone around your neck. Or if you must publish it for heaven's sake do it under another name.'[42]

Back in London, Ian sat on the book. It was not until May that he got around to showing it to William Plomer, the South African novelist and poet who he had known since 1929. They met for lunch at the Ivy Restaurant; Plomer had worked at NID as a specialist writer during the war, a post Ian had recommended him for. By then he was a reader and literary advisor to Jonathan Cape. Ian prevaricated, talking about old times, and asked an odd question about how to get cigarette smoke out of a woman who has taken a 'deep lung full'. He thought 'exhales' a poor word and 'puffs it out' even worse. Plomer now guessed what it was all about: 'You've written a book.'

It was hardly a book, said Ian, merely a *Boy's Own Paper* story. Plomer asked to see the manuscript, but it took two months and reminders before Ian sent it to him. 'He forced Cape to publish it,' Ian later wrote. There was something in this, as Jonathan Cape and his editorial director did not like it. However, Plomer and Daniel George, another reader at Cape, with the added influence of Peter Fleming, who Cape much admired, pushed it through. Plomer would go on to edit all the Bond books.[43]

Ian Fleming claimed his creation was 'a mere entertainment'. He inscribed one of his later books, given to his old friend Paul Gallico, the American thriller writer, with: 'To Paul who has always seen the joke.'[44] Yet Gallico was full of praise for *Casino Royale*. After reading the manuscript by Cape he said: 'The book is a knockout. I thought I had written a couple of pretty fair torture scenes, in my day, but yours beats anything I ever read. Wow!'[45] In 1955, Raymond Chandler wrote to Ian: 'I cannot imagine what I can say to you about your books that will excite your publisher. What I do say in all sincerity is that you are probably the most forceful and driving writer, of what I suppose still must be called "thrillers" in England.'[46]

On Monday, 13 April 1953, *Casino Royale* was published by Jonathan Cape. Like the following thirteen Bond books penned by Ian Fleming, and published by Cape, they were all set in the Cold War era, but firmly rooted in the Second World War. Those six years spent at Naval Intelligence were the highlight of his life, even given his later success; no wonder he called his house in Jamaica Goldeneye after Operation Golden Eye, the nearest he came to being a secret agent. In *Thunderball*, Bond reflects with Felix Leiter: 'The war just doesn't seem to have ended for us ...' It never really did for Ian Fleming either.[47]

Fleming had been suffering heart problems since his heart attack in 1961, against medical advice he continued to smoke and drink far more than was good for him; he was determined to live life to the full. On 11 August 1964, he went to his golf club for lunch. That evening after dinner he collapsed and an ambulance was called, which took him to Kent and Canterbury Hospital. During the journey he talked to ambulance man James Parker: 'I am sorry to trouble you chaps. I don't know how you get along so fast with the traffic on the roads these days.'[48]

Ian died of a massive haemorrhage at 0130 on 12 August; he was only 56. He was buried in the cemetery of the Parish Church of St James, Sevenhampton, near Highworth in Wiltshire, only three days later. Fleming wrote fourteen Bond books and numerous short stories about 007, two non-fiction books and the children's book *Chitty Chitty Bang Bang*, which became a classic in its own right. At the time of his death these books had sold 30 million copies. The films based on the books have taken more than $5 billion at the box office.

His epitaph could be no better than those words written for Bond by Mary Goodnight in *You Only Live Twice*: 'I shall not waste my days trying to prolong them. I shall use my time.'[49]

IAN FLEMING'S JAMES BOND BOOKS AND THEIR SECOND WORLD WAR CONTENT

Casino Royale

Publication Date 13 April 1953, published by Jonathan Cape (all the Bond books were published by Cape), 213 pages. Cover conceived by Ian Fleming.

Main plot based on Fleming's visits to Lisbon and the casino at Estoril during his missions to evaluate Operation Golden Eye, a stay-behind scheme in the event of the German invasion of the Iberian Peninsula.

The villain Le Chiffre is based on Aleister Crowley, the 'Great Beast'. Ian met him in 1940 in relation to the 'Hess' affair.

SMERSH Soviet counter-intelligence organisation formed in 1943, absorbed into the NKGB in 1946. Le Chiffre is a SMERSH agent eliminated by them for his failure and loss of funds.

Scenes: Fleming used his own experience with William Stephenson breaking into the Japanese Consul in New York in 1941. Used as the setting for 007 killing a Japanese cipher expert. The attempted assassination of 007 by the 'Bulgarians' based on the attempt on the life of the German Ambassador Franz von Papen and his wife in Ankara in 1942.

Other smaller items: Walking stick gun as used by SOE. La Chiffre torture of Bond based on similar techniques used in Vichy French North Africa against British agents: the steel string of a mandolin was used to slice the scrotum.

Live and Let Die (Original title: The Undertaker's Wind)
Publication date 5 April 1954, 234 pages. Cover conceived by Ian Fleming and completed by Kenneth Lewis.

The villain 'Mr Big' is another SMERSH agent working to destabilise the West by funding agents in the USA with buried treasure, believed to be from a hoard buried in Jamaica by the Welsh Pirate Sir Henry Morgan.

Fleming first went to the island in 1943 for a conference about U-boat activities in the Caribbean. Mr Big's background includes service with OSS in Marseilles during the war against Vichy collaborators. He met a Soviet agent on the same mission who indoctrinated him with communist ideals. He then defected to Moscow after the war.

Scenes: Bond's use of the limpet mine and underwater swimming based on the exploits of Italian Naval Commandos Decima MAS (X MAS) in the Second World War and the countermeasures used by Commander Lionel Crabb, who fought the Italians at Gibraltar. Fleming was also an accomplished swimmer in his own right, having dived with Jacques Cousteau.

Other smaller items: Use of time pencils in mines. Use of the name Bryce as cover name for Bond during the train journey to Florida.

Moonraker (Other possible titles: Mondays are Hell, Wide of the Mark, Out of the Clear Sky, The Inhuman Element)
Publication date 5 April 1955, 255 pages. Cover conceived by Ian Fleming and completed by Kenneth Lewis.

Main plot based on the German V-2 rocket. Both the USA and USSR adopted the V-2, updating it to a ballistic intercontinental weapon. The first photograph of the earth from space was taken from a V-2. Ian Fleming learned a lot about the V-1 and V-2 programmes from 30AU. The character in the book Dr Walter is based on Hellmuth Walter, the German submarine expert captured by 30AU.

Villain Hugo Drax is given a Nazi background; he has served in the Brandenburg Regiment, the RSHA Foreign Intelligence Service of the SS, with Otto Skorzeny's 150th Panzer Brigade in the Ardennes and with the guerrilla stay-behind Werewolves. All his staff are former Nazis. Drax is another closet SMERSH agent and, far from building the Moonraker for Britain, he intends to use it against London. He is regarded by many as the best of Fleming's villains.

Moonraker is littered with snippets of the Second World War. Drax's men often throw in the odd 'Heil Hitler'. The Germans are working for the Soviets as they hold relatives in the Soviet Union whose lives could be used as blackmail. There is mention of the 'Cicero Affair' in Ankara, in which the British Ambassador's valet sold secrets to the Germans. The Werewolves were credited with shooting dispatch riders in the Ardennes.

Diamonds are Forever

Publication date 26 March 1956, 257 pages, cover by Pat Marriott.

The fourth Bond book was one of the least reliant on his Second World War background. Fleming went with Ernest Cuneo to Saratoga Springs, New York state, for the race meeting, although he had no interest in horse racing. Later they went on to Las Vegas and then Los Angeles. Bond is sent to investigate diamond smuggling, which starts in French Guinea and ends in Las Vegas.

Yet even in this book there are passages that relate to the Second World War. The helicopter pilot early in the book is former Luftwaffe, having served with 'Galland' (Lieutenant General Adolf Galland, renowned German fighter pilot of the Second World War). We learn a little about Bond's travels around Europe during the war. Also, he recalls the liner *Queen Elizabeth* dodging the U-boats when used as a troop ship. Fleming often sailed on one of the *Queens*, *Mary* or *Elizabeth*, to cross the Atlantic, which took five days on his trips to Jamaica via New York. During the war most of his Atlantic crossings were by air, usually by the US Clipper service from Lisbon.

Fleming's fascination with treasure led him to write the non-fiction book *The Diamond Smugglers*, also published by Jonathan Cape, in November 1957.

From Russia with Love

Publication date 8 April 1957, 253 pages, the first iconic cover by Richard Chopping.

Ian Fleming thought this his best book and it was a favourite of President John F. Kennedy.

The first third of the book takes place mainly in the Soviet Union at the SMERSH training camp in the Crimea and then in Moscow. First we are introduced to one of two villains in the book, Donovan Grant, 'Chief Executioner of SMERSH'. He is Irish with an IRA background. He served in the Royal Corps of Signals at the end of the war but defected to the Soviets from Berlin. He uses the alias Captain Norman Nash, former Royal Engineer, to get close to Bond. The other villain is Rosa Klebb, a colonel in SMERSH. They plan to assassinate Bond as revenge against the SIS, with Grant as the tool. They plan to lure Bond to Istanbul, where a beautiful Soviet cipher expert wants to defect; she will also bring with her a 'Spektor' coding machine. This is clearly based on the German Enigma machine, the machine Fleming was trying to obtain when he was at NID in 1940 in an operation code-named Ruthless.

The book has a wealth of Second World War material. The choice of Istanbul and the story of a defection, although it is a trap in the book, have many parallels in the Second World War. The Cicero case, although based in Ankara, had plenty of scenes in Istanbul.

Probably one of the most famous defections took place in the city in 1944 when the Vermehrens, husband and wife who worked for the Abwehr, went over to the British. Hitler was so furious it led to the demise of the Abwehr as an effective service. Shortly after this, Cornelia Kapp, a secretary at the German Embassy who worked for the controller of Cicero, defected to the OSS, to whom she revealed the spy at the British Embassy. Delays in handing her over to the British allowed Elyesa Bazna, valet to the British Ambassador, to escape the SIS agents closing in on him.

The story of Eugene Karpe, a US naval attaché travelling on the Orient Express from Budapest to Paris in 1950, also influenced Fleming. He was carrying important papers and was killed by Soviet assassins. His body was found in a railway tunnel south of Salzburg.

Dr No (Original title: The Wind Man)
Publication date 21 March 1958, 256 pages, cover by Pat Marriott, the first book to be filmed.

The Villain Dr Julius No, part Chinese, part German, lives on Crab Key, a small island off Jamaica, where his business is mining guano for fertiliser. However, the fertiliser business is a front, although a profitable one, for he is a Soviet agent, and from an elaborate base built into a mountain he is disrupting US missile tests at nearby Cape Canaveral. Dr No is also interested in human behaviour under stress, and greatly admires the German experiments on live humans during the war. The inspiration for Crab Key was Fleming's visit with Ivar Bryce to the flamingo colony on Great Inagua near the Bahamas.

The rock galleries built into the mountain on Crab Key have clear similarities to the tunnels inside the Rock of Gibraltar. Also, Fleming was directly involved in Operation Tracer, the stay-behind plan to leave an observation team inside the Rock if the Germans had taken Gibraltar.

Crab Key is patrolled by Dr No's government surplus motor torpedo boat, which mounts German Spandau machine guns, both Second World War vintage. Bond recalls the sound of the Spandau gun from the Ardennes in 1944.

Goldfinger (Original title: The Richest Man in the World)
Publication date 23 March 1959, 318 pages, Fleming's longest book, cover by Richard Chopping. Dedication: 'To my gentle Reader William Plomer.'

Auric Goldfinger is the paymaster of SMERSH and hatches a plot to steal the gold in Fort Knox. This was inspired by the BSC plan to obtain the Vichy French gold on Martinique in 1941, by instigating a mutiny within the French Navy ships there. One of these, a cruiser, had brought the gold reserves to the island in the first place.

Among the Second World War influences, Goldfinger intends to use GB Trilane, a German nerve poison developed in 1943 but not used by the Wehrmacht, which the Soviets captured at the end of the war. He will use it in the water supply to deal with the guards at Fort Knox and the local population. This equates with Sarin, which was developed in the 1930s and supplied to the German Army in 1939. It was never used in the Second World War, and has the NATO designation GB. Goldfinger also uses former Luftwaffe pilots and intends to use a Soviet cruiser on a goodwill visit to the US to take the gold away.

Ian Fleming had a lifelong fascination with gold, even to the extent of obtaining a gold-plated typewriter in 1952.

For Your Eyes Only

Publication date 11 April 1960, 252 pages, cover Richard Chopping. Collection of five short stories, outlined below:

From a View to a Kill

This story was originally conceived as an earlier tale about Hugo Drax, who appears in *Moonraker*. This would have been part of his background during the Second World War as a motorbike assassin in the Ardennes. It was largely based on elements of Operation Tracer in Gibraltar, and Peter Fleming's work with the Auxiliary Units, in preparation for a German invasion in 1940. There are also attacks by both sides on dispatch riders, which was perfected by SOE. Bond even refers to some of this in the story where he foils Soviet attacks on NATO dispatch riders. It is the only time Fleming's Bond rides a motorbike, in this case a BSA M20.

For Your Eyes Only

This is set on the US–Canadian border, with elements of Fleming's visit to Canada in 1944 and his later holidays at Ivar Bryce's Black Hollow Farm in Vermont. The villain von Hammerstein is a former Gestapo man. Colonel Johns RCMP served with Monty (General Montgomery) in the Ardennes. Bond assassinates von Hammerstein in revenge for killing M's friends, the Havelocks, in Jamaica.

Quantum of Solace

Not a Secret Service story. Bond is told a story of love and betrayal by the Governor of the Bahamas when he attends a dinner at Government House. With a twist on the title, when consideration from one of the partners to the other dies in a relationship the governor says he has 'invented a rather high-sounding title for this basic factor in human relations. I have called it the Law of the Quantum of Solace'.

Risico

This was inspired by Commander Lionel Crabb's time in Venice clearing German mines at the end of the war, for which he was awarded the George Medal. Enrico Colombo, a gangster, helps Bond destroy a rival gang run by Kristatos, who is supposed to be a CIA agent but in fact is running a drugs ring backed by the Soviets. Colombo was based on Lucky Luciano, the Mafia boss who ensured Atlantic convoys were not sabotaged by the Dockers Union. Fleming covered this while he was at NID.

The Hildebrand Rarity

More a murder mystery than spy story, whereby Bond meets Milton Krest, an obnoxious American millionaire, and his wife and they set off on his motor cruiser *Wavekrest* looking for rare fish. Bond finds Krest dead with one of the rare fish stuffed in his mouth, a Hildebrand Rarity. He throws him overboard, making it look like he fell to draw attention away from the wife and her possible lover, one of whom killed him.

Thunderball

Publication date 27 March 1961, 253 pages, cover Richard Chopping. Title taken from US military personnel witnessing atomic bomb tests describing the fireball and mushroom cloud. Dedication: 'To Ernest Cuneo Muse.'

Bond's first encounter with SPECTRE, headed by the villain Ernst Stavro Blofeld. Another character with his roots set in the Second World War, he has worked for the Abwehr but, when things turn against the Germans, works for the Americans. He amasses a fortune and, with the war ending, slips off to South America. Now he wants to become the greatest criminal of all time. Fleming even gave him his own birthday, 28 May 1908. SPECTRE is thought to have been based on the Switz Gang, a Soviet-backed organisation centred on Paris in the 1930s.

The leader, American Robert Gordon Switz, was arrested by the French Secret Service in 1933 on spying charges, which was more akin to industrial espionage, along with twenty-nine others including the Romanian Octave Dumoulin. Later, the American Arvid Jacobson was arrested in Finland as part of the same Soviet-backed group.

Bond tangles with Emilio Largo, Blofeld's lieutenant, who is one of the better looking of Fleming's villains. A Roman, his name is taken from Key Largo, south of Miami. The plot centres on the stealing of a Vindicator bomber (a Vulcan is used in the film) with its nuclear bombs, to hold the world to ransom. Largo then uses this motor yacht, the *Disco Volante*, to recover and move the bombs.

Fleming took a lot of inspiration from the exploits of the Italian Naval Commandos X MAS. Even *Olterra*, the ship the Italian frogmen used as a base from which to attack shipping in Gibraltar, is mentioned in the book. Commander Lionel Crabb was another aspect used. His loss in April 1956 while examining the hull of the Soviet cruiser *Ordzhonikidze* would have been fresh in Fleming's mind.

Giuseppe Petacchi, the pilot who steals the Vindicator after the crew are poisoned, is given a detailed Second World War background. He serves in the Italian Air Force seconded to the Luftwaffe and steals a Focke-Wulf Fw 200, which he delivers to the Allies complete with the new German pressure mines after shooting the crew. After the war he stays in the Air Force but his expensive tastes make him easy prey for SPECTRE.

The Spy Who Loved Me

Publication date 16 April 1962, 198 pages, cover Richard Chopping. The book has been described as not a secret service thriller. Fleming later explained that he wrote this book to show Bond in a bad light to discourage his younger readers from making him a hero.

The heroine Vivienne Michel, a Canadian, returns to Canada disillusioned with Europe after some failed relationships. She sets out on a road trip on a Vespa scooter to Florida but gets no further than the Dreamy Pines Motor Court in New York State. There she witnesses and helps Bond deal with some gangsters.

Fleming visited Quebec in 1944 for a conference, so he knew the area through which Michel travels. Given his attention to detail, it is likely he travelled much of her route.

On Her Majesty's Secret Service

Publication date 1 April 1963, 288 pages, cover Richard Chopping. Dedication: 'For Sable Basilisk Pursuivant and Hilary Bray who came to the aid of the party.'

The plot centres on the Schloss Mittersill, a sporting club in the Austrian Alps. In 1940 the Nazis took over the club. It was then used to study inferior Asiatic races and to store human parts in the guise of scientific research to show the superiority of Hitler's Aryan race. Fleming changed the name to Piz Gloria. Since *Thunderball*, Bond has been trying to find Blofeld for a year. Marc-Ange Draco, head of the Unione Corse, the French Mafia, agrees to help Bond if he will help his daughter Tracy di Vicenzo, who has suicidal tendencies. Bond tracks down Blofeld to the Piz Gloria and finds out he is trying to use a biological agent against Britain. Bond destroys the base but Blofeld escapes. Bond marries Tracy but she is killed when they set off on their honeymoon and their car is ambushed by Blofeld.

Other Second World War references include the mention of M's ship HMS *Repulse*, his last sea-going command. Admiral Godfrey commanded *Repulse*, the battlecruiser that was sunk by the Japanese in 1941. Rommel's gold is mentioned, which is thought to lie in the sea near Corsica. The gold was looted in North Africa and sent back to Europe in a submarine that sank. Fleming had personal experience of avalanches when he was in Austria in the 1930s.

You Only Live Twice

Publication date 16 March 1964, 255 pages, cover Richard Chopping. Dedication: 'To Richard Hughes and Tarao Saito But for whom etc.'

After the death of Tracy, Bond suffers depression and M sends him to Japan to snap him out of it. His mission is to try and obtain Japanese help in decoding Soviet radio traffic with their Magic 44 system. They agree but only if Bond kills a mysterious Dr Shatterhand, who runs a 'Garden of Death' for suicides. Bond recognises Shatterhand as Blofeld, whose wife Bunt is with him. He infiltrates their castle, kills Blofeld and the castle explodes; Bond is injured and suffers amnesia.

The main Second World War content is that Tiger Tanaka, the head of the Japanese Secret Service who works with Bond, was a former Kamikaze pilot and once an aid to Admiral Ohnishi. Reprieved by Hiroshima, he really regrets not going on that final mission and being part of the 'Divine Wind'. It often feels like he is back fighting the war. Bond sympathises as he also is 'haunted by the forest of memory'.

Commander James Bond CMG, RNVR's *Times* obituary is in the book, which says he had 'the Nelson touch'. However, it says little about his service as it is covered by the Official Secrets Act.

The Man with the Golden Gun

Publication date 1 April 1965, 221 pages, cover Richard Chopping. Published posthumously, manuscript polished by Kingsley Amis, although his suggestions were not used. He would write the first non-Fleming Bond book, *Colonel Sun*, in 1968.

Bond returns from Vladivostok brainwashed by the KGB and tries to kill M with a poison spray pistol. However, he is restored to health and turned against the Soviets. He is sent to Jamaica to assassinate Francisco 'Pistols' Scaramanga, a SMERSH agent who has been killing SIS men in the Caribbean using the Golden Gun, a long-barrelled, single-action Colt. 45.

Mary Goodnight has been posted to Kingston, so Bond comes across one of his old flames. She is possibly based on Clare Blanchard. Also, Fleming uses the name Hugill for one of the characters, harking back to John Hugill from 30AU and NID.

Octopussy and The Living Daylights

Publication date 23 June 1966, 94 pages, cover Richard Chopping. This book contained two short stories. (The later edition also had the short stories *The Property of a Lady* and *007 in New York*.)

Octopussy

This has major Second World War content. Former Commando Major Dexter Smythe RM obtained two bars of Nazi gold at the end of the war while working for the Miscellaneous Objectives Bureau in the Austrian Alps. However, in so doing he killed his guide, Hannes Oberhauser, who led him to the gold's location. Years later the body is found and Bond comes looking for Smythe, who is living on Jamaica. Rather than face justice, Smythe commits suicide via the sting of the scorpion fish and his pet octopus begins to eat him. Bond's interest lies in Oberhauser, who years before the war taught him to ski.

The Living Daylights (Original title: Trigger Finger)

Bond is sent to Berlin to cover an escape, which has been set up, covering the border area using his sniper skills. A Soviet sniper is ready to kill the escapee, but when Bond sees it is a beautiful woman through the telescopic sight he shoots the butt of her rifle instead of killing her.

The story was inspired by Pat Reid's *Escape from Colditz Castle*.

OTHER WRITERS OF BOND BOOKS AND THEIR BOOKS

Kingsley Amis

Glidrose Publications, publishers of the James Bond novels, first approached James Leasor to write a continuation novel but he declined. Kingsley Amis agreed and wrote *Colonel Sun* under the pseudonym of Robert Markham. *Colonel Sun* was published in March 1968 by Jonathan Cape. The book received good reviews and sold well. Amis also wrote the non-fiction book *The James Bond Dossier* in 1965.

John Pearson

In 1973 Glidrose allowed John Pearson, who had written a biography of Ian Fleming, to publish *James Bond: The Authorised Biography of 007*. Written in the first person, James Bond tells his own story, and it was Fleming that made him famous by embellishing his career.

Christopher Wood

In 1977, Eno Production got Christopher Wood to write a book based on their film, *James Bond: The Spy Who Loved Me*, due to the stark contrast between the film and original book. The same was done with *James Bond: Moonraker* in 1979, in which a character is called Hugo Drax. Both were published by Jonathan Cape and received favourably.

John Gardner

Sixteen Bond novels were written by the prolific author John Gardner. Two, like Wood, were novelisations of Eno Productions, *Licence to Kill* and *GoldenEye*.

Gardner did see action in the Second World War; he served in the Fleet Air Arm before transferring to the Royal Marine Commandos. He was with 42 Commando in the Far East but considered himself 'the worst Commando in the world'.

He wrote mainly thrillers and created his own spy, Boysie Oakes, writing eight books about him. He brought Bond into the 1980s and *Licence Renewed*, his first 007 book, was published in 1981. Others were more tuned toward an American audience, with mixed results. In *Licence Renewed* he even has Bond driving a Saab 900 Turbo, after the character's previous loyalty to British cars, although Fleming himself loved American cars. Gardner's bringing Bond into the modern age met with mixed results. In 1996 he stopped writing due to ill health.

Raymond Benson

The American author Raymond Benson took up the 007 mantle in 1997 after Gardner. He had already written *The James Bond Bedside Companion* in 1984. He followed Gardner's model in bringing Bond up to date. Most reviewers looked on his work favourably. Also, he did restore to Bond a British car, a Jaguar XK8. He wrote six novels, three novelisations and three short stories, the last in 2002.

Sebastian Faulks

Ian Fleming Publications approached Lee Child twice but he declined their offers to write a Bond novel. In 2008 Sebastian Faulks accepted and he produced *Devil May Care*. He returned Bond to the 1960s and put him behind the wheel of a battleship-grey 1967 T series Bentley. He was true to the Fleming background.

Jeffery Deaver

The next to be commissioned was the American author Jeffery Deaver, who produced *Carte Blanche* in 2011.

This book returned Bond to the modern age.

William Boyd

In 2013 William Boyd's James Bond novel *Solo* was published, in which he returned 007 to 1969, when, observing the timeline, he made him 45. It took him eighteen months to write the book and there was some friction with the Fleming estate over the character of Bond. *Solo* received mixed reviews, although it sold well.

In Boyd's 2002 novel *Any Human Heart*, the hero Logan Mountstuart is recruited into NID by Ian Fleming. He is given the job to monitor the Duke and Duchess of Windsor.

Anthony Horowitz

In 2015, *Trigger Mortis* was published by Orion, in which Horowitz returns Bond to 1957. The story is set two weeks after *Goldfinger*. It also featured previously unpublished Ian Fleming material. He used *Murder on Wheels* as Chapter 7, in which Bond drives in a grand prix, which to his credit worked seamlessly. *Trigger Mortis* received mainly good reviews.

In 2018, Horowitz's second Bond novel, *Forever and a Day*, was published by Jonathan Cape, Fleming's old publisher. A prequel to *Casino Royale*, set in 1950, again he was able to use unpublished Fleming material. This book also received good reviews, one finding it 'fiendishly inventive'.

Young Bond

A series of Young Bond novels were published in 2005–17 for younger readers. They were written by Charlie Higson, Kevin Walker and Stephen Cole.

NOTES

United Kingdom National Archive References, Kew.

Admiralty Records
ADM/196/62   Officers' service records [WWI].
ADM/196/147   Officers' service records.
ADM/223/213/214 30 Assault Unit, operations & history of the unit.
ADM/223/464/463 Naval Intelligence Department history & Operation Tracer.
ADM/223/480/481 Naval Intelligence Department & SOE.
ADM/223/490   Naval Intelligence Department Portugal, Spain & Operation
        Golden Eye.
ADM/223/478   Naval Intelligence Department Reports & NID deception.
ADM/223/500   Naval Intelligence Department & 30AU.
ADM/223/794   Naval Intelligence Department operational intelligence.

SOE
HS/6/970   SOE Agents in Spain.
HS/6/987   SOE relations with Portugal.
HS/6/976   Shipping in Spain.

Security Services
KV/2/845/846   Tricycle (Dusko Popov) in Portugal.
KV/2/1685   SIS/MI6 German Files Rudolf Hess.
KV/4/185-186   Policy Files (Liddell diary).
HW/4   Government Code & Cipher School Far East HMS *Anderson*.

Foreign Office
FO/371/26565-26566   Flight of Rudolf Hess.
FO/371/55930   Albrecht Haushofer & Rudolf Hess.

The following abbreviations have been used:
Central Intelligence Agency Library/OSS CIAL
Cambridge Churchill Archives Centre CCAC
Imperial War Museum IWM
National Archives (USA) US/NA
The National Archives KEW (UK) TNA

All references to Ian Fleming's Bond books are taken from the Penguin Modern Classics editions, unless otherwise stated.

Introduction

1   Ian Fleming, *From Russia with Love*, p. 95. 'The blubbery arms ...'
2   Ian Fleming, *Casino Royale*, p. 181. 'This is 007 ...'
3   Duff Hart-Davis, *Peter Fleming*, p. 329. 'Once again ...'
4   BBC Radio Interview, Ian Fleming and Raymond Chandler, 1958.

Chapter 1 Lunch at the Carlton Grill

1   Patrick Beesly, *Very Special Admiral*, p. 95. '*Repulse* was due ...'
2   Ian Fleming, *On Her Majesty's Secret Service*, Chapter 20, M En Pantoufles, p. 190. 'These thoughts ran ...'
3   Donald McLachlan, *Room 39*, p. 13. 'All that was ...'
4   Ibid., p. 14. 'Godfrey decided ...'
5   Beesly, p. 4. 'Like his brothers ...'
6   Ibid., p. 39. 'When he returned ...'
7   Ibid., pp. 38–39. 'On the way ...'
8   David Ramsay, *Blinker Hall*, p. 18. 'Physically, Hall ...'
9   McLachlan, pp. 17–18. 'However, none of this ...'
10   John Pearson, *The Life of Ian Fleming*, pp. 103–104. 'When Admiral Godfrey ...'
11   Hart-Davis, p. 354. 'His loyalty was ...'
12   Pearson, p. 28. 'It was three ...'
13   Original blurb on the cover of *Casino Royale* 1953 starting: 'Ian Fleming is 44, ...'
14   Ian Fleming, *You Only Live Twice*, Chapter 21, Obit., p. 200.
15   Hart-Davis, p. 51. 'The odd thing ...'
16   Andrew Lycett, *Ian Fleming*, p. 22. 'Having qualified ...'
17   Ibid., p. 27. 'Ian still refused ...'
18   Hart-Davis, p. 55. 'Peter went to ...'
19   Pearson, pp. 37–38. 'On the surface ...'
20   Ian Fleming, *Thrilling Cities*, p. 189. 'I remember ...'
21   Pearson, p. 46. 'During the first year ...'
22   Fleming, *Casino Royale*, Chapter 5, The Girl From Headquarters, p. 30. 'Bond's car was ...'
23   Pearson, p. 48. 'Arnold remembers ...'

24 Ian Fleming, *Moonraker*, Chapter 20, Drax's Gambit, pp. 195–197. 'Drax took the ...'
25 Pearson, p. 49. 'During his early ...'
26 Fleming, *On Her Majesty's Secret Service*, Chapter 17, Bloody Snow, p. 162. 'The ground shook ...'
27 Pearson, p. 59. 'His Majesty's ...'
28 Lycett, p. 52. 'Luckily for Ian ...'
29 Ibid., p. 52. 'The editor-in-chiefs ...'
30 Ibid., p. 52. 'To reach Munich ...'
31 Ibid., p. 53. 'On the last ...'
32 Donald Healey, *My World of Cars*, p. 52. 'On one of the ...'
33 Lycett, p. 57. 'Ian's itinerary ...'
34 Pearson, pp. 61–62. 'Night-falls ...'
35 Fergus Fleming, *The Man with the Golden Typewriter*, p. 4. 'He later joined ...'
36 Lycett, p. 59. 'The caviar took its ...'
37 Ibid., p. 63. 'Ian was deeply ...'
38 Ben Macintyre, *For Your Eyes Only*, p. 40. 'Fleming's distinctive ...'
39 Pearson, p. 83. 'In fact ...'
40 Lycett, p. 97. 'After five days ...'
41 Ibid., p. 97. 'Back in London ...'
42 Pearson, p. 102. 'Not that Fleming ...'
43 Ibid., pp. 105–106. 'A few days after ...'

Chapter 2 Naval Intelligence Division, 1912–39

1 Ramsay, p. 177. 'In his unpublished ...'
2 Ibid., p. 178. 'Because of this ...'
3 Ibid., p. 43. 'Tyron selected ...'
4 Ibid., p. 45. 'In 1909 ...'
5 Barbara Tuchman, *The Zimmermann Telegram*, pp. 9–10. 'Before the sun ...'
6 Franz von Papen, *Memoirs*, p. 30. 'On my return ...'
7 Paul Gammon, *Inside Room 40*, p. 27. 'One military ...'
8 Ibid., p. 36. 'No time ...'
9 Ibid., p. 33. 'According to ...'
10 Ibid., p. 38. 'Even in August ...'
11 Ibid., p. 39. 'Churchill described ...'
12 Ramsay, p. 32. 'Four days later ...'
13 Gammon, p. 41. 'Although the naval ...'
14 Ibid., p. 43. 'With the return ...'
15 Patrick Beesly, *Very Special Intelligence*, pp. 1–2. 'Room 40's activities ...'
16 Ramsay, pp. 75–76. 'Had instructed ...'
17 Ibid., p. 76. 'On 13 March ...'
18 Ibid., pp. 76–77. 'Hall immediately ...'
19 Ibid., p. 77. 'Hall had kept ...'
20 Ibid., p. 125. 'At the Naval ...'
21 Ibid., p. 126. 'When Hall examined ...'
22 Christopher Andrew, *Secret Service*, p. 114. 'Through Hall's ...'
23 Ramsay, pp. 130–132. 'The episode ...'

24   Andrew, pp. 114–115. 'Through Hall's …'
25   Ramsay, p. 133. 'On April 9 …'
26   Andrew, pp. 246–247. 'After investigating …'
27   Ibid., p. 247. 'Hall probably …'
28   Ramsay, p. 136. 'Evidence suggests …'
29   Philip Vickers, *Finding Thoroton*, p. 64. 'His first move …'
30   Ibid., p. 61. 'Also in 1915 …'
31   Andrew, p. 116. 'Within Spain itself …'
32   Vickers, p. 84. 'From this it …'
33   Andrew, p. 116. 'Mason sometimes …'
34   Vickers, p. 99. 'In his book …' & p. 106. 'On several occasions …'
35   Ibid., pp. 104–105. 'Thoroton's commentary …' Report No. 7 24/10/16.
36   Andrew, p. 117. 'Hall's Spanish …'
37   TNA/HW 3/6 & Ramsay, p. 162. 'W.F. Clarke …'
38   TNA/HW 3/6, 3/177.
39   Andrew, pp. 93–94. 'The very success …'
40   Penelope Fitzgerald, *The Knox Brothers*, p. 126. 'Under his …'
41   Ibid., p. 127. 'You needed I.D.25 …'
42   Ramsay, p. 190. 'Hall wrote …'
43   US/NA.
44   Andrew, p. 109. 'Hall almost …'
45   Ramsay, p. 193. 'On the following …'
46   Andrew, pp. 110–111. 'For over …'
47   Ibid., p. 112. 'The Zimmermann …'
48   Ibid., p. 113. 'Hall was …'
49   Lycett, p. 112. 'According to Minshall's …'
50   Ramsay, p. 222. 'Wellington famously …'
51   Ibid., p. 283. 'In one other …'
52   Gammon, pp. 244–245. 'A memo preserved …'
53   Ramsay, p. 301. 'The Division's …'
54   Beesly, *Very Special Intelligence*, p. 9. 'For most …'
55   Ibid., pp. 9–10. 'He had good …'
56   McLachlan, p. 55. 'What specially …'
57   Ibid., p. 56. 'The Munich …'
58   Beesly, pp. 1–18. 'Munich finally …'

Chapter 3 The Phoney War

1   McLachlan, p. 1. 'To pay a call …'
2   Ibid., p. 61. 'For 18 months …'
3   Ibid., p. 2. 'For the man …'
4   Lycett, p. 101. 'So it was …'
5   McLachlan, p. 8. 'If not the …'
6   Anthony Cave Brown, *'C'*, p. 13. 'With the death …'
7   Andrew Cook, *Ace of Spies*, pp. 285–87. 'Documents purporting …'
8   Ibid., p. 139. 'Sinclair was …'
9   Keith Jeffery, *MI6*, p. 328. 'The sixty-six …'

10 Brown, p. 13. 'Sinclair's death …'
11 Jeffery, pp. 328–329. 'Despite Sinclair's efforts …'
12 TNA/KV4/185 Liddell diary 24/11/1939.
13 Walter Schellenberg, *The Memoirs of Hitler's Spymaster*, p. 83. 'Further information …'
14 Ibid., p. 85. 'Captain Best …'
15 Ibid., pp. 85–86. 'The British …'
16 Brown, p. 215. 'Afterwards Best claimed …'
17 Ibid., pp. 218–219. 'Hitler's second …'
18 Schellenberg, p. 94. 'I had taken …'
19 Ibid., pp. 99–100. 'On November 11 …'
20 Jeffery, p. 383. 'But if Stevens …'
21 Ibid., p. 385. 'Beyond the wider …'
22 Brown, pp. 221–222. 'Churchill tried …'
23 Beesly, *Very Special Admiral*, p. 123. 'All three tasks …'
24 McLachlan, p. 9. 'Fleming suffered not …'
25 Beesly, pp. 138–139. 'Even further removed …'
26 Lycett, pp. 108–109. 'This stimulated …'
27 Pearson, p. 116. 'A lot …'
28 Ibid., p. 115. 'This idea of …'
29 Ian Fleming, *For Your Eyes Only (From a View to a Kill)*, pp. 32–33. 'Now from the direction …'
30 Ibid., p. 37. 'It was another …'
31 Beesly, p. 143. 'A country which …'
32 Winston Churchill, *The Second World War, Vol. 2: Their Finest Hour*, p. 412. 'The attitude of …'
33 TNA/ADM 223/490. 'It would be …'
34 Beesly, p. 144. 'The A1 Spanish …'
35 Merlin Minshall, *Guilt Edged*, pp. 138–140. 'Before trying …'
36 Ibid., p. 20. 'I find it …'
37 *The Times*, 23 September 1987.
38 North American Singer Owners Club.
39 Ian Fleming, *Thunderball*, Chapter 5, SPECTRE, p. 47. 'And now Ernst …'
40 Minshall, pp. 102–104. 'The official …'
41 Ibid., pp. 69–70. (The British naval attaché in Budapest told him [Minshall] that Lisa Kaltenbrunner was an Abwehr agent and he had got her into Austria prior to the Anschluss.)
42 Ibid., p. 142. 'Did you say …'
43 Ibid., p. 207. 'Admiral Godfrey …'
44 TNA/ADM 223/213 26/3/1942.
45 Minshall, p. 153. 'Yet the cool …'
46 Hart-Davis, pp. 221–224. 'Peter did not …'
47 Ibid., p. 227. 'Unshakable though …'
48 Ibid., p. 229. 'Dear Mr Dawson …'
49 Ibid., p. 231. 'Norway was a …'
50 Ibid., p. 232. 'Everything about …'
51 Ibid., pp. 232–233. 'After dark …'

Chapter 4 Find the Admiral

1   IWM-No. 7183 Private papers Lt-Commander A.F. Whinney, pp. 18–19.
2   Ibid., p. 69.
3   Ibid., p. 60.
4   Ibid., p. 24.
5   Beesly, pp. 157–158. 'On another occasion ...'
6   IWM-No. 7183 Whinney, p. 47.
7   Jeffery, pp. 199–200. 'From the mid-1920s ...'
8   Ian Fleming, *Goldfinger*, Chapter 6, Talk of Gold, p. 61. 'Colonel Smithers eyes ...'
9   *Daily Telegraph* Naval obituaries, 10 June 2006.
10 Ian Fleming, *Goldfinger*, Chapter 6, Talk of Gold, p. 54. 'Commander Bond ...'
11 Geoffrey Cox, *Countdown to War*, pp. 197–199. 'By Saturday ...'
12 Ibid., p. 186. 'Never was Paris ...'
13 Ian Fleming, *Thrilling Cities*, p. 161. 'Every capital city ...'
14 Ian Fleming, *For Your Eyes Only* (*From a View to a Kill*), p. 9. 'Sitting in Fouquet's ...'
15 Kingsley Amis, *The James Bond Dossier*, p. 76. 'Where Mr Fleming ...'
16 IWM-No. 23941 Private papers Commander M. Mackenzie, p. 10.
17 IWM-No. 8489 Private papers Nurse Miss R. Andrew.
18 IWM-No. 7183 Whinney, p. 73.
19 Cox, p. 203. 'The rest of the road ...'
20 Pearson, p. 119. 'By the time ...'
21 Beesly, *Very Special Admiral*, pp. 157–158. 'The very heavy ...'
22 Ian Fleming, *Goldfinger*, Chapter 7, Thoughts in a DBIII, p. 69. 'The car was ...'
23 Ibid., Chapter 12, Long Tail on a Ghost, pp. 135–136. 'At eleven-forty-five ...'
24 Ibid., Chapter 12, Long Tail on a Ghost, p. 140. 'Bond motored ...'
25 Cox, pp. 202–203. 'For miles we ...'
26 Pearson, p. 118. 'This was practically ...'
27 IWM-No. 23941 Mackenzie, p. 10.
28 IWM-No. 7183 Whinney, pp. 81–82.
29 Lycett, p. 116. 'Having finally accomplished ...'
30 IWM-No. 7183 Whinney, p. 82.
31 Ian Fleming, *Diamonds are Forever*, Chapter 25, The Pipeline Closes, p. 225.
    'Down among the ...'
32 IWM-No. 8489 Andrew, p. 3 & *Sunday Times*.
33 IWM-No. 7183 Whinney, pp. 90–91.
34 Churchill, p. 197. 'The edition of the French ...'
35 Ibid., p. 195. 'For the rest ...'
36 Major General I.S.O. Playfair, *The Mediterranean and Middle East Vol. 2*, p. 136.
    'At times it seemed ...'

Chapter 5 Operation Golden Eye

1   Neill Lochery, *Lisbon*, p. 43. 'Initial estimates ...'
2   Samuel Hoare, *Ambassador on Special Mission*, p. 18. 'Once again my ...'
3   Pearson, p. 112. 'It would be ...'
4   IWM-No. 23941 Mackenzie, pp. 11–12. No. 7183 Whinney pp. 111–113. No. 8489
    Andrew, p. 5.

5   Duff Hart-Davis, *Man of War*, p. 70. 'In the autumn ...'
6   Ibid., p. 79. 'He was placed ...'
7   TNA/ADM 196/147.
8   Hart-Davis, pp. 77–78. 'I, Alan Hugh ...' & *The Times*, 3 September 1926.
9   Ibid., p. 136. 'The novel was ...'
10   CCAC/Godfrey Papers GBR/0014/GDFY/1, 5.
11   Hart-Davis, p. 203. 'After flying to ...'
12   Ibid., p. 203. 'One of the brightest ...'
13   Macintyre, pp. 170–171. 'In some ways ...'
14   TNA/ADM 233/490.
15   Ibid.
16   TNA/SOE HS9/61.
17   Lycett, p. 123. 'Ian himself ...'
18   Pearson, p. 128. 'It began in ...' (The single page courier's passport was sold at Sotheby's in 2000 for £15,525.)
19   Ian Fleming, *From Russia with Love*, Chapter 13, BEA Takes you There, p. 113. 'Q Branch had ...'
20   Maurice Harvey, *Gibraltar*, pp. 140–141. 'Gibraltar was fortunate ...'
21   Ian Fleming, *Dr No*, Chapter 13, Mink-Lined Prison, pp. 137–138. 'Bond answered ...'
22   TNA/ADM 223/490.
23   Paul Bowles, *Too Far from Home*, p. 314.
24   Warner Brothers, *Casablanca*, 1942.
25   TNA/ADM 223/490 757/48/N 17/4 & 29/4/41.
26   Ian Fleming, *Diamonds are Forever*, Chapter 14, We Don't Like Mistakes, pp. 124–125. '"Okay," Leiter pushed ...'
27   Hoare, p. 82. 'As a result ...'
28   TNA/ADM 223/490 24/4/41.
29   TNA/ADM 223/490 17/4/41.
30   McLachlan, p. 227. 'So Donovan was ...'
31   Alex Danchev, *Establishing the Anglo-American Alliance*, p. 62. 'Donovan came around ...'
32   Ibid., p. 61. 'A local gale ...'
33   Ibid., p. 62. 'Quare had made ...'
34   TNA/ADM 223/490.
35   Danchev, p. 62. 'I sat with ...'
36   TNA/ADM 223/480 3/4/41.
37   Hart-Davis, p. 207. 'Alan himself ...'
38   TNA/ADM 223/490.
39   TNA/SOE HS 6/970.
40   Alan Hillgarth, *The Role of the Naval Attaché*, 1946.
41   Ibid., *Relations with SIS and SOE*.
42   Jeffery, p. 404. 'There was some ...'
43   Ibid., pp. 404–405. 'What then happened ...'
44   Ian Fleming, *Goldfinger*, Chapter 1, Reflections in a Double Bourbon, p. 4. 'Bond looked down ...'
45   Jeffery, p. 405. 'There was some ...'
46   Ibid., pp. 404–405. 'But it was ...'

47 Ibid., pp. 406–407. 'The second affair …'
48 Hart-Davis, p. 221. 'He claimed he …'
49 TNA/ADM 223/490.
50 Ibid.
51 Ibid., 7 April 1941.
52 Ibid.
53 Lycett, p. 125. 'Golden Eye proved …'

Chapter 6 Operation Ruthless

1   Noble Frankland & Christopher Dowling, *Decisive Battles of the Twentieth Century*, p. 121. 'On the 15 August …'
2   Peter Fleming, *Invasion 1940*, p. 252. 'Planning for the …'
3   Ibid., p. 298. 'The foregoing chapters …'
4   Churchill, p. 472. 'A far graver …'
5   TNA/ADM 223/464, p. 38.
6   Ibid., p. 39.
7   Ibid., p. 39.
8   Ian Fleming, *Thunderball*, Chapter 5, SPECTRE, p. 47. 'And now Ernst …'
9   Mark Simmons, *Agent Cicero*, p. 102. 'It was certainly …'
10 Ian Fleming, *Thunderball*, Chapter 5, SPECTRE, p. 44. 'The man's name …'
11 Ibid., Chapter 13, My Name is Emilio Largo, p. 143. 'Same as you …'
12 Ibid., Chapter 5, SPECTRE, p. 50. 'The founder …' & Chapter 7, Fasten Your Lap Strap, p. 70. 'The aircraft was …'
13 Ibid., Chapter 9, Multiple Requiem, p. 85. 'Giuseppe Petacchi …'
14 www.navweops.com
15 Ian Fleming, *Thunderball*, Chapter 9, Multiple Requiem, p. 86. 'But he was …'
16 Ibid., p. 88. 'They had said …'
17 Ibid., pp. 93–94. 'Now No 1's …'
18 Ibid., Chapter 8, Big Fleas Have Little Fleas, p. 77. 'M looked …'
19 Ian Fleming, *Casino Royale*, Chapter 5, The Girl from Headquarters, p. 34. 'She did not …'
20 Ian Fleming, *Moonraker*, Chapter 14, Itching Fingers, p. 130. 'Commander Bond …'
21 Ian Fleming, *You Only Live Twice*, Chapter 21, Obit, p. 200. 'The Times …'
22 Marshall Pugh, *Commander Crabb*, p. 159. 'It has been …'
23 Ian Fleming, *Thunderball*, Chapter 16, Swimming the Gauntlet, p. 175. 'Now he swam …'
24 Peter Wright, *Spycatcher*, pp. 72–73. 'The Soviet Leaders …'
25 Pugh, p. 160. 'Commander Crabb …'
26 Ibid., p. 163. 'He would …'
27 Ibid., p. 160. 'When time passed …'
28 Wright, p. 74. 'A thankful John Henry …'
29 Pugh, pp. 165–166. 'On the 14 May …'
30 Ian Fleming, *The Man with the Golden Gun*, Chapter 2, Attentat!, p. 22. 'They were …'
31 Jonathan Haslam, *Near and Distant Neighbours*, p. 178. 'Inevitably improvisation …'
32 Matthew Parker, *Goldeneye*, p. 213. 'Predictably, there were …'
33 *The Independent*, 4 January 2006.

34 John le Carré, *Call for the Dead* (Lamplighter edition, 1992) & Adam Sisman, *John le Carré*, p. 208. 'The second novel …'

35 Pearson, p. 236. 'There are plenty …'

Chapter 7 The Hess Affair, May 1941

1   TNA/WO 167/806 Oxfordshire & Buckinghamshire Light Infantry.

2   Hart-Davis, *Peter Fleming*, pp. 237–238. 'For him by …'

3   Jeffery, p. 353. 'Over the summer …'

4   Ibid., p. 353. 'Jebb was …'

5   TNA/ADM 223/480 3/4/41.

6   Mark Simmons, *Ian Fleming & Operation Golden Eye*, p. 105. 'It came …'

7   TNA/ADM 223/490 3/4/41.

8   TNA/ADM 223/464.

9   Beesly, *Very Special Admiral*, pp. 111–112. 'Satisfied that he …'

10 Ian Fleming, *The Man with the Golden Gun*, Chapter 1, Can I Help You? p. 10. 'James Bond frowned …'

11 Ian Fleming, *On Her Majesty's Secret Service*, Chapter 20, M En Pantoufles, p. 190. 'These thoughts ran …'

12 Brian Lett, *Ian Fleming and SOE's Operation Postmaster*, pp. 18–21. 'Colin Gubbins was …'

13 Christopher Andrew, *MI5*, p. 217. 'During the first …'

14 Derek Tangye, *The Way to Minack*, pp. 163–164. 'Yet I had …'

15 Anthony Masters, *The Man Who was M*, p. 158. 'Fleming knew the …'

16 Hart-Davis, p. 219. 'At the end …'

17 Peter Fleming, *The Flying Visit*, p. 78. 'He began to …'

18 Peter Padfield, *Hess, Hitler & Churchill*, pp. 38–39. 'One of my first …'

19 Lynn Picknett, Clive Prince, & Stephen Prior, *Double Standards*, pp. 142–143. 'Common sense dictates …'

20 Bodleian Papers Oxford, Lord Simon interview transcript, 9 June 1941.

21 Padfield, p. 83. 'This was noticed …'

22 Andrew, *MI5*, p. 225. 'Anna Wolkoff was …'

23 Masters, p. 158. 'Ironically, Sir Barry …'

24 TNA/INF 1/192 1500 28.

25 TNA/KV/2/1685, Dec, 57A.

26 TNA/FO 371/26542 C1118/324/18.

27 Sir Hughe Knatchbull-Hugessen, *Diplomat in Peace and War*, p. 152. 'Nor did he …'

28 TNA/FO 371/26542 C6101324/18.

29 TNA/FO 371/613141 C2505/324/18F75.

30 John Colville, *The Fringes of Power*, p. 383.

31 Padfield, p. 156. 'This is hugely …'

32 TNA/FO 25/4/41 No. 148 C4613/306/41.

33 Padfield, p. 124. 'The difficulty …'

34 Ibid., p. 340 'The indications over …'

35 Masters, p. 90. 'Knight and Crowley …'

36 Ibid., p. 159. 'But, at first …'

37 Pearson, p. 127. 'All his life …' & Masters, p. 160. 'Once Hess was …'

38 Picknett, Prince, & Prior, p. 297. 'The Admiralty document …'

39   Pearson, p. 128. 'It is a pity …'
40   Ian Fleming, *Casino Royale*, Chapter 10, The High Table, p. 67. 'Bond had just …'
41   Ibid., Chapter 11, Moment of Truth, p. 71. 'Le Chiffre looked …'
42   Martin Booth, *A Magick Life*, p. 10. 'As a child …'
43   Henry Chancellor, *James Bond: The Man and his World*, p. 119. 'One likely …'
44   *Birmingham Mail*, Mike Lockley article, 28 May 2017.
45   Chancellor, p. 119. 'Crowley-the Great Beast …'
46   Ian Fleming, *Thrilling Cities*, p. 59. 'I am not …'
47   Ian Fleming, *Live and Let Die*, Chapter 3, A Visiting Card, p. 23. 'This extraordinary book …'
48   Artemis Cooper, *Patrick Leigh Fermor*, p. 223. 'Paddy became …'
49   Lycett, pp. 85–86. 'Sex inevitably …'
50   Ian Fleming, *Casino Royale*, Chapter 17, My Dear Boy, p. 112. 'Le Chiffre came …'
51   Ibid., p. 113. 'My dear boy …'
52   Ian Fleming, *Books & Bookmen*, May 1963.
53   BBC interview, 13–14 May 1941.
54   Padfield, p. 186. 'Hess went on …'
55   Picknett, Prince, & Prior, p. 229. 'At the end …'
56   TNA/INF 1/912 & Picknett, Prince, & Prior, p. 232. 'It is officially …'
57   Alan Bullock, *Hitler: A Study in Tyranny*, p. 547. 'Hitherto Hitler …'
58   Pearson, p. 128. 'It was a pity …'
59   Andrew, *MI5*, p. 258. 'Through the security …'
60   Brown, p. 308. 'Popov arrived …'
61   Ibid., pp. 309–310. 'Menzies took one …'
62   TNA/KV2/895.
63   KV2/845.
64   Dusko Popov, *Spy Counter Spy*, p. 115. 'I couldn't help …'
65   Padfield, p. 283. 'How Philby obtained …' & Vadim to Moscow, No. 378, 18/5/41; NKVD file No 20566.
66   Ibid., p. 361. 'If so, the answer …'

Chapter 8 Architect of US Intelligence

1   TNA/ADM 223/490.
2   Lochery, p. 126. 'On May 20 …'
3   Ibid., pp. 58–59. 'Lourenço's loyalty …'
4   Pearson, p. 131. 'The reality seems …'
5   Ian Fleming, *Casino Royale*, Chapter 1, The Secret Agent, p. 1. 'The scent and …'
6   Ibid., p. 1. 'James Bond suddenly …'
7   *Sunday Telegraph*, 16 May 1964.
8   KV2/849.
9   Ibid.
10   Popov, p. 125. 'When the Germans …'
11   Ibid., pp. 125–126. 'Then I went …'
12   David & Sybil Eccles, *By Safe Hand*, p. 303. 'My darling love – Ian …'
13   Popov, p. 126. 'I don't know …'

14 Ibid., p. 127. 'Fleming was ...'

15 Ian Fleming, *Casino Royale*, Chapter 12, The Deadly Tube, p. 79. 'Bond swallowed ...'

16 Russell Miller, *Codename Tricycle*, pp. 188–189. 'Plan Midas ...'

17 Popov, p. 125. 'I'm told that ...'

18 Ian Fleming, *Live and Let Die*, Chapter 1, The Red Carpet, p. 1. 'There are ...'

19 Popov, pp. 128–129. 'The big flying ...'

20 Peter Smithers, *Adventures of a Gardener*, p. 19. 'With Lord Lothian ...'

21 Ian Fleming, *Thrilling Cities*, p. 2. 'We climbed on ...'

22 Ibid., *For Your Eyes Only* (*Quantum of Solace*), p. 104. 'James Bond said ...'

23 Ibid., *From Russia with Love*, Chapter 13, BEA Takes you There, pp. 117–118. 'Bond smelt ...'

24 CCAC, Godfrey papers.

25 Pearson, p. 133. 'Fleming was ...'

26 William Stevenson, *A Man Called Intrepid*, p. 270. 'The truth was ...' (This book is not regarded as the most reliable of sources. However in most quotes from it I have cross referenced with other sources.)

27 Ibid., pp. 270–271. 'To Stephenson ...'

28 Ian Fleming, *Casino Royale*, Chapter 20, The Nature of Evil, p. 134. 'Well, in the ...'

29 CCAC, Godfrey papers.

30 Stevenson, p. 235. 'Suppose the Bismarck ...'

31 Kim Philby, *My Silent War*, p. 54. 'Stephenson actually ...'

32 Pearson, p. 132. 'Hoover, a chunky ...'

33 Smithers, p. 20. 'My tiny frame ...'

34 Philby, pp. 53–54. 'Stephenson like ...'

35 Pearson, p. 132. 'However, Hoover ...' & Lycett, p. 129. 'Ian and Godfrey ...'

36 McLachlan, p. 223. 'This was not ...'

37 CCAC, Godfrey papers.

38 Ibid.

39 Beesly, *Very Special Admiral*, p. 183. 'Godfrey makes ...'

40 Ibid., p. 179. 'Before this happened ...'

41 Jeffery, p. 449. 'In his memory ...'

42 Eccles, p. 251. 'Wednesday 2 April ...'

43 Ibid., p. 283. '24 June 1941 ...'

44 Ivar Bryce, *You Only Live Once*, p. 158. 'At that time ...'

45 Bill Macdonald, *The True Intrepid*, p. 48. 'Donovan asked ...'

46 Lycett, p. 131. 'On 18 July ...'

47 Eccles, p. 303. 'He came straight ...'

48 TNA/ADM 223/490 17/4/41 Greenleaves report.

49 Ibid.

50 Ibid.

51 Ibid.

52 Ibid.

53 Ibid.

54 Ibid., 19/8/41.

Chapter 9 Gibraltar

1   Harvey, p. 98. 'Although his north ...'
2   Ladislas Farago, *The Game of Foxes*, p. 559. 'The service action ...'
3   J. Valerio Borghese, *Sea Devils*, pp. 44–45. 'The mission was ...'
4   Ibid., pp. 65–69. 'Report of Gino Birandelli ...'
5   Marc Antonio Bragadin, *The Italian Navy in World War II*, pp. 282–285. 'Even before the attempt ...'
6   TNA/ADM 223/463, p. 268.
7   Ibid.
8   Nigel West, *Historical Dictionary of Naval Intelligence*, p. 213.
9   Royal Geographical Society, *With Scott to the Pole*, p. 62.
10 TNA/ADM 223/463 p. 269 25/1/42.
11 Ian Fleming, *For Your Eyes Only (From a View to a Kill)*, p. 31. 'Bond's breath ...'
12 Hart-Davis, *Peter Fleming*, p. 233. 'Immediately after ...'
13 Peter Fleming, *Invasion 1940*, pp. 269–270. 'He accordingly ...'
14 Ibid., p. 271. 'There were in all ...'
15 Ibid., p. 272. 'The underground ...'
16 Ian Fleming, *For Your Eyes Only (From a View to a Kill)*, pp. 33–34. 'Bond let out ...'
17 Neill Rush, *Operation Tracer – Stay behind cave*, www.aboutourrock.com
18 TNA/ADM 223/463, p. 268.
19 Neill Rush, *Operation Tracer – Stay Behind Cave*, www.aboutourrock.com
20 TNA/ADM 223/463, p. 269.
21 Ibid.
22 McLachlan, p. 61. 'For 18 months ...'
23 *Daily Telegraph* obituary, 3 January 2011.
24 Ibid.
25 TNA/ADM 223/463 p. 270.
26 Bundesarchiv/OKW No. 55455/42 8/3/42.
27 TNA/ADM 223/463, p. 270.
28 Ewen Montagu, *Beyond Top Secret Ultra*, pp. 88–89. 'Another German activity ...'
29 Paul Kemp, *Underwater Warriors*, pp. 40–41. 'But how should ...'
30 Borghese, p. 212. 'At the villa ...'
31 Ibid., p. 128. 'A new name ...'
32 Ibid., p. 214. 'Lieutenant Visintini ...'
33 Ibid., p. 215. 'They included ...'
34 Ian Fleming, *Live and Let Die*, Chapter 18, Beau Desert, pp. 181–182. 'Quarrel cooked ...'
35 Ibid., Chapter 19, Valley of Shadows, pp. 191–194. 'It was while ...'
36 Stevenson, p. 188. 'The land was ...'
37 Pearson, pp. 128–129. 'The training staff ...' & Lycett, p. 149 & Rankin, p. 223 cast some doubt on the story Pearson supports at Camp X.
38 Pugh, p. 13. 'His partner ...'
39 Ibid., pp. 19–20. 'Now that Crabb ...'
40 Ibid., pp. 23–31. 'Each day ...'
41 Ibid., pp. 39–42. 'Commander Handcock ...'
42 Ibid., pp. 123–125. 'There is one reason ...'
43 Royal Navy Submarine Museum & Kemp, p. 46. 'The net had ...'

44   IWM/Sound Records interview with Frank Goldsworthy SR 11245/11.
45   Ibid.
46   Pugh, p. 77. 'On a morning …'
47   Lycett, p. 150. 'The sextant Conference …'
48   Pugh, p. 78. 'In the summer …'
49   Amis, pp. 100–101. 'Every so often …'
50   Lycett, p. 241. 'Once again …'

Chapter 10 Is Your Journey Really Necessary?

1   Lycett, p. 132. 'In the wake …'
2   Ibid., p. 132. 'Godfrey however …'
3   McLachlan, pp. 4–5. 'Not least of …'
4   Robert Harling, *Ian Fleming: A Personal Memoir*, p. 48. 'Fleming arrived …'
5   Ibid., p. ix. 'What I have …'
6   Ibid., pp. 15–16. 'An obliging RN …'
7   Lycett, p. 133. 'Leonard Miall …'
8   Ibid., p. 134. 'Ian's boyish …'
9   Ian Fleming, *Moonraker*, Chapter 19, Missing Person, p. 180. 'Bond sat …'
10   Ian FLeming, *Diamonds are Forever*, Chapter 3, Hot Ice, p. 20. 'Bond's face …'
11   Montagu, pp. 92–93. 'We learned …'
12   David Nutting, *Attain by Surprise*, pp. 13–14. 'That German Unit …'
13   Lycett, p. 136. 'While Ian …'
14   Ian Fleming, *Live and Let Die*, Chapter 17, The Undertaker's Wind, p. 177. 'By the end …'
15   Chancellor, pp. 133–134. 'I think education …'
16   Beesly, *Very Special Intelligence*, pp. 119–121. 'The short cut …'
17   Ibid, p. 123. 'It was a …'
18   Lycett, p. 137. 'Over dinner …'
19   TNA/ADM 223/500.
20   Ian Fleming, *Talk of the Devil*, p. 44. 'The night passed …'
21   Nicholas Rankin, *Ian Fleming's Commandos*, p. 5. 'Straight ahead …'
22   J.C. Beadle, *The Light Blue Lanyard*, p. 26. 'The commando assembled …'
23   Ian Fleming, *Talk of the Devil*, pp. 46–47. 'During this period …'
24   Ibid., p. 51. 'Incidentally, this …'
25   Ibid., pp. 56–57. 'At about 1900 …'
26   TNA/ADM 223/500.
27   Ian Fleming, *Talk of the Devil*, p. 57. 'It had been …'

Chapter 11 Change of Command

1   Ian Fleming, *Talk of the Devil*, p. 57. 'It had been …'
2   Churchill, *The Second World War, Vol. 3: The Grand Alliance*, p. 509. 'We must however …'
3   Lycett, p. 137. 'Ian had little …'
4   TNA/ADM 223/481.
5   IWM/Gubbins Collection 12618.

6   Ian Fleming, *The Man with the Golden Gun*, Chapter 11, Ballcock and other Trouble, p. 125. 'He went and ...'
7   Ian Fleming, *On Her Majesty's Secret Service*, Chapter 15, Heat Increases, p. 143. 'Bond laughed out ...'
8   Jeffery, p. 358. 'Whatever the day ...'
9   Lett, pp. 49–50. 'In fairness ...'
10 Lycett, pp. 141–142. 'As much detailed ...'
11 Beesly, *Very Special Admiral*, pp. 229–230. 'Find that ...'
12 Andrew Browne Cunningham, *A Sailors Odyssey*, p. 458. 'As may be ...'
13 Ibid., pp. 463–464. 'Finally we got ...'
14 Beesly, *Very Special Admiral*, pp. 229–230. 'Godfrey himself ...'
15 Stevenson, pp. 166–167. 'The fascination ...'
16 Lycett, p. 143. 'Cuneo observed ...'
17 Ian Fleming, *Diamonds are Forever*, Chapter 14, We Don't Like Mistakes, p. 120. '"Sure," said Leiter ...'
18 Ibid., Chapter 18, Night Fall on the Passion Pit, p. 151. 'Ernie Cureo's voice ...'
19 Roald Dahl, *Boy & Going Solo*, p. 401. 'I had been ...'
20 Stevenson, pp. 168–169. 'A graphic account ...'
21 Donald Sturrock, *Storyteller*, p. 224. 'Shortly after Dahl ...'
22 Stevenson, p. 169. 'Dahl was ...'
23 Roald Dahl, *Lamb to the Slaughter*, first published by Harpers in 1953. Transmitted as part of *Tales of the Unexpected* by ITV, 14 April 1979.
24 Sturrock, pp. 433–434. 'Dahl's script ...'
25 Smithers, p. 22. 'Now a British ...'
26 Bryce, pp. 69–70. 'A high-level ...'
27 Beesly, *Very Special Intelligence*, pp. 108–109. 'Godfrey had no ...' & McLachlan, p. 238. 'Winn was sent ...'
28 Ian Fleming, *Live and Let Die*, Chapter 9, True or False? p. 83. 'Pennsylvania Station ...' & *Dr No*, Chapter 13, Mink-Lined Prison, p. 136. 'Your name please ...'
29 Ibid., Chapter 8, No Sensayuma, pp. 67–68. 'Mr Big reflected ...'
30 Bryce, pp. 70–71. 'The date arrived ...'
31 Ibid., pp. 71–73. 'In those days ...'
32 Ian Fleming, *Dr No*, Chapter 7, Night Passage, p. 69. 'They were at ...'
33 Bryce, p. 74. 'Our goodbyes ...'
34 Beesly, *Very Special Admiral*, p. 240. 'It might have ...'
35 John Pearson papers interview with Joan Saunders 24/3/65 & Rankin, p. 142.
36 Hart-Davis, *Man of War*, p. 210. 'In the event ...'
37 TNA/ADM 223/490. 'Golden Eye experience ...'
38 Ibid., 25/4/41.
39 Ibid., 20/11/41.

Chapter 12 30AU Get their Knees Brown

1   TNA/ADM 223/463.
2   TNA/ADM 223/214.
3   Pearson, p. 146. 'At this stage ...'
4   Nutting, p. 25. 'After this meeting ...'
5   Ibid., p. 26. 'During the remaining ...'

6   Commando Pocket Manual, p. 120. '1 Explain …'
7   Nutting, p. 26. 'Our small party …'
8   John H. Waller, *The Unseen War in Europe*, p. 252. 'Operation Torch …'
9   Nutting, p. 27. 'On arrival …'
10 John Pearson papers interview with Dunstan Curtis & Rankin pp. 152–153. &
    note p. 359.
11 Nutting, p. 33. 'Under the guidance …'
12 Mavis Batey, *Dilly the Man who Broke Enigma*, p. 189. & Nutting, p. 35.
13 Ian Fleming, *From Russia with Love*, Chapter 12, A Piece of Cake, p. 109.
    'She had a …'
14 Ibid., Chapter 2, The Slaughterer, p. 15. 'It was about …'
15 Ibid., Chapter 20, Orient Express, p. 192. 'Bond reached up …'
16 Chancellor, pp. 96–97. 'The death of …'
17 Churchill, *The Second World War, Vol. 3: The Grand Alliance*, p. 572. 'I regard these …'
18 Brown, pp. 447–449. 'As Giroud came …'
19 Jeffery, pp. 495–496. 'Algiers was the …'
20 Brown, pp. 447–449. 'By mid November …'
21 Ibid., p. 449. 'In what was …'
22 Ibid., p. 451. 'Whatever the …'
23 Ibid., pp. 451–453. 'Coon also admitted …'
24 Raymond Chandler, 'Trouble is my Business', *Dime Detective Magazine*,
    August 1939.
25 Ian Fleming, *Casino Royale*, Chapter 8, Pink Lights and Champagne, p. 51.
    'He stripped the …'
26 Lett, p. 156, 'March-Phillipps …'
27 Fergus Fleming, p. 141. Letter of G. Boothroyd, 23/5/1956.
28 Ibid., p. 141. 'I really am …'
29 Ian Fleming, *Dr No*, Chapter 2, Choice of Weapons, p. 17. 'M took his …'
30 Montagu Papers 13/9/1964 & Ben Macintyre, *Operation Mincemeat*, p. 31.
31 Macintyre, *Operation Mincemeat*, p. 31. 'Before placing Montagu …'
32 Ewen Montagu, *The Man Who Never Was*, p. 11. 'It all really …'
33 TNA/ADM 223/478.
34 David Kahn, *Hitler's Spies*, pp. 453–454. 'A Royal Navy postmaster …'
35 Ibid., p. 454. 'But their suspicions …'
36 TNA/ADM 223/794.
37 Pearson, p. 125. 'Occasions like these …'
38 Hart-Davis, *Peter Fleming*, p. 285. 'Besides devising …'
39 Lycett, pp. 143–144. 'Running the …'
40 Stevenson, p. 187. 'Camp X was near …'
41 Ibid., p. 189. 'Factories grew for …'
42 Ian Fleming, *Live and Let Die*, Chapter 22, Terror By Sea, p. 220. 'Sixty yards to
    go …'
43 Stevenson, p. 193. 'The chances …'
44 Pearson, p. 139. 'He got his …'
45 Lycett, p. 149. 'Ian's attendance …'
46 Rankin, pp. 222–223. 'Ian Fleming made …'
47 David Stafford, *Camp X*, pp. 277–278. 'As noted earlier …'
48 Macdonald, p. 183. 'De Chastelain had …'

49   Ibid., p. 146. 'Following Stephenson's death …'
50   Ibid., p. 286. 'Pat Bayly …'
51   Ibid., pp. 330–331. 'Bayly thought …'
52   Stevenson, pp. 193–194. 'He went through …'
53   Ian Fleming, *For Your Eyes Only*, p. 72. 'Bond spent the …'
54   Ibid., p. 60. 'M said shortly …'
55   Ibid., p. 71. 'Colonel John's closed …' & p. 65. 'The headquarters….'
56   Fergus Fleming, p. 297. Letter to Michael Howard, 19/4/1962.
57   Ian Fleming, *The Spy Who Loved Me*, Chapter 6, Go West Young Woman, p. 69. 'Route 2 from …'
58   Amis, p. 147. Reference Guide *The Spy Who Loved Me*.
59   Bryce, pp. 109–110. 'Jo has made …'
60   Stafford, p. 282. 'Brooker and Skilleck …'
61   Pearson, p. 139. 'He got his …'
62   Nutting, p. 47. 'We got into …'
63   Ibid., p. 105. 'We went to …'
64   Artemis Cooper, *Cairo*, p. 282. 'Everything about this …'
65   Lycett, p. 150. 'The Sextant Conference …'

Chapter 13 Back to France

1   Nutting, p. 37. 'There used to be …'
2   Patrick Dalzel-Job, *From Arctic Snow to Dust of Normandy*, p. 115. 'Our boss …'
3   Nutting, p. 181. 'This decision …'
4   Ibid., p. 244. 'So it was …'
5   TNA/ADM 223/213.
6   Ibid.
7   Nutting, p. 160. 'At a meeting …'
8   Ibid., p. 160. 'Although this formation …'
9   See Anthony Rogers' book, *Churchill's Folly*.
10   TNA/WO 32/11430.
11   Nutting, p. 59. 'This ended …'
12   Jack Webster, *Alistair MacLean*, pp. 92–93. 'That however …'
13   Pearson, p. 150. 'He was summoned …'
14   Lycett, pp. 151–152. 'The unreality …' & Pearson, p. 150.
15   Harling, pp. 83–84. 'I left on the …'
16   Ian Fleming, *Diamonds are Forever*, Chapter 22, Love and Sauce Bearnaise, p. 194. 'And you'd marry …'
17   Ian Fleming, *From Russia with Love*, Chapter 11, The Soft Life, pp. 98–99. 'That morning …'
18   Ian FLeming, *On Her Majesty's Secret Service*, Chapter 27, All the Time in the World, pp. 258–259. 'Ten minutes later …'
19   Ian Fleming, *You Only Live Twice*, Chapter 22, Sparrows Tears, p. 204. 'When Kissy saw …'
20   Nutting, pp. 160–161. 'So we followed …'
21   Ibid., p. 165. 'Back again …'
22   Harling, p. 55. 'Pamela nodded …'
23   Nutting, p. 172. 'This went on …'

24 Ibid., p. 180. 'By now the ...'
25 Dalzel-Job, p. 115. 'I met Ian's ...'
26 Ibid., p. 118. 'We were still ...'
27 Harling, p. 73. 'To our disbelief ...'
28 Ibid., p. 70. 'So with one ...'
29 Ibid., p. 77. 'Within an hour ...'
30 Ibid., pp. 78–89. 'Mapping the ...'
31 Ibid., p. 81. 'Within a couple ...'
32 Ian Fleming, *Thunderball*, Chapter 11, Domino, p. 114. 'Bond settled ...'
33 Ian Fleming, *The Spy Who Loved Me*, Chapter 4. Dear Viv. p. 47. 'I was lucky ...'
34 Harling, p. 357. '30AU by that ...'
35 Nutting, p. 204. 'Capt Ward RA ...'
36 Ian Fleming, *Moonraker*, Chapter 12, The Moonraker, p. 109. 'It was like ...'
37 J.A.C. Hugill, *The Hazard Mesh*, p. 60. 'One of the Admiralty ...'
38 Ian Fleming, *The Man with the Golden Gun*, Chapter 4, The Stars Foretell, pp. 53–54. 'The car's outside ...'
39 Dalzel-Job, p. 122. 'In the late ...'
40 TNA/AIR 20/2629.
41 Harling, pp. 92–93. 'Patton received us ...'
42 Ibid., pp. 93–97. 'The day was ...'
43 Hugill, pp. 101–104. 'Five minutes later ...'
44 Nutting, pp. 218–219. 'Our first target ...' & TNA/ADM 391/44 Glanville's report 25/10/44.
45 Dalzel-Job, p. 139. 'After that ...'
46 Nutting, p. 222. 'We returned ...'

Chapter 14 The Final Push

1   TNA/HW4 HMS *Anderson* Records.
2   Hart-Davis, *Man of War*, pp. 277–278. 'In Colombo ...'
3   Lycett, pp. 154–155. 'As soon as ...'
4   TNA/ADM 223/480 (Contains most of Iann Fleming's reports).
5   Lycett, p. 155. 'After the festivities ...'
6   Hart-Davis, *Peter Fleming*, p. 283. 'D Division's ...'
7   Ian Fleming, *Man of War*, pp. 278–279. 'In January ...' (Ian Fleming's letter Hillgarth family collection.)
8   Ian Fleming, *The Man with the Golden Gun*, Chapter 17, Endit, p. 190. 'James Bond ...'
9   Ian Fleming, *On Her Majesty's Secret Service*, Chapter 6, Bond of Bond St, p. 54. 'Bond's replacement ...'
10 Nutting, p. 249. 'The first possible ...'
11 Ibid., p. 250. 'Dr Walter ...'
12 Ibid., pp. 244–252. 'One of the most ...'
13 Ibid., p. 256. 'I got to know ...'
14 Ian Fleming, *Moonraker*, Chapter 11, Policewoman Brand, p. 102. 'My right hand ...'
15 Amis, p. 59. 'For my ...'
16 Ian Fleming, *Moonraker*, Chapter 22, Pandora's Box, pp. 207–208. 'Yes my dear Bond ...'

17 Ibid., pp. 209–210. 'Drax's spoke …'
18 Ibid., Chapter 3, Belly Strippers, Etc, p. 25. 'Yes James …'
19 Nutting, p. 257. 'The German …'
20 TNA/ADM 223/214.
21 Nutting, pp. 259–260. 'A special party …'
22 Ibid., pp. 261–262. 'The library contained …'
23 Harling, p. 188. 'In the course …'
24 Ian Fleming, *Thrilling Cities*, pp. 152–155. 'I was altogether …'
25 Ian Fleming, *Octopussy and the Living Daylights*, pp. 20–21. 'Here Major …'
26 OSS/CIAL Nazi war crimes disclosure ID 168130425 CIA report.
27 Ian Fleming, *Octopussy and the Living Daylights*, pp. 30–33. 'The impact …'
28 Ibid., pp. 38–39. 'The Smythes met …'
29 Ibid., p. 44. 'James Bond looked …'
30 Ian Fleming, *On Her Majesty's Secret Service*, Chapter 5, The Capu, p. 40. 'The Union Corse …'
31 Ian Fleming, *Goldfinger*, Chapter 19, Secret Appendix, p. 219. '"GB" is the …'
32 Stevenson, p. 311. 'The most exotic …'
33 Ibid., pp. 321–328. 'Captain Brousse …' & Macdonald, pp. 176–177. 'De Chastelain usually …'
34 Mark Simmons, *The Battle of Matapan 1941*, pp. 152–153. 'Hyde's book …'
35 Harling, p. 190. 'And what …'
36 Ibid., pp. 190–193. 'I enjoyed …'
37 Pearson, p. 162. 'When Commander Ian …'

Chapter 15 Casino Royale

1   Pearson, p. 164. 'But again …'
2   Ian Fleming, *From Russia with Love*, Chapter 11, The Soft Life, p. 95. 'The blubbery arms …'
3   Lycett, p. 159. 'Hugo Pitman …'
4   Bryce, pp. 78–81. 'No sooner …'
5   *Noel Coward Diaries*, p. 107. Note 3. 'Where Ian …'
6   Bryce, p. 83. 'I agreed …'
7   Ibid., p. 87. 'She was …'
8   Lycett, p. 168. 'Each working …'
9   Ian Fleming, *Diamonds are Forever*, Chapter 22, Love and Sauce Bearnaise, p. 187. 'Sitting in his …'
10 Harling, pp. 109–110. 'In this manner …'
11 Pearson, p. 212. 'I thought Ian …'
12 Harling, p. 128. 'Her gift for …'
13 Parker, p. 15. 'Ann continued her …'
14 Pearson, pp. 213–214. 'My first day …'
15 Parker, p. 38. 'On around 17 February …' & Mark Amory, *The Letters of Ann Fleming*, p. 108.
16 Pearson, pp. 184–185. 'During the first …'
17 Parker, p. 128. 'On around 17 February …'
18 Bryce, pp. 96–97. 'This was …'
19 Pearson, p. 223. 'James Bond was born …'

20 Lycett, pp. 216–217. 'In a diary fragment ...'

21 IWM-No. 17063 Private papers Lt Commander J.A.C. Hugill, pp. 26–27.

22 Pearson, p. 230. 'Ivar Bryce ...'

23 Ian Fleming, *Casino Royale*, Chapter 5, The Girl from Headquarters, pp. 28–29. 'Royale-les-Eaux ...'

24 Ibid., Chapter 10, The High Table, p. 70. 'Bond lit a ...'

25 Ibid., p. 67. '*Bond had* ...' & Chapter 11, Moment of Truth, p. 71. 'During this ...'

26 Ibid., Chapter 2, Dossier For M, pp. 13–14. 'In my case ...'

27 Haslam, p. 124. 'Evidence of Stalin's ...'

28 Jeffery, pp. 665–666. 'SIS sources ...'

29 Ian Fleming, *From Russia with Love*, Authors note & Chapter 4, The Moguls of Death, p. 28. 'The headquarters ...'

30 Fergus Fleming, p. 139. Letter to Ross Napier, 11/11/1961.

31 Ian Fleming, *Casino Royale*, Chapter 20, The Nature of Evil, p. 134. 'Well in the last ...'

32 Papen, pp. 485–489. 'Amid those minor ...'

33 Ian Fleming, *Casino Royale*, Chapter 6, Two Men in Straw Hats, p. 37. 'What a ghastly ...'

34 Ibid., Chapter 22, The Hastening Saloon, p. 148. 'Every day ...'

35 Ian Fleming, *Moonraker*, Chapter 25, Zero Plus, pp. 243–244. 'The 1953 Mark VI ...'

36 Ian Fleming, *Thunderball*, Chapter 7, Fasten Your Lap Strap, p. 67. 'But Bond refused ...'

37 Bryce, pp. 106–107. 'Casino Royale was ...'

38 Ian Fleming, *Casino Royale*, Chapter 5, The Girl from Headquarters, p. 32. 'Her Hair ...'

39 Ibid., Chapter 27, The Bleeding Heart, p. 181. 'This is 007 ...'

40 Hart-Davis, *Peter Fleming*, p. 329. 'Once again ...'

41 Cook, p. 10. 'The idea of writing ...'

42 Chancellor, p. 5. 'Having finished ...'

43 Fergus Fleming, p. 12. 'This approach was ...' & Lycett, p. 226. 'It was not until ...'

44 Parker, p. 141. 'This is one ...'

45 Fergus Fleming, p. 23. Letter to Jonathan Cape 29/10/1952.

46 Ibid., p. 225. Letter from Raymond Chandler, 4/6/1955.

47 Ian Fleming, *Thunderball*, Chapter 14, Sour Martinis, p. 153. 'The drinks came ...'

48 Lycett, pp. 442–443. 'Any additional ...'

49 Ian Fleming, *You Only Live Twice*, Chapter 21, Obit, p. 203. 'M.G. Writes ...'

BIBLIOGRAPHY

Ian Fleming's Books, all published by Jonathan Cape
The Bond Books
Casino Royale (1953)
Live and Let Die (1954)
Moonraker (1955)
Diamonds are Forever (1956)
From Russia with Love (1957)
Dr No (1958)
Goldfinger (1959)
For Your Eyes Only (1960)
Thunderball (1961)
The Spy Who Loved Me (1962)
On Her Majesty's Secret Service (1963)
You Only Live Twice (1964)
The Man with the Golden Gun (1965)
Octopussy and The Living Daylights (1966)

Children's Fiction
Chitty Chitty Bang Bang (1964–65)

Non-Fiction
The Diamond Smugglers (1957)
Thrilling Cities (1963)

Books

Amis, Kingsley, *The James Bond Dossier* (New American Library, 1965)

Amory, Mark, *The Letters of Ann Fleming* (Harvill Press, 1985)

Andrew, Christopher, *Secret Service* (Heinemann, 1985)

_____, *The Defence of the Realm: The Authorised History of MI5* (Allen Lane, 2009)

Beadle, Major J.C., *The Light Blue Lanyard* (Square One, 1992)

Beesly, Patrick, *Very Special Admiral* (Hamish Hamilton, 1980)

_____, *Very Special Intelligence* (Greenhill Books, 2000)

Booth, Martin, *A Magick Life* (Hodder & Stoughton, 2000)

Borghese, J. Valerio, *Sea Devils: Italian Naval Commandos in World War II* (United States Naval Institute, 1995)

Bowles, Paul, *Too Far From Home: The Selected Writings of Paul Bowles* (Eco Press, 1991)

Bragadin, Commander Marc Antonio, *The Italian Navy in World War II* (United States Naval Institute, 1957)

Brown, Anthony Cave, *'C': The Secret Life of Sir Stewart Menzies, Spymaster to Winston Churchill* (Macmillan, 1987)

Bryce, Ivar, *You Only Live Once* (Weidenfeld & Nicolson, 1984 revised edition)

Bullock, Alan, *Hitler: A Study in Tyranny* (Oldham Press, 1953)

Cabell, Craig, *Ian Fleming's Secret War* (Pen & Sword, 2008)

Chancellor, Henry, *James Bond: The Man and His World* (John Murray, 2005)

Churchill, Winston, *The Second World War* (Reprint Society, 1949)

Colville, John, *The Fringes of Power* (W.W. Norton, 1986)

Colvin, Ian, *Canaris, Chief of Intelligence* (George Mann, 1973)

Conant, Jennet, *The Irregulars* (Simon & Schuster, 2008)

Cook, Andrew, *Ace of Spies* (History Press, 2002)

Cooper, Artemis, *Cairo: In the War 1939–1945* (Hamish Hamilton, 1989)

_____, *Patrick Leigh Fermor* (John Murray, 2012)

Cox, Geoffrey, *Countdown to War* (William Kimber, 1988)

Cunningham, A.B., *A Sailor's Odyssey* (Hutchinson, 1951)

Dahl, Roald, *Boy & Going Solo* (Jonathan Cape, 1992)

Dalzel-Job, Patrick, *From Arctic Snow to Dust of Normandy* (Nead-an-Eoin, 1992)

Danchev, Alex, *Establishing the Anglo-American Alliance* (Brassey's, 1990)

Eccles, David & Sybil, *By Safe Hand: The Letters of David & Sybil Eccles 1939–1942* (Bodley Head, 1983)

Farago, Ladislas, *The Game of Foxes* (David Mckay, 1971)

Fitzgerald, Penelope, *The Knox Brothers* (Putnam, 1978)

Fleming, Fergus, *The Man with the Golden Typewriter* (Bloomsbury, 2015)

Fleming, Peter, *The Flying Visit* (Charles Scribner's & Sons, 1940)

_____, *Invasion 1940* (Rupert Hart-Davis, 1957)

Frankland, Noble, & Dowling, Christopher, *Decisive Battles of the Twentieth Century* (Sidgwick & Jackson, 1976)

Gammon, Paul, *Inside Room 40: The Codebreakers of WWI* (Ian Allen, 2010)

Haining, Peter, *The Mystery of Rommel's Gold* (Robson Books, 2004)

Harling, Robert, *Ian Fleming: A Personal Memoir* (Robson, 2015)

Hart-Davis, Duff, *Peter Fleming* (Jonathan Cape, 1974)

_____, *Man of War* (Century, 2012)

Harvey, Maurice, *Gibraltar* (Spellmount, 1996)

Healey, Donald, *My World of Cars* (Patrick Stephens, 1989)

Hemming, Henry, *'M': Maxwell Knight, MI5's Greatest Spymaster* (Penguin, 2007)

Hinsley, F.H., *British Intelligence in the Second World War* (HMSO, 1993)

Hoare, Sir Samuel, *Ambassador on a Special Mission* (Collins, 1946)

Hugill, J.A.C., *The Hazard Mesh* (Faber & Faber, 2011)

Jeffrey, Keith, *MI6: The History of the Secret Intelligence Service 1909–1949*
    (Bloomsbury 2010)

Kahn, David, *Hitler's Spies* (Arrow Books, 1980)

Kemp, Paul, *Underwater Warriors* (Brockhampten Press, 1996)

Knatchbull-Hugessen, Sir Hughe, *Diplomat in Peace and War* (John Murray, 1949)

Le Carré, John, *Call for the Dead* (Lamplighter, 1992)

Lett, Brian, *Ian Fleming and SOE's Operation Postmaster* (Pen & Sword, 2012)

Lochery, Neill, *Lisbon* (Public Affairs, 2011)

Lycett, Andrew, *Ian Fleming* (Weidenfeld & Nicolson, 1993)

Macdonald, Bill, *The True Intrepid* (Raincoast Books, 2001)

Macintyre, Ben, *For Your Eyes Only: Ian Fleming and James Bond* (Bloomsbury, 2008)

_____, *Operation Mincemeat* (Bloomsbury, 2010)

Masterman, J.C, *The Double Cross System* (Folio Society, 2007)

Masters, Anthony, *The Man Who Was M* (Basil Blackwell, 1984)

McCormick, Donald, *The Life of Ian Fleming* (Peter Owen, 1993)

McLachlan, Donald, *Room 39: Naval Intelligence in Action 1939–45* (Weidenfeld &
    Nicolson, 1968)

Miller, Russell, *Codename Tricycle* (Secker & Warburg, 2004)

Minshall, Merlin, *Guilt Edged* (Bachman & Turner, 1975)

Montagu, Ewen, *The Man Who Never Was* (Penguin Books, 1955)

_____, *Beyond Top Secret Ultra* (Coward, McCann & Geoghegan, 1978)

Nutting, David, *Attain by Surprise* (David Colver, 2003)

Padfield, Peter, *Hess, Hitler & Churchill* (Icon Books, 2013)

Papen, Franz von, *Memoirs* (Andre Deutsch, 1952)

Pearson, John, *The Life of Ian Fleming* (Aurum Press, 2003)

Philby, Kim, *My Silent War* (Macgibbon & Kee, 1968)

Picknett, Lynn, Prince, Clive & Prior, Stephen, *Double Standards: The Rudolf Hess
    Cover-up* (Little Brown, 2001)

Playfair, Major-General I.S.O., *The Mediterranean & Middle East Vol. II* (The Naval &
    Military Press, 2004)

Popov, Dusko, *Spy Counter Spy* (Weidenfeld & Nicolson, 1974)

Pugh, Marshall, *Commander Crabb* (Macmillan, 1956)

Ramsay, David, *Blinker Hall Spymaster* (Spellmount, 2008)

Rankin, Nicholas, *Ian Fleming's Commandos* (Faber & Faber, 2011)

_____, *Defending the Rock* (Faber & Faber, 2017)

Schellenberg, Walter, *The Memoirs of Hitler's Spymaster* (Andre Deutsch, 2006)

Simmons, Mark, *The Battle of Matapan 1941* (Spellmount, 2011)

_____, *Agent Cicero* (Spellmount, 2014)

_____, *Ian Fleming & Operation Golden Eye* (Casemate, 2018)

Sisman, Adam, *John le Carré* (Bloomsbury, 2015)

Smith, Michael, *The Secret Agents, Bedside Reader,* (Biteback, 2014)

Smithers, Peter, *Adventures of a Gardener* (Harvill Press, 1993)

Stafford, David, *Camp X: Canada's School for Secret Agents 1941–45* (Lester & Orpen Dennys, 1986)

Stevenson, William, *A Man Called Intrepid* (Macmillan, 1976)

Sturrock, Donald, *Storyteller: The Life of Roald Dahl* (Harper Collins, 2010)

Tangye, Derek, *The Way to Minack* (Michael Joseph, 1968)

Tuchman, Barbara, *The Zimmermann Telegram* (Folio Society, 2004)

Vickers, Philip, *Finding Thoroton: The Royal Marine Who Ran British Naval Intelligence in the Western Mediterranean in World War One* (Royal Marines Historical Society, 2013)

Waller, John H., *The Unseen War in Europe* (Random House, 1996)

Webster, Jack, *Alistair MacLean* (Chapmans, 1991)

West, Nigel, *Historical Dictionary of Naval Intelligence* (Scarecrow Press, 2010)

_____, *GCHQ: The Secret Wireless War 1900–1986* (Weidenfeld & Nicolson, 1986)

Wigg, Richard, *Churchill and Spain* (Sussex Academic Press, 2008)

Wright, Peter, *Spycatcher* (Viking, 1987)

Archives

BBC Archives (UK)

Bodleian Library, Oxford (UK)

Bundesarchiv (Germany)

Central Intelligence Agency Library (USA)

Imperial War Museums (UK)

Littlehampton Museum

National Archives (USA)

The National Archives, Kew (UK)

Royal Marines Historical Society

Royal Navy Submarine Museum

United States Navy Historical Centre

Viscount Templewood Papers, Cambridge (UK)

Winston Churchill Archive, Cambridge (UK)

Journals & Newspapers

Birmingham Mail

Daily Telegraph

Dime Detective Magazine

The Globe & Laurel Magazine: Journal of the Royal Marines

The Independent

Medal News

Sunday Telegraph

Sunday Times

The Times

World War II Quarterly Magazine

Websites

www.commandoveterans.org
www.literary007.com
www.ianfleming.com
www.30AU.co.uk
www.navweops.com
www.aboutourrock.com

ACKNOWLEDGEMENTS

My sister, Jane, enabled my interest in James Bond to begin with by getting me into a cinema because she was over 15 to watch *From Russia with Love* – thanks to her. Ian Lancaster Fleming, through his writing, kindled my interest in writing. Having re-read all his Bond books and some of his non-fiction for this book and my previous book *Ian Fleming and Operation Golden Eye,* it is a testament to him how well his work has stood the test of time.

Tom Cull my literary agent has been one of the main driving forces behind this work, always helpful and constructive. He is also a devotee of Ian Fleming's work, running the online-site Artistic Licence Renewed. Sincere thanks to Anthony Horowitz for his introduction.

I am grateful to the staff at various libraries and museums, including: the BBC, Bletchley Park, the Churchill Archives Centre Cambridge, Ian Fleming Publications, the Imperial War Museum London, The Royal Marines Historical Society, the Public Records Office at Kew, the Royal Navy Museum and the Royal Navy Submarine Museum.

Overseas museums and libraries have been equally helpful: the Central Intelligence Agency Library, United States Library of Congress, United States National Archives and Records Administration and the Bundesarchiv-German Federal Archives.

For help and ideas with the manuscript I thank Mark Beynon at The History Press, Group Captain L.E. (Robbie) Robins CBE, AE, DL for his help over many years and projects, and John Sherress. Thanks to my magazine editors, who have always been helpful and free with their time: Iain Ballantyne, John Mussell and Flint Whitlock. Thank you to Denny Lane for insights into the life of his stepfather, Peter Smithers, and for the use of family photographs.

The memories of many friends and colleagues, published and unpublished, of Ian Fleming have proved a veritable gold mine: R. Andrew, Patrick Beesly, Ivar Bryce, Roald Dahl, Patrick Dalzel-Job, David & Sybil Eccles, Peter Fleming, Robert Harling, J.A.C. Hugill, S.M. Mackenzie, Donald McLachlan, Merlin Minshall, Ewen Montagu, David Nutting, Dusko Popov, Peter Smithers and Patrick Whinney.

The biographers of Ian Fleming have been invaluable: Kingsley Amis, Henry Chancellor, Fergus Fleming, Andrew Lycett, Ben Macintyre, Matthew Parker and John Pearson.

Also, the expertise and work of the following have been helpful: Christopher Andrew, Martin Booth, J. Valerio Borghese, Marc Antonio Bragadin, Anthony Cave Brown, Jennet Conant, Geoffrey Cox, Alex Danchev, Paul Gannon, Duff Hart-Davis, Paul Johnson, Keith Jeffery, David Kahn, Paul Kemp, Brian Lett, Neill Lochery, Bill Macdonald, Anthony Masters, Anna Mosley, Peter Padfield, Lynn Picknett, Clive Prince, Stephen Prior, Marshal Pugh, David Ramsay, Nicholas Rankin, Walter Schellenberg, Michael Smith, David Stafford, William Stevenson, Donald Sturrok, Philip Vickers, John H. Waller and Andrew Webb.

Finally, as always and most important, my wife, Margaret, gave her wholehearted support to the nuts and bolts of building a book, with proof reading, finding her way through the labyrinth of strange and unfamiliar names, and my creative misspelling of them. Thanks to all. Any mistakes or errors are mine alone.

INDEX

IF YOU ENJOYED THIS TITLE FROM THE HISTORY PRESS ...

Mark Simmons weaves together personal accounts by the leading characters and information from top-secret files from MI5, MI6 and the CIA to tell the astonishing story of Agent Cicero.

978 0 7509 5286 6

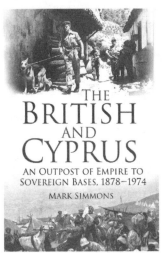

Using previously unpublished letters and personal interviews, *The British and Cyprus* is told through the words of the people who served the British Crown on Cyprus – civil and military – and includes fascinating accounts of the dramatic fight against EOKA in the 1950s, who pressed for an end to British rule on the island.

978 0 7509 6070 0

The destination for history
www.thehistorypress.co.uk